"It is a privilege to commend thi   n
Galatians by my teacher and friend Grant Osborne. Grant rightly envisions profitable use of it in personal devotions, church Bible study, and as a sermon aid. His encyclopedic knowledge of the New Testament literature and his lucid writing style make this commentary a joy to read. Highly recommended!"

—**Andreas J. Köstenberger**, senior research professor of New Testament and biblical theology, Southeastern Baptist Theological Seminary, and founder of Biblical Foundations™ (www.biblicalfoundations.org)

"I am very excited about Grant Osborne's series of New Testament commentaries! The Galatians commentary is a wonderful resource for pastors and Bible study leaders. Osborne brings to bear his many years of experience as a professor and pastor as he explains and applies each passage in clear and substantive ways without getting bogged down in minor details or more technical discussions. Osborne's careful blend of accessibility and depth is what marks out this commentary as particularly useful. I hope many people will get this book and use it."

—**Ray Van Neste**, professor of biblical studies, director of the R. C. Ryan Center for Biblical Studies, Union University

"As a student of Dr. Osborne's, I taped many of his lectures because of their deep and profound insight into New Testament Scripture. It is a marvelous blessing that he has found time to provide a verse-by-verse exposition of Paul's letter to the Galatians. This excellent work will save pastors, professors, and speakers hours of study and preparation time, since the thorough and unique presentation totally eliminates the need to look anywhere else for deeper understanding. This is an outstanding, superb, one-stop shop commentary on the book of Galatians."

—**Raleigh B. Washington**, president and CEO, Promise Keepers

"Grant Osborne is an eminent New Testament scholar and warm-hearted professor who loves the word of God. The volumes in this accessible commentary series help readers understand the text clearly and accurately. But they also draw us to consider the implications of the text, providing key insights on faithful application and preaching that reflect a lifetime of ministry experience. This unique combination of scholarship and practical experience makes this series an invaluable resource for all students of God's word, and especially those who are called to preach and teach."

—**H. Wayne Johnson**, associate academic dean and associate professor of pastoral theology, Trinity Evangelical Divinity School

Praise for the Osborne New Testament Commentaries

"For years I have found Grant Osborne's commentaries to be reliable and thoughtful guides for those wanting to better understand the New Testament. Indeed, Osborne has mastered the art of writing sound, helpful, and readable commentaries and I am confident that this new series will continue the level of excellence that we have come to expect from him. How exciting to think that pastors, students, and laity will all be able to benefit for years to come from the wise and insightful interpretation provided by Professor Osborne in this new series. The Osborne New Testament Commentaries will be a great gift for the people of God."

—**David S. Dockery**, president, Trinity International University

"This is a set of commentaries by one of the premier New Testament commentators of our day—a reputation earned over many years of teaching, preaching, and writing. Dr. Osborne brings a full understanding of the Old Testament and Second Temple literature to bear on a careful and profound reading of the New Testament. In this series his previous exegetical commentary writing comes to a full expository expression that will be of great benefit to students, preachers, and teachers alike."

—**Richard E. Averbeck**, director of the PhD program in theological studies, professor of Old Testament and Semitic languages, Trinity Evangelical Divinity School

"One of my most valued role models, Grant Osborne is a first-tier biblical scholar who brings to the text of Scripture a rich depth of insight that is both accessible and devotional. Grant loves Christ, loves the Word, and loves the church, and those loves are embodied in this wonderful new commentary series, which I cannot recommend highly enough."

—**George H. Guthrie**, Benjamin W. Perry Professor of Bible, Union University

"With this new series, readers will have before them what we—his students—experienced in all of Professor Osborne's classes: patient regard for every word in the text, exegetical finesse, a preference for an eclectic resolution to the options facing the interpreter, a sensitivity to theological questions, and most of all a reverence for God's word."

—**Scot McKnight**, Julius R. Mantey Chair of New Testament, Northern Seminary

GALATIANS

Verse by Verse

GALATIANS

Verse by Verse

GRANT R. OSBORNE

LEXHAM PRESS

Galatians: Verse by Verse
Osborne New Testament Commentaries

Copyright 2017 Grant R. Osborne

Lexham Press, 1313 Commercial St., Bellingham, WA 98225
LexhamPress.com

Print ISBN 9781683590361
Digital ISBN 9781683590378

Lexham Editorial Team: Elliot Ritzema, Joel Wilcox
Cover Design: Christine Christophersen
Back Cover Design: Brittany Schrock

CONTENTS

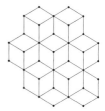

SERIES PREFACE

There are two authors of every biblical book: the human author who penned the words, and the divine Author who revealed and inspired every word. While God did not dictate the words to the biblical writers, he did guide their minds so that they wrote their own words under the influence of the Holy Spirit. If Christians really believed what they said when they called the Bible "the word of God," a lot more would be engaged in serious Bible study. As divine revelation, the Bible deserves, indeed demands, to be studied deeply.

This means that when we study the Bible, we should not be satisfied with a cursory reading in which we insert our own meanings into the text. Instead, we must always ask what God intended to say in every passage. But Bible study should not be a tedious duty we have to perform. It is a sacred privilege and a joy. The deep meaning of any text is a buried treasure; all the riches are waiting under the surface. If we learned there was gold deep under our backyard, nothing would stop us from getting the tools we needed to dig it out. Similarly, in serious Bible study all the treasures and riches of God are waiting to be dug up for our benefit.

This series of commentaries on the New Testament is intended to supply these tools and help the Christian understand more deeply the God-intended meaning of the Bible. Each volume walks the reader verse-by-verse through a book with the goal of opening up for us what God led Matthew or Paul or John to say to their readers. My goal in this series is to make sense of the historical and literary background of these ancient works, to supply the information that will enable the modern reader to understand exactly what the biblical writers were saying to their first-century audience. I want to remove the complexity of most modern commentaries and provide an easy-to-read explanation of the text.

But it is not enough to know what the books of the New Testament meant back then; we need help in determining how each text applies to our lives today. It is one thing to see what Paul was saying his readers in Rome or Philippi, and quite another thing to see the significance of his words for us. So at key points in the commentary, I will attempt to help the reader discover areas in our modern lives that the text is addressing.

I envision three main uses for this series:

1. **Devotional Scripture reading.** Many Christians read rapidly through the Bible for devotions in a one-year program. That is extremely helpful to gain a broad overview of the Bible's story. But I strongly encourage another kind of devotional reading—namely, to study deeply a single segment of the biblical text and try to understand it. These commentaries are designed to enable that. The commentary is based on the NIV and explains the meaning of the verses, enabling the modern reader to read a few pages at a time and pray over the message.

2. **Church Bible studies.** I have written these commentaries also to serve as guides for group Bible studies. Many Bible studies today consist of people coming together and sharing what they think the text is saying. There are strengths in such an approach, but also weaknesses. The problem is that God inspired these scriptural passages so that the church would understand and obey *what he intended the text to say.* Without some guidance into the meaning of the text, we are prone to commit heresy. At the very least, the

leaders of the Bible study need to have a commentary so they can guide the discussion in the direction God intended. In my own church Bible studies, I have often had the class read a simple exposition of the text so they can all discuss the God-given message, and that is what I hope to provide here.

3. *Sermon aids.* These commentaries are also intended to help pastors faithfully exposit the text in a sermon. Busy pastors often have too little time to study complex thousand-page commentaries on biblical passages. As a result, it is easy to spend little time in Bible study and thereby to have a shallow sermon on Sunday. As I write this series, I am drawing on my own experience as a pastor and interim pastor, asking myself what I would want to include in a sermon.

Overall, my goal in these commentaries is simple: I would like them to be interesting and exciting adventures into New Testament texts. My hope is that readers will discover the riches of God that lay behind every passage in his divine word. I hope every reader will fall in love with God's word as I have and begin a similar lifelong fascination with these eternal truths!

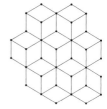

INTRODUCTION TO GALATIANS

S everal years ago Harold Lindsell, the editor of *Christianity Today* from 1968 to 1978, called for a "battle for the Bible." In this remarkable letter Paul is engaged in "the battle for the gospel"—the first great theological battle in the history of the church. It took place when a group of conservative Jewish Christians became upset over the Gentile mission that had begun with Peter and Cornelius (Acts 10-11) and continued with Paul's first missionary journey (Acts 13-14). They were bothered that Peter and Paul had been converting Gentiles without mandating that they become Jews by being circumcised and following the Mosaic law. These "Judaizers" visited some of the churches Paul had established, telling the members that they had to become Jewish proselytes before they could become Christian converts. Paul learned that many in the Galatian churches were starting to accept that teaching, and his alarm led him to pen this letter.[1] This helped produce the Jerusalem Council of Acts 15 in which the church officially decided that Gentiles did not need to be circumcised and follow the law to become Christians.

---

1. See "Recipients and Date" below for arguments regarding its early date.

AUTHOR

Galatians has always been considered one of Paul's chief letters (with Romans and the Corinthian correspondence), and virtually no one has ever doubted that "Paul an apostle" (Gal 1:1) wrote it. There are so many signs of his hand in the letter, such as his emphasis on the centrality of the gospel and on justification by faith. The first two chapters are almost autobiographical in nature, detailing four key episodes in Paul's early Christian life: his conversion and early ministry in Arabia (1:13–17); his first Jerusalem visit, when he was accepted by James and Peter (vv. 18–24); his second visit, when his apostolic ministry was accepted by "the pillars" of the church (2:1–10); and the incident of his having to correct Peter to preserve the essence of the gospel (vv. 11–21).

Virtually all of Paul's letters were written by an **amanuensis**,[2] a scribe who wrote down Paul's message. This was likely due to Paul's poor eyesight (see commentary on 4:13–15), with Paul personally signing the letter to authenticate that it was indeed his own (6:11). Frequently in the Roman world an amanuensis would add a good deal of supplementary material, but with this letter the task certainly amounted to dictation—the letter is so personal that we can only conclude that all of the content stemmed from Paul himself. This is not to suggest that the freedom to fill in explanatory material was never used by an amanuensis in New Testament letters. In later volumes of this series I will argue that this may have been the case in the Pastoral Letters and also in 1 Peter.

RECIPIENTS AND DATE

The debate over the recipients and date has consumed nearly everyone who has studied this letter, because so much of the background context changes depending on which view you choose. The letter is addressed to "the churches of Galatia" (1:2; 3:1), and there

---

2. Terms in bold type are discussed in the glossary (page 222).

are two main theories regarding who these Galatians were: the North Galatian hypothesis and the South Galatian hypothesis. The difference hinges on whether "Galatians" is meant to describe the people ethnically or geographically. Ethnically, the Galatians were the Gauls (= "Gaulatians") who had migrated into the northeast part of modern-day Turkey in the third century BC, which would make North Galatia more probable. If the North Galatian hypothesis is true, the letter would have been written during Paul's third missionary journey (AD 52-57).

However, Rome had established the geographical province of Galatia in 25 BC. It was located in the eastern half of modern-day Turkey and extended from the Mediterranean to the Black Sea, encompassing several ethnic groups. In this case, Paul would have thought of the cities of the first missionary journey as part of Galatia, since they occupied the southern portion of this Roman province. This would mean that the letter was written to the churches established on Paul's first missionary journey, just prior to the Jerusalem Council of Acts 15.

The North Galatian Hypothesis

This view is generally preferred for several reasons, beginning with the term "Galatia" itself, which points to the Gaulic tribes of the north (so the "foolish Galatians" of 3:1 would not have been people of the southern cities). Also, when Luke speaks of "the region of Phrygia and Galatia" in Acts 16:6, it would be natural to assume he is speaking geographically, thus of northern Galatia. Phrygia and Galatia seem to be two distinct areas, which would go against the southern hypothesis.

Against this view the term "Galatians" was used in the first century to speak of people in the southern region; indeed, there was no other term Paul could have used of them. Paul's travels through the region also call the North Galatian hypothesis into question. His ministry to the southern cities is extensively described in Acts 13-14, while the northern area seems to be mentioned only in passing on the second journey in Acts 16:6 ("traveled throughout the region of Phrygia and Galatia") and in 18:23 at the start of the third journey ("traveled from place to place throughout the region of Phrygia and Galatia"). However, a growing number of scholars interpret 16:6 and 18:23 as referring to the Roman province and therefore to ministry in south Galatia, and that may be preferable in light of the arguments in favor of the south Galatian hypothesis. Therefore South Galatia receives extended coverage in Acts, while North Galatia, as I have noted, gets hardly any mention at all. It seems that if North Galatia merited a major letter, it would have received more coverage in Acts.

THE SOUTH GALATIAN HYPOTHESIS

One of the strongest arguments for this position is the absence of firm material in either Acts or Paul's letters for a ministry in the northern part of the province (as noted above). Moreover, that area did not have much Roman influence and lacked Roman roads, and Acts seems to indicate that Paul tended to follow the Roman roads in his missionary journeys. Further, Paul in his letters tended to use Roman imperial names for cities and regions, which would have meant that "Galatia" would refer in his writing to the Roman province and rather than to the ethnic territory in the north.

The mention of Barnabas in Galatians 2:13 would also favor the south. There is no evidence that Barnabas ever reached the northern area, since he and Paul split up at the beginning of the second journey (Acts 15:36-40). Finally, the events described in Galatians 1-2 fit much better with the time prior to the Jerusalem Council in Acts 15.

While there are strong arguments for both positions, and we will never have certainty, I am convinced that the southern hypothesis is the closer fit and that the background material in Galatians 1-2 supports that view. Therefore, it is my conclusion that this letter was written to the Gentile churches that Paul had established in the southern region of the Roman province of Galatia between his first missionary journey in Acts 13:1–14:20 and the Jerusalem Council in Acts 15:1–21—thus about AD 48. Whichever hypothesis is chosen, though, it is certain that Paul's opponents were a group of Jewish Christian false teachers who were demanding that Gentiles be circumcised and follow the Mosaic law.

OCCASION AND OPPONENTS

Paul's ministry method that guided him throughout his life was established on his first missionary journey. He went first to the synagogues and proclaimed Christ to his Jewish countrymen, as well as to the "God-fearers," Gentiles who were seriously interested in Judaism. Then, when Jewish "jealousy" (Acts 13:45; 17:5) over the success of his mission stirred up serious opposition, he switched his attention to the Gentiles. This of course is stated directly as his mission method in Romans 1:16.

During that first journey groups of converts, mainly Gentiles, were established into a thriving set of churches. After Paul had returned from this journey a group of Jewish Christian opponents visited all of the churches he had established, teaching that Gentiles had to become Jews—be circumcised (6:12) and submit to the Mosaic law (3:5)—before they could be saved. The converts would have been familiar with this expectation, since as God-fearers many of them had previously accepted the Mosaic law and had seriously contemplated submitting to circumcision. These teachers were "disturbing" or "agitating" the new converts (1:7; 5:12), but not for a good cause; their true goal was not really to make them followers of God but to gather followers for themselves so they could brag about their success (4:17; 6:13). Also, they desired to avoid persecution (6:12) and did not wish to be viewed as part of a radical new movement challenging mainline Judaism. So their heresy was not **christological** (having to do with the doctrine of Christ) but **soteriological** (related to the doctrine of salvation). They accepted Jesus as both Messiah and Son of

God, but circumcision and law were for them at the heart of the gospel—and that message constituted false teaching. Theirs was not Christian but "a different gospel" (1:6).

In addition to impugning Paul's gospel, these teachers were calling his apostolic authority into question, telling the Galatian churches that Paul was not a true apostle like the Twelve. Paul responded in Galatians 1 that his apostolic commission was not secondary or derivative, coming from the other apostles, but primary, conferred on him directly from Christ. In chapter 2 he showed that his gospel also came directly from Christ and was affirmed by the other apostles as identical to their own.

These opponents belonged to a movement that began in reaction to the universal gospel proclaimed first by Peter, after the conversion of Cornelius in Acts 11, and then by Paul. At first nearly everyone agreed with Peter's defense in Acts 11:4-17 of the coming of the Spirit on the Gentile God-fearer Cornelius, recognizing that "even to Gentiles God has granted repentance that leads to life" (Acts 11:18). Very quickly, however, a group, many of them former Pharisees and all of them completely committed to the necessity of circumcision and following the Torah for Gentile as well as Jewish converts to Christianity, began to dispute this. They were called the Judaizers—those who wanted to make all Christians followers and practitioners of Judaism.

After Paul had disputed this position in his Galatian letter, the Jerusalem Council decided against the Judaizers in Acts 15. Still, they continued to reject that decision and travel around to the Gentile churches, insisting that the Gentile believers become Jewish before they could be Christian (as in Phil 3:1-4:1). In Galatians 1:6, 8 Paul insisted that these Judaizers were proclaiming "a different gospel" and were "under God's curse." To follow their teaching, he declared, was to fall into apostasy and to stop being Christian. So these enemies of the gospel, though claiming to be Christians, were unbelievers—as, by extension, were their followers.

A small minority of scholars, drawing support from the material on freedom in Christ in 5:13-6:10, has argued that Paul's opponents were libertines. However, there is little evidence that Paul was addressing a different religious movement in that passage from the one he argues against in the rest of the letter. It is much more likely that Paul was repudiating a possible misuse of Christian freedom. In short, Paul was using a free/slave distinction against the Judaizers, contending that they were turning Gentile converts into slaves to the law rather than pointing them in the direction of freedom in Christ. That led Paul to explain how Christian liberty could be misused in a libertine—an immoral—manner.

A more substantial recent argument related to the Christ versus Torah issue behind Galatians comes from the movement called the "new perspective on Paul." E. P. Sanders reinterpreted "the works of the law" in Galatians to mean that salvation for the Jews came through divine grace on the basis of their corporate election as a covenant people; the issue for them, then, was not one of "getting in" but of "staying in." The Jewish view, Sanders argued, was based not on salvation by works—legalistic salvation—but on salvation by God's grace, and the goal for the Jews was that of maintaining their place in the covenant. This perspective has come to be known as the "covenantal nomism" view. J. D. G. Dunn built on it, positing that the problem addressed in Galatians was the Jewish use of the works of the law as boundary markers to maintain Jewish separation from Gentiles. In this view Paul was opposed not to a legalistic religion but to a divide between Jew and Gentile in the church.[3]

This movement has led to a significant reassessment of the belief that the Jews of Paul's day believed in works righteousness. Judaism was not in this view a purely legalistic religion, devoid

---

3. See E. P. Sanders, *Paul and Palestinian Judaism: A Comparison of Patterns of Religion* (Philadelphia: Fortress, 1977); and J. G. D. Dunn, *The New Perspective on Paul: Collected Essays* (Tübingen: Mohr Siebeck, 2005).

of grace. On this Sanders was correct. Nevertheless, there were
distinct legalistic aspects of first-century Judaism, and the whole
tenor of Galatians shows that the Judaizers' movement was a
legalistic one. Paul was indeed opposed to the separation of Jew
and Gentile, but he was even more opposed to a works-oriented
religion (Gal 3:10; 5:1–3). While he did not regard Old Testament
Judaism as a legalistic religion, it had become legalistic in light of
the salvation-historical shift to faith in Christ. The **eschatological**
salvation the Jews anticipated has become a reality in Christ, and
in light of this development trust in the law has become works
righteousness, since it involves a rejection of faith in Christ.

OUTLINE

I. The false gospel and the true gospel (1:1–2:21)
- A. Introduction: the centrality of the cross (1:1–10)
  - 1. Greeting to the church (1:1–5)
    - a. The author and recipients of the letter (1:1–2)
    - b. The salutation and power of the cross (1:3–5)
  - 2. The occasion of the letter: the dangers exposed (1:6–10)
    - a. The danger: turning to a false gospel (1:6–7)
    - b. The invocation of the divine curse (1:8–9)
    - c. Paul's model: not trying to please people (1:10)
- B. The divine source of Paul's gospel (1:11–24)
  - 1. Thesis: the origin of Paul's gospel in a revelation from Christ (1:11–12)
    - a. Not of human origin (1:11–12a)
    - b. The true source: revelation from Jesus Christ (1:12b)
  - 2. Paul's conversion and early failure to consult others (1:13–17)
    - a. His past animosity (1:13–14)
      - i. Persecution of the church (1:13)
      - ii. Zeal for Judaism (1:14)

b. His apostolic call (1:15–16a)

c. His decision not to consult others (1:16b–17)

3. Paul's first Jerusalem visit: not seeking the approval of the apostles (1:18–24)

    a. Time in Jerusalem: met only Cephas and James (1:18–20)

        i. Very short time with the two apostles (1:18–19)

        ii. Oath regarding the truth of Paul's claims (1:20)

    b. Time in Judea and Syria: unknown to these people (1:21–24)

        i. Not recognized in either region (1:21–22

        ii. Known only by report (1:23–24)

C. The pillars accept Paul as an apsotle (2:1–10)

1. The trip with Barnabas to Jerusalem (2:1–5)

    a. The purpose: presentation of his gospel to the Gentiles (2:1–2)

    b. Circumcision not required (2:3–5)

2. The approval of the pillars (2:6–10)

    a. Nothing added to Paul's gospel (2:6)

    b. The validity of Paul's Gentile and Peter's Jewish ministries (2:7–8)

    c. The right hand of fellowship from the pillars (2:9)

    d. Request to remember the poor (2:10)

D. Conflict with Peter and the essence of the gospel (2:11–21)

1. Rebuke and the defense against Peter (2:11–14)

    a. The rebuke at Antioch (2:11)

    b. The situation: withdrawal from the Gentiles (2:12a)

    c. The reason: pressure from the circumcision group (2:12b–13)

A. Paul's signature: the impor-
   tance of the conclusion (6:11)
B. The closing exhortations (6:12–15)
   1. The danger of the circumcision group (6:12–13)
      a. Their erroneous motivation (6:12)
      b. Their sinful purpose (6:13)
   2. The true basis for pride (6:14–15)
      a. The centrality of the cross and
         the crucified life (6:14)
      b. The centrality of the new creation (6:15)
C. The prayer-wish for the New Israel (6:16)
D. Proof of Paul's ministry: the marks of Jesus (6:17)
E. Closing benediction (6:18)

THE THEOLOGY OF THE LETTER
The Triune Godhead

While Galatians does not explicitly enumerate the persons of the Trinity (though see 4:6), it has a strong theology of each member of the Triune Godhead. As would be expected in this letter, God the Father is the God of the Old Testament, who is sovereign over his world and Creator of all. Yet he is also the God who brought about the new creation and sent his Son to produce the salvation-historical switch to the new covenant reality of salvation by faith rather than by works. He is the God who revealed his power by raising Christ from the dead and brought salvation to the Gentiles through the cross, commissioning Paul as his apostle to the Gentiles to proclaim this new message of salvation. His new creation includes a new family of God, with Jew and Gentile united in a new Israel, and he intends them to have a new life of freedom in Christ.

The "Lord Jesus Christ" (this combination occurs three times in the letter, with "Christ" appearing more than thirty times) is royal Messiah and Lord of all, revealed to Paul on the Damascus road (1:16) and bringing salvation to all by dying on the cross as our substitute for the remission of our sins. The sonship of Jesus is emphasized (1:16; 2:20; 4:6), as is his lordship (1:3; 5:10; 6:14, 18). Salvation is secured only by faith in him (2:16; 3:5, 7, 9), and by faith believers become one "in Christ" (1:24; 2:17; 3:26, 28). The cross is central in this letter and has replaced the law at the apex of God's salvation. The death of Christ for sins, which has defeated the dark cosmic powers (1:4), renders the Judaizers' teaching null and void (3:1). In union with Christ believers are crucified to the world (2:20; 6:14).

The Spirit, together with the cross, is the sign of the reality of the new age. Our Christian life begins when we receive the Spirit (3:2–5). In fact, the coming of the Spirit marks the beginning of the new age in salvation history and the beginning of each believer's life in Christ. The Spirit keeps us in Christ until we reach the final consummation of all things (5:5). The Christian life is defined by receiving the Spirit (3:2), being led by the Spirit (5:18), and then walking in step with the Spirit (vv. 16, 25), enabling us to exemplify the fruit of the Spirit (vv. 22–23).

THE GOSPEL

(1) *The truth of the gospel*. The core of this letter is the stability of the true Christian gospel. Even though the noun ("gospel") and the verb ("preach the gospel") occur primarily in the first two chapters (thirteen times out of fifteen in the letter), the issue permeates the whole. In fact, Paul defines the gospel in 3:1–4:11. The basis of the war over "the truth of the gospel" (2:5, 14) is made clear in the opening chapters. Paul proves that the Judaizers' attempt to replace the cross with circumcision and the law constitutes heresy. It is anathema to the gospel, which centers on salvation by grace through faith (see below). When salvation in Christ is claimed to be attainable by works rather than by faith, the gospel is not merely threatened but destroyed.

(2) *Salvation history*. The basic problem with these Jewish Christian opponents is their failure to understand that Christ

did more than come to be Messiah. "When the set time had fully come" (4:4) he brought about a fundamental change in God's economy of salvation by inaugurating the switch from the old covenant age of the law to the new covenant age of salvation in Christ. Circumcision and the law, the signs of the old covenant, had reached their nadir, and their purpose had been fulfilled by Jesus, rendering them obsolete as means of salvation (Rom 10:4). Thus, they have ended, and the new age of salvation by faith, rather than by works, has begun. The promises of Abraham are fulfilled in Christ, and so Abraham's faith replaces Moses' works (Gal 3:16, 19). We are now living in the last days, when the hopes of the ages are in the process of being consummated, making us people of future hope (5:5). The **apocalyptic** reality in Christ has come.

(3) *Justification by faith alone.* In opposition to works righteousness is justification by faith. Justification deals with the forgiveness of sins and the reception of salvation. The verb "justify," meaning to "declare righteous," is a forensic term describing God on his judgment seat declaring a person to be in a right standing before himself. On the basis of Jesus' willingly allowing himself to be placed on the cross and bearing our sins as our substitute, God declares us innocent, forgiven, and righteous in his sight. If we could earn this right standing with God by keeping the law or doing good works, Jesus' death would be worth nothing (2:21). That is the point of this letter.

(4) *Freedom and the Christian walk.* In Galatians 5:13–6:10 Paul explores walking in the Spirit as the way the believer experiences freedom in the Spirit. For him the Christian life consists of keeping in step with the Spirit (5:25), and that mandates a lifestyle that turns away from the libertine desires of the flesh (vv. 16–18). In other words, it rejects enslavement to sin and finds freedom in Christ. After the Spirit enters believers, he leads and empowers them, guiding them to meet God's standards and live a life pleasing to him (v. 24; 6:8). This is a life of obedience, not to the law (external works) but to the Spirit's leading (internal faith).

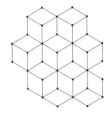

THE CENTRALITY OF
THE CROSS (1:1–10)

Nearly all New Testament letters are constructed according to the first-century pattern followed by Jewish, as well as **Hellenistic**, letters: They begin with the identification of the writer, followed by acknowledgment of the recipients and a greeting in the form of a prayer-wish. This is a very ancient form, as evidenced in Daniel 4:1: "King Nebuchadnezzar, To the nations and peoples of every language, who live in all the earth: May you prosper greatly!"

In his greeting Paul goes beyond the statements of typical first-century letters and provides an introduction to the main themes of his letter. In Galatians there are two:

1. Paul was an apostle not by human appointment but by divine commissioning (1:1a). This leads into the opening of the body of the letter and to Paul's defense of his apostolic office (vv. 11–24).

2. Christ offered himself as a sacrifice on the cross to rescue us from evil (v. 4). Paul stresses this to prepare for the central part of his letter, defending the gospel and the cross against the attempts of the **Judaizers** (see vv. 6–7) to declare the law the basis of salvation (3:1–4:7).

One critical aspect of this greeting is the absence of the customary thanksgiving and prayer, which are replaced here by Paul's rebuke of the Galatians for being taken in by the false arguments of the Judaizers. The only other of Paul's letters to make this change is Titus, which also centers on the dangers of heresy.[1] The impression we get from such a substitution is that the situation in Galatia was so fraught with danger that there was not much for which Paul could be thankful. Paul was stressing the seriousness of the problem. The Galatians needed to repent and correct their course immediately, before it was too late.

PAUL GREETS THE GALATIAN CHURCHES (1:1–5)

THE AUTHOR AND RECIPIENTS OF THE LETTER (1:1–2)

As in each of Paul's letters, he begins by identifying himself as "Paul," the Hellenized form of his Jewish name, Saul (Acts 7:58). He always calls himself Paul in his letters, probably to stress that God has called him to be the apostle to the Gentiles (Acts 26:17–18). As in most of his letters he also includes his title as "apostle," the Greek word *apostolos*, indicating that he has been "sent" by God and given divine authority to speak for the Lord. Behind this is the Old Testament idea of the *shaliach* sent with the authority of God as his official spokesman (note, for example, the role of Ahijah in 1 Kgs 14:6). There is the air of a prophet behind the concept, and here Paul is emphasizing the divine commission underlying his office in the church. Jesus, who called his twelve disciples "apostles" from the beginning (Luke 6:13), also designated Paul an apostle on the Damascus road, a fact Paul will stress in verses 2–17.

The Judaizers were challenging Paul's apostolic office, so here at the outset he points out that he has been "sent [*apostellō*] not from men or by a man, but by Jesus Christ and God the Father." It is unusual to stress both plural and singular—"not from men nor by a man," and by so doing Paul is emphasizing that neither

---

1. See also Hebrews, James, 2 Peter, and 1 John for this omission. All are dealing with extremely serious issues involving the danger of apostasy.

any human source (the church) nor human individual agent (for instance, James or Peter, vv. 18–19) was responsible for his office.[2] The change in prepositions stresses this even more strongly. The source (*apo*: "from") and agent (*dia*: "by") of Paul's apostolic office were in no sense human. In stressing that he was neither inferior nor superior to the Twelve but equal to them, Paul is neither denigrating his own status nor placing himself above the others or trying to usurp their authority. In verses 18–19 he reports that he had traveled to Jerusalem after his conversion to get to know them (see Acts 9:27–28).

The true agents behind Paul's apostolic authority were Christ (God the Son) and God the Father. Paul is always trinitarian in his theology (the Spirit is implied), picturing the Godhead acting in concert at all times. Notice that Christ and the Father are found twice in this greeting—as joint agents of Paul's apostolic commission (1:1) and as the true greeters of the Galatians (v. 3). In his other greetings Paul tends to mention them only in the latter sense, so the authority issue underlying this letter is a special emphasis here. Everything Paul will say stems from the Three-in-One. To the Greek way of thinking any superior could send an apostle (a "sent one"), but Paul makes it absolutely clear that it was God and Christ who had sent him, and they alone. His apostleship is not of human origin but is derived entirely from divine action.

Further, his authority comes from the God "who raised [Christ] from the dead" (v. 1) The center of Paul's theology is not the Mosaic law or circumcision, as is the case with his opponents, but the Risen One. Behind his gospel is the power of the resurrection. The power in the true gospel is exclusively centered on the Lord, who was raised as the firstfruits for God's people (1 Cor 15:20, 23) and inaugurated the new age of the Spirit and the church. When the Galatians surrendered to the false teachings of the Judaizers and

---

2. Ananias (Acts 9:10–19) and Barnabas (Acts 9:27) clarified Christ's message to Paul, but neither commissioned him.

returned to the law, they were rejecting this new age and the law's fulfillment in Christ for the mere promise of the Mosaic ordinances.

Paul frequently greets his readers on behalf of one or more associates (for instance, 1 Cor 1:1; 2 Cor 1:1). Only here in verse 2, however, does he send greetings from "all the brothers and sisters with me," an amorphous group rather than a list of specific individuals. This could refer to all his associates, which would make sense since he regularly mentions his ministry team in the salutations of his letters. However, "brothers and sisters" elsewhere in Paul's letters always refers to all the saints. Construed in this way, this would suggest that Paul is talking about all the believers, including those in Jerusalem who would soon side with him at the Jerusalem Council (Acts 15). He wants to present a united front as he addresses the problems in Galatia.

In other letters Paul commends his readers and describes them further; see, for example, 1 Corinthians 1:2, "to those sanctified in Christ Jesus and called to be his holy people." Here his address is "to the churches in Galatia"—the churches of South Galatia that Paul had founded on the first missionary journey (Acts 13–14).[3] His terse identification of his audience is likely an implicit rebuke, suggesting in effect that there was little for which he could commend them at that point.

THE SALUTATION AND POWER OF THE CROSS (1:3–5)

This was Paul's first letter, and the salutation he uses here would become standard in all his letters. It builds on the basic pattern in ancient greetings, with "grace" (*charis*) the Greco-Roman hello and "peace" (*eirēnē*, the Greek version of the Hebrew *shalom*) the Jewish hello. Paul infuses both with Christian content and turns them into fulfilled promises, saying in effect, "The grace you have always wanted and the peace you have always hoped for are now offered to you by God and Christ." Grace is the New Testament

3. See "Recipients and Date" in the introduction.

concept at the heart of God's plan ("It is by grace you have been saved," Eph 2:5, 8), and peace plays a similar role, summarizing the Old Testament promises of shalom, as well as the New Testament hope ("Peace I leave with you; my peace I give you," John 14:27). In Christ, all human yearning and hope can finally be realized.

A key phrase in Galatians is "God the Father," which appears three times in this opening section (1:1, 3, 4). Paul emphasizes that the saints have become the children of God through adoption and now have a loving, merciful Father who cares for them and is involved deeply in their lives (Rom 8:14-17). Paul next stresses the lordship of Christ, who is sovereign over his creation (see Col 1:16, 20 for Christ as the agent of creation).

In verse 4 Paul makes clear that the only hope for sinful humankind lies in Christ's atoning sacrifice, and it is he who will bring this evil world to its deserved end and open the gates of eternity for the faithful. The gospel is encapsulated in the trumpet call of victory and salvation: "who gave himself for our sins." This is the means by which God's grace and peace are made available to us, echoing Isaiah 53:6 ("the LORD has laid on him the iniquity of us all") and 53:12 ("he poured out his life unto death ... [and] bore the sin of many").

This is one of the primary themes of the letter—that salvation comes to us not by means of the law but entirely by the atoning sacrifice of Christ on the cross. Paul's words here could be a fragment of an early Christian creed, but it is more likely that Paul himself wrote them to emphasize the voluntary nature of Christ's sacrifice. Jesus died "for our sins"; while the preposition (hyper) could mean "on behalf of," in material like this it often incorporates the idea of substitution. This is the basis of the doctrine of substitutionary atonement—that Jesus, the only righteous One, died on the cross as our substitute, so that our sins could be forgiven based on his sinlessness.

Christ did this to "rescue us from the present evil age." The idea of rescue is taken from the exodus, which is often spoken of as God "delivering" or "saving" his people from the Egyptians (see, for example, Exod 18:8-10). Later the terminology came to be used of God's future delivery of his people in the messianic age to come (Isa 31:5). Here that promise comes to full fruition, for in Jesus God has rescued his people "from the present evil age."

Scripture speaks of "this age" (as opposed to "the age to come," see Eph 1:21), the present age that remains under the control of evil and the ways of this world (Eph 2:2). The difference Christ's sacrifice and resurrection have made, however, even in this age, is that God's people have been granted authority over the cosmic forces of evil (Mark 3:15; 6:7) and given divine strength to overcome these opposing forces (Rom 8:37; Eph 6:10-12). Paul's reference to the present evil age foreshadows his argument in the central section of the book (Gal 3-4), in which he will clarify that the law belongs to the old dispensation that the age of Christ has culminated (or "ended," Rom 10:5). Christ has fulfilled the law (see Matt 5:17-20), and believers live in Christ rather than under the law.

This rescue from the present age has been accomplished "according to the will of our God and Father" (Gal 1:4) The incarnation of Christ, his redemptive and atoning death on behalf of humanity, and his victorious resurrection all resulted from God's will. When God created this world he knew that it would succumb to evil, and he predestined the coming of Christ to save it from the power of sin. The entire Bible is dedicated to tracing God's rescue of this world by first giving the law and then detailing its fulfillment in the coming, death, and resurrection of Christ, which together constitute a single redemptive event in salvation history.

As often happens when Paul makes a key point that gets at the core of the gospel, here in verse 5 he is overcome by the enormity of the truth and breaks out in doxological praise. After discussing the love and grace of God and the redemptive sacrifice of Christ, he lifts his voice in worshipful praise to the glory of God for his gift of salvation in Christ.

The glory of God is a defining theme of Scripture, as the heavenly scenes of Isaiah 6 and Revelation 4 demonstrate. All that he has done in creation and redemption attests to his majesty and splendor. The concept of **Shekinah**, seen during the time of the Israelites' wilderness wanderings in the pillar of fire by night and the cloud by day, indicated the glory of God "dwelling" (Hebrew: *shakan*) among his people. When the tabernacle was dedicated, a cloud covered it (Num 9:15–23), signifying the Shekinah glory entering God's house. In John 1:14, this divine glory is pictured as having dwelt among us in Christ: "The Word became flesh and made his dwelling [or 'tabernacled'] among us." Paul's prayer here is for this glory to be eternal, "forever and ever," reflected in the eradication of evil and the wondrous eternal glory of the heavenly home awaiting.

PAUL IS WRITING TO EXPOSE THE DANGER TO THE GALATIANS (1:6–10)

THE DANGER: TURNING TO A FALSE GOSPEL (1:6–7)

Paul expresses horror at the disturbing news he has received about the Galatians, using an expression of amazement: "I am astonished." In the Gospels this verb describes the awe or wonder of those who witness the miracles of Jesus, but here Paul uses it negatively to convey his shock at hearing about their abandonment of the true faith. When he speaks of the Galatians "so quickly deserting," he probably means so soon after their conversion. This echoes Exodus 32:8, where after the golden calf incident God condemned the people who had been so "quick to turn away from what I commanded." Similarly, in Judges 2:17 the Israelites "prostituted themselves to other gods" and "quickly turned from the ways of their ancestors." Like the Israelites, the Galatians had become a new set of wilderness wanderers.

They were not simply deserting Paul's gospel teaching but were turning away from "the one who called you to live in the grace of Christ"—from God the Father, whose will in verse 4 led to their rescue from evil. It is one thing to turn from Paul but quite another to turn away from (the meaning of "desert") God, who in his mercy had seen fit to call them from the sin of this world to the grace of Christ. While they assumed that their strict adherence to the law would draw them nearer to God, it was having the opposite effect! The grace of God in Christ is at the center of the doctrine of salvation in this letter, and this salvation centers on the cross. By turning away from God the Galatians were not living in the grace of Christ as they had been called to do.

The key problem of the Galatians was that through being swayed by the Judaizing false teachers they were in the process of "turning to another gospel." Note the progress of the action in verse 6—they were not only "turning away" from God but "turning to"[4] another gospel. As we will see in verse 7, this "gospel" of Paul's opponents was not truly a gospel, though it was being proclaimed as such, and the Galatians were beginning to accept it as truth. Paul demands that they realize it has no connection with the gospel of Christ and is actually "another gospel."

The word "gospel" in its noun and verb form occurs fifteen times in Galatians (five times in this introductory section alone: 6, 7, twice in 8, 9). In both Hellenistic and Jewish contexts the term meant "good news." In the Old Testament it refers to the proclamation of new kingdom realities, and is prominent in Isaiah (40:9; 41:27; 52:7–10; 60:6; 61:1). Both there and in the New Testament it refers not only the coming of salvation in Christ but also to the arrival of the kingdom of God, and both thrusts are present here. God is altogether absent from the so-called gospel of these heretics; in reality, the gifts of salvation and the kingdom blessings come only through Christ and the cross, not through the law.

---

4.   The change does not come from separate verbs but from a change of prepositions—they were turning "from" (*apo*) God "to" (*eis*) another gospel. The NIV paraphrase "and are turning to" captures this well.

I have earlier described the history and purpose of the Juda-izers,[5] but a summary will prove helpful here as well. The descrip-tive term "Judaizers" is used of a group of Jewish Christians who wanted to make all Christians practitioners of Judaism.[6] Rejecting the conclusion of the Jerusalem Council in Acts 15, they continued to believe that Gentile converts to Christianity had to become Jews before they could become Christians. For them, becoming circum-cised and following all Torah (the Mosaic law) regulations was necessary for Christians to attain salvation. In effect, they were replacing the cross with the law. This group had sent missionar-ies to the Christians in Asia Minor whom Paul had evangelized on his first missionary journey (Acts 13–14) to convince them that Paul was wrong and to get them to join the Judaizing movement in the church.

In response to all of this, in verse 7 Paul goes so far as to strongly correct even his own language in verse 6. Theirs was not simply a "different gospel" but was "really no gospel at all." There is in fact nothing "good" about the "news" they have brought. There is only one true gospel, and its declaration of good news is clear in all apostolic proclamation (as preserved for us in the pages of the New Testament). To replace the atoning sacrifice of Christ on the cross with anything else—even the law—as the basis for salvation is heresy.[7] This is critically important for us today, when many so-called churches are looking to alternate sources—such as good works or adherence to certain church practices—for salvation. It is imperative that we center on the cardinal truths of Christian doctrine and continue to fight the good fight (1 Tim 1:18; 2 Tim 4:7)

---

5.   See "Occasion and Opponents" in the introduction.

6.   The closest we come to this term is in Gal 2:14, where "to follow Jewish customs" is *ioudaïzein*, rendered "to Judaize." This means the Judaizers wanted to compel Gentiles to "follow Jewish customs" or "live like Jews."

7.   The word "heresy" comes from the Greek *heteros*, meaning "another." Any "other" claim to salvation is by definition heresy.

for sound doctrine (1 Tim 1:10; 2 Tim 4:3). This will be an application theme throughout this commentary.

The Judaizers were doing two things: "throwing you into confusion and ... trying to pervert the gospel of Christ." The first verb (*tarassō*) means to "trouble" or "disturb" others. These people had become agitators. They had infiltrated these Galatian churches, claiming to wield authority from the Jewish Christian leaders in Jerusalem, and brought confusion. In doing this they were trying to "pervert" or "distort" the true gospel of the cross of Christ. Paul's language shows that they had not yet fully succeeded but were in the process of winning over many of the Galatians. The "gospel of Christ" likely carries here a double meaning: both the gospel that Christ proclaimed and the gospel about Christ. These opponents were preaching a false gospel, distorted by their replacement of Christ's sacrificial death on the cross with the centrality of circumcision and the law as the basis for salvation.

THE INVOCATION OF THE DIVINE CURSE (1:8–9)

In this verse Paul strongly portrays the severity of the heresy, trying to get across how serious the situation had become. It is critical that the church differentiate between doctrinal disagreement, on which we debate but agree to disagree, and teaching that is clearly false, against which we as orthodox Christians must go to war. Actual heresy alters and distorts (v. 7) the true gospel and undermines the very basis of the Christian faith. Paul is convinced that the Judaizing movement is heretical, and so he strongly states the consequences. The Judaizers knew the "gospel of Christ," for it had been clearly explained to them in the apostolic preaching of Paul and his team. There was no doubt about the truth of the gospel, and anyone who deviated from divine truths would "be under God's curse." This translates the Greek *anathema*, which has become an English term for "accursed." In Scripture it includes being cut off from the community and condemned and destroyed at the judgment seat of God (Exod 22:20; Lev 27:29; 1 Cor 16:22). Nothing could be more serious.

This law is so sacred that it covers even the heavenly realm, for Paul includes angels from heaven in the divine curse for preaching another gospel. Some think this means that these opponents had claimed to receive their message directly from angels, but there is no indication of this in the text. A likely parallel from 3:19, "the law was given through angels," refers to the Jewish belief that angels mediated the giving of the Torah on Sinai. Paul could also have had in mind the fallen angels; Revelation 12:4 says that one third of the angels followed Satan in rebellion and were cast from heaven to earth as their prison house. Other New Testament texts regard the philosophies of false teachers to be demonically inspired, and these fallen angels, still active in their rebellion against divine truth, are even today operating in earth's false religions and in heresies like that of the Judaizers (2 Cor 11:13-14; 1 Tim 4:1; Jas 3:15).

Paul is saying that these Judaizers and their followers are no longer Christians and will come under eternal punishment at the last judgment. This is just as serious a warning for us today. We dare not allow a shallow theology in our churches that makes it possible for some to pursue serious deviations from divine revelation.

Paul's Model: Not Trying to Please People (1:10)

The final part of Paul's rebuke implicitly charges the Galatians with lowering their standards by trying to please the agitators rather than God. Paul makes himself a model for his readers, asking, "Am I now trying to win the approval of human beings, or of God?" Paul would never allow himself to be influenced by a desire to be liked and to curry favor with others. Truth was infinitely more important to him than popularity. So he asks a second time, "Am I trying to please people?" The implied answer is clear: "Not in any way." The implication is that the Galatians were doing just that in acceding to the Judaizers' heresy.

Yet Paul's opponents *were* accusing him of aiming to please people. They charged that he was failing to preach the full gospel (which they believed had to center on circumcision and the law, as well as on Christ) in order to please Gentiles—an accusation he emphatically denied. If any charge were to have been baseless and ridiculous from the beginning, this would have been the one. Paul lived, heart and soul, to please the Lord and challenged others to do the same, referring to the issue frequently (as in Rom 12:1-2; 1 Cor 7:32; 1 Thess 4:1).

This is his point in the last part of this verse: "If I were still trying to please people, I would not be a servant of Christ." A better translation than "servant" of the word *doulos* in this context would be "slave." Paul not only refrained in every way from seeking to please others but, quite to the contrary, completely surrendered himself to Christ as a bond-slave—a person who chose slavery over freedom and voluntarily gave himself over to his master. Romans 6:20-22 tells us that Christ's death has redeemed us from the slavery of sin and purchased us to be "slaves of God." Sin had been an evil, torturous taskmaster, but God is a loving, caring master, so that we, too, place ourselves in willing servitude to him as his bond-slaves. Just as slaves were part of the family of their owner, we become members of the family of God.

While subservience is part of Paul's point, there was also in his day an elevated air to calling oneself the *doulos* of someone great, for high government officials viewed themselves as slaves of the emperor. Paul showed his preference for serving God by relinquishing his high status in Judaism (see Phil 3:4-7) to become a persecuted preacher of the Christian gospel and to suffer egregious abuse for his Lord and for his faith (Gal 5:11; 6:17; 2 Cor 11:23-27). This was not a person who lived for the plaudits of others.

———

The opening of this letter, while following ordinary letter-writing protocol, goes far beyond to highlight both the authority of Paul as apostle (speaking with authority from God) and salvation by Christ alone via his death on the cross (not by the law). In Christ the new age has arrived, and with him this world moves toward its intended end. The glory of God is uppermost, and God's people must center upon that which leads to the praise and pleasure of God and Christ rather than of self or others. Based on their capitulation to the false views of the Judaizers, the Galatians were not doing this. In our day, too, we must make certain that we do not allow false theology to destroy our usefulness to God and endanger our relationship with him.

Paul's rebuke of the Galatians begins with verses 6–10. The issues could not have been more important. Failing to guard the essential doctrines of the faith and allowing alternative teachings about Christ and salvation to sneak in to the church will destroy the Christian faith and lead both the purveyors and the adherents of false religion to eternal judgment. There is no such thing as a "different" gospel; anything that departs from the one true gospel is no gospel at all. It is heresy.

Paul's message to those of us in Christian leadership positions is that we *must* become teachers of God's truths and lead our churches into the exciting world of biblical teaching. There is far too much shoddy preaching from Christian leaders who seek to entertain rather than to train. Those who do this are preaching to "itching ears" (2 Tim 4:3), telling the congregation what they want to hear rather than what God would have them hear.

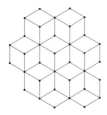

THE DIVINE SOURCE OF PAUL'S GOSPEL (1:11–24)

In verses 6-10 Paul began the transition to the body of his thesis. He introduces his primary argument in two stages: first he asserted that the gospel of the **Judaizers** was no gospel at all but a distorted pack of lies (vv. 6-10); now he states that the gospel he preaches is of divine origin, the result of revelation f God (vv 11-12). He proves this in the rest of this section by tracing his own history (1) from his Damascus road vision (vv. 13-17); (2) to his initial failure to seek the approval of others, including the disciples (vv. 18-24), proving that his authority was from God rather than of human derivation; (3) to its recognition and acceptance by the three pillars of the church (2:1-10); and (4) to its substantiation when Paul corrected Peter in Antioch (vv. 11-21). Paul proclaims "the gospel of Christ" (1:7) as the only gospel.

PAUL'S GOSPEL ORIGINATED IN A REVELATION FROM CHRIST (1:11–12)

NOT OF HUMAN ORIGIN (1:11–12A)

Paul connects this paragraph to verses 6-10 with a *gar* ("for"), which could be causal (giving a reason for his previous point) or explanatory (clarifying his previous point). The latter is more likely. The opening "I want you to know [about] the gospel I preached" closely parallels the creedal quote of 1 Corinthians 15:1:

"I want to remind [literally, 'make known to'] you of the gospel I preached to you." He is saying that this gospel of Christ (Gal 1:7) is not optional or subject to change. It is at the heart of all Christian truth, stemming from God and recognized by the church as creedal and essential. It is not "of human origin" but comes entirely from the Godhead. As I pointed out at verse 10, Paul's language here may reflect a charge the Judaizers had made against him—that he had made up his own gospel to curry favor with the Gentiles, who would not then have had to be circumcised or follow the law. He denies this vociferously. There is nothing human about his gospel; it is divine truth.

The next phrase, "I did not receive it from any man" (v. 12), seems to contradict 1 Corinthians 15:3, "what I received I passed on to you"—code language among rabbis for the passing on of official tradition. Paul's point is that his gospel did not derive from church tradition, nor had he received it secondhand from the Jerusalem apostles, as he had the stories of Jesus' appearances from eyewitnesses (1 Cor 15:3–8). The gospel he proclaimed came straight from God himself, with no intervening steps. To reinforce this point he adds, "nor was I taught it." Paul is not implying that he had learned nothing from the other apostles; indeed, throughout his letters he frequently quotes church teaching he has received. He is specifically stating that he has not been taught the gospel itself through any human agency. His apostolic commission and his reception of the truths of the gospel came directly from the Lord, with no involvement from the other apostles.

THE TRUE SOURCE: REVELATION FROM JESUS CHRIST (1:12B)

Paul had sat in no classes, nor had he sat under any Christian teacher. The gospel had been given to him directly by "revelation from Jesus Christ." There is a question whether this should be interpreted as general revelation or as a specific revelation. The latter is more likely, referring to the specific revelation Paul had received from Jesus on the Damascus road (Acts 9, 22, 26). There is also a question whether this was "a revelation from Jesus" (subjective, emphasizing Christ's message in the vision) or "a revelation about Jesus" (objective, emphasizing the vision itself). It is likely that Paul is using here a "general genitive" in the Greek, where both aspects are emphasized. The objective is seen in verse 16, where Paul claims that God had revealed Jesus to him, and the subjective in Jesus' giving of the gospel to Paul.

It is difficult to determine how much meaning to read into "revelation" (*apokalypsis*), since this word normally has **eschatological** overtones dealing with the unveiling of God's heavenly secrets about the last days. It is unlikely that Paul was thinking here of the second coming and the end of this age. Rather, he appears to be saying that the giving of the gospel is part of the inauguration of the age to come, the age that began with Christ's incarnation. In the back of his mind may have been the kingdom truths represented by Mark 1:15, which summarizes Jesus' message as "The time has come. The kingdom of God has come near. Repent and believe the good news!" The main emphasis here, however, is on the Damascus road vision of Christ, who called Paul to be an apostle and revealed to him these gospel truths.

PAUL RECOUNTS HIS CONVERSION AND EARLY FAILURE TO CONSULT OTHERS (1:13–17)

His Past Animosity (1:13–14)

These verses begin with another *gar* ("for"), showing that Paul is continuing his explanation from verse 11, clarifying that his gospel is not of human origin. In order to prove that only God could have brought about his conversion and commission as the apostle to the Gentiles. Paul recalls his history of devotion to Judaism and his hostility toward everything Christian, reminding the Galatians that they had heard the story before and were already quite familiar with his personal history. He had told them of his past persecution when he founded the church in Galatia.

Persecution of the church (1:13)

Paul had made a clean break with his previous attitudes and actions, which he considered to be entirely in his past. That, in fact, is one of his main points: The Judaizers and their views are part of that past, and he wants the Galatians to know that their views have no part in the present life or beliefs of the church. But when Paul speaks of his "previous way of life in Judaism" he does not mean that he stopped being Jewish and became a Gentile. In fact, Acts 21:26-29 shows that he continued to observe many aspects of the sacrificial system and never repudiated his Jewish background. Rather, he was a *Jewish Christian*. The law had stopped having salvific force, and he was part of the new covenant reality rather than the old. When he performed a sacrifice or followed a purity law, he did so from the perspective of one who followed the Messiah.

Paul had been deeply committed to the Judaism of his day, with its beliefs and practices. As an extremely zealous and strict orthodox Jew (Acts 26:5) he had considered Christianity an aberration and an abomination. As long as Paul and others allowed this upstart and dangerous new sect to exist, he had reasoned, God would look upon the nation with extreme displeasure. So Paul had felt impelled to so "intensely persecute the church of God"[1] as to "destroy it." Paul's zealous oppression of the Christians is often chronicled in Acts. We see it in Acts 7:58-8:1 (the stoning of Stephen); 8:1-3 (the great persecution in Jerusalem); and 9:1-2, 13-14 (his possession of letters from the Sanhedrin allowing him to lead the persecution outside Palestine). He was even instrumental in the imprisonment and execution of several believers (22:4, 19; 26:10-11), leading the charge in such attempts until his conversion on the Damascus road. No wonder many Christians were afraid to trust his conversion (9:26), certain that it was a ruse to suck them in and leave them vulnerable to even more persecution.

---

1. By adding "of God" Paul shows that in reality the church, rather than Judaism, belonged to God; the church, not the Judaism of his day, was "of God."

Zeal for Judaism (1:14)

Paul's deep commitment to his Jewish heritage had undoubtedly begun in his childhood. Students began preparing for rabbinic training while small children and then went into formal training after the age of thirteen, when they had reached maturity according to Jewish custom. Paul was gifted enough to qualify for rabbinic training under the tutelage of Gamaliel (Acts 22:3), the grandson of Hillel (the leading rabbi of first-century Judaism) and to assume leadership in higher circles while he was still quite young.

The reason for Paul's rapid advancement is that he "was extremely zealous for the traditions of my fathers." This does not mean that he was a Zealot, a member of the group of Jewish rebels (political insurgents more than religious leaders) whose activities would eventually lead to the First Jewish Revolt in AD 66–70. Paul was instead speaking of religious zeal for Jewish traditions, including not just the Mosaic regulations but also the oral Torah (the "tradition of the elders" of Mark 7:3, 5)—that set of extra laws developed by the scribes and Pharisees to enable adherents to apply the general laws more specifically to different situations. Being zealous for the law meant being jealous for Judaism, and Paul's ardent persecution of Christians was a natural outgrowth of this zeal. This same fanatical fervor had led orthodox Jews to the Maccabean revolt in 167 BC, to the development of both Pharisaism and the Qumran movement (the keepers of the Dead Sea Scrolls), and to Paul's own extreme activities against Christians.

HIS APOSTOLIC CALL (1:15–16A)

Paul returns to the issue of his apostolic authority and adds detail to his proof that he was not subordinate to the Twelve and did not derive his ministry from their authority. Rather, he was independent of Jerusalem and equal to the other apostles; like them he derived his authority directly from Christ. Paul's authority began with his election, as he testifies that God "set me apart from my mother's womb and called me by his grace" to his apostolic ministry. This is a prophetic motif throughout Scripture for those who receive special calls for specific ministries, echoing Isaiah's declaration, "Before I was born the LORD called me; from my mother's womb he has spoken my name" (Isa 49:1), as well as Jeremiah 1:5, "Before I formed you in the womb I knew you, before you were born I set you apart." Paul recognized the prophetic aspects of his call and believed that God had brought him into this world for a single purpose. His sense of divine commissioning could hardly have been more pronounced.

While our callings may differ from Paul's, those Christians who assume that God is uninvolved in their lives could not be more wrong. Each of us is special to him and "called according to his purpose" (Rom 8:28). Paul's emphasis here is on the One who has "called me by his grace." Paul was well aware of how little he deserved his calling and acceptance as God's child; like him, we all must remind ourselves that "God does not need me; I need him." God's grace is totally beyond our capacity to understand. God, knowing in advance all the terrible things that Paul would do, had still called him before he was even born. He was not only forgiven but given a ministry he could never have imagined. That is the case with each of us if we will but surrender to God's calling and will for our lives, as Paul did.

The grace-gift is now specified (v. 16a): God was "pleased to reveal his son in me," a reference to Paul's Damascus road vision of Acts 9. It brought God pleasure to call Paul to himself (compare 1 Thess 2:8, "delighted to share with you"). Note the stages of revelation: God revealed Christ in the redemptive vision on the road to Damascus (Gal 1:12), and then Christ revealed to Paul the gospel and his mission to the Gentiles (v. 16). Paul was hardly able to recognize Christ on his own; he had majored in anti-Christian activity for several years and had convinced himself that Jesus was the anti-messiah. But God in his infinite mercy and grace revealed the full reality of the One Paul opposed, proving to Paul that he was deeply loved by the very One he so hated.

It is an interesting question whether *en emoi* in verse 16 should be translated as "*in me*" (the literal thrust of the Greek) or as "*to me*" (more natural in the context). Is the emphasis on the internal change in Paul (*in me*) or on the vision itself (*to me*)? Likely the revelation to Paul is implicit in the verb itself, and the unusual language "in me" should be taken literally as a reference to the internal change in Paul—his conversion. It is hard to imagine a more complete transformation. Paul was transformed from a Christ-hater to a Christ-believer, then to a Christ-worshipper, and finally to a missionary to the despised Gentiles—all as the result of a single vision! No wonder he had to spend the next three days blind and isolated in Damascus (Acts 9:8–9). It had taken him that long just to begin to process the radical alteration of everything he had ever stood for and thought.

Paul's calling was not only to come to Christ but also to "preach him among the Gentiles." The emphasis here is not ontological (his becoming a Christ-follower), but functional (to proclaim the gospel to the Gentiles). There were three stages to this call to the Gentiles: (1) Jesus in the Damascus vision called him to be a "witness" and stated that he would be sent to the Gentiles "to open their eyes and turn them from darkness" (Acts 26:15–18). (2) In Damascus Ananias showed Paul that Christ had made him his "chosen instrument to proclaim my name to the Gentiles" (9:15). And (3) during his later visit to Jerusalem God confirmed this in a temple vision, saying, "Go, I will send you far away to the Gentiles" (22:21). This last revelation must have come as more of a shock to Paul than had his own response of turning from Judaism to Christianity, for Jewish aversion to Gentiles could not have been more deeply ingrained—it was religious, ethnic, political, and as ancient as Israel's very founding as a people.

It took quite a while for the church to understand and accept God's will regarding the Gentiles. Early Jewish Christians interpreted the Great Commission (Matt 28:18–20) to "go disciple the nations" through the lens of Jewish proselyte theology. This

understanding led them to remain in Jerusalem (Acts 1–7) waiting for the Gentiles to come to them via Isaiah's procession of the
nations to Zion (Isa 60:1–11). God had to send them out in spite of
their entrenched reluctance through various means: the persecution of Acts 8:1–3, the mission to the Samaritans (vv. 4–25), the
conversion of the Ethiopian eunuch (vv. 26–40), the conversion of
Saul/Paul as the apostle to the Gentiles (Acts 9), and the conversion of Cornelius (Acts 10). Paul was commissioned to spearhead
a radical change of heart on the part of the Jerusalem Christians.
This in itself separated him from the Twelve; for a long time they
had no clue about the Gentile mission, as the steps toward it in
Acts 7–11 make clear.

His Decision Not to Consult Others (1:16b–17)

After his conversion and its astonishing revelation one would
think that Paul would have looked up the apostles and other
Christian leaders to get their advice and confirmation of this total
turnaround that God had demanded of him. It is quite surprising
that he didn't, and this must have been due to the leading of the
Lord. Paul's point here is that both the content of the message
and the affirmation of his call came strictly from God and were
so clear that he needed no help in the process of coming to understand them. So he didn't need to "consult" (Greek: *prosanatithēmi*)
anyone, with the verb meaning not only to seek advice to interpret
it properly but also to legitimate its authenticity. Both of these
capacities came from Christ, and he needed nothing further.

Moreover, he did not "go up to Jerusalem" to meet with the
other apostles. At one level the Christians of Jerusalem were not
ready to meet their archenemy who was behind so much of the
misery, imprisonment, and death they had experienced. When
Paul did make his way to Jerusalem three years later (v. 18), many
were still terrified of him and could not accept the reality of his
conversion (Acts 9:26). While true, that is not Paul's point here. His

point is that he needed no confirmation or further interpretation from them, for the vision itself provided all he needed.

Rather, he set out in the opposite direction and "went into Arabia," returning to Damascus about three years later (v. 18). The Arabia spoken of here surrounded Palestine to the north, east, and south and included parts of Syria, Transjordan, and the Negev. The term would especially have indicated the kingdom of the Nabatean Arabs, a Roman colony whose king, Aretas, acted against Paul in 2 Corinthians 11:32. Some think that Paul went to Arabia to put some distance between himself and his former life and to meditate on his new relationship to God and Christ, as well as on his calling to proclaim the gospel to the Gentiles. In particular, many speculate that he spent time at Mount Sinai, reflecting on the relationship between the Mosaic law and the new, kingdom truths of Christ. Certainly this may have been part of the picture, but there had to have been more to account for the lengthy duration of his stay, leading most interpreters to agree that Paul also began his missionary preaching ministry there.

ON HIS FIRST JERUSALEM VISIT, PAUL DID NOT SEEK THE APPROVAL OF THE APOSTLES OR THE CHURCH (1:18–24)

This lengthy stay in Arabia probably began as a period of reflection on Christ's call and the new life for Paul that this astounding revelation had unlocked. After these early stages he put Christ's plan into effect as missionary to the Gentiles, beginning with those in Arabia. Acts does not include this time in Arabia, preferring to center on Paul's stay in Damascus as a bridge to his return to Jerusalem. Acts 9:19–25 relates events that occurred on his return to Damascus, especially his preaching in the synagogues and debates with the Jews. Paul was in a sense continuing Stephen's ministry from Acts 7.

TIME IN JERUSALEM: MET ONLY CEPHAS AND JAMES (1:18–20)

After Paul was forced to leave Damascus he did go to Jerusalem (Acts 9:26), where many of the believers were still afraid of him. The "three years" could mean either two or three (by Jewish reckoning it could mean "in the third year"), leading many to believe that Paul was converted in AD 32/33 and went to Jerusalem in about 34/35. This section reinforces the point from verse 10 that he did not seek anyone's approval, for all that mattered to him was pleasing God. Far from being subordinate to and dependent on the Twelve, as the Judaizers claimed, Paul had limited contact with them and did not even meet them until two or three years after his conversion and the official beginning of his ministry. And then his purpose was simply to meet with Peter.

Very short time with the two apostles (1:18–19)

"Cephas," the Aramaic term for "rock," translates the Greek *Petros* ("Peter"). Paul preferred the Aramaic form and used it often (1 Cor 1:12; 3:22; 9:5; 15:5),[2] possibly to stress Peter's Jewish background. He is emphasizing that his purpose in meeting with Cephas was to get to know him, not to be taught by him. Still, it would have been wonderful to be a fly on the wall as they shared their experiences and insights. What a fifteen days that must have been!

The only other apostle Paul mentions meeting was James, the Lord's brother (v. 19),[3] who is included among the four brothers and several sisters of Jesus mentioned in Mark 6:3. These could have been children of a previous marriage of Joseph but more

---

2. The only place in his writings Paul uses "Peter" is Gal 2:7, 8.

3. This could not have been James, John's brother who was martyred in Acts 11. Nor would it have been James the Younger, one of the Twelve (Mark 15:40), or James the father of Judas (Luke 6:16). Neither of these latter individuals was prominent enough to have warranted such exclusive recognition from Paul, who at any rate clearly identifies James here as "the Lord's brother."

likely were born of Mary as well and so would have been younger than Jesus. Mary was likely about fourteen years of age when Jesus was born—a normal age for marriage in that setting. James had by this point become the head elder and leader of the Jerusalem church, with a remarkable ministry to Christians and Jews alike. It must have felt strange to Paul to actually seek the acquaintance of these two former archenemies, the leaders of the church. I can only imagine that Paul was enamored with James, asking him question after question about having grown up with Jesus. The two men would have had a lot in common, for James, like Paul, had not become a believer until a resurrection appearance (1 Cor 15:7). James had gone through his childhood and early adulthood rejecting Jesus, as had Paul (John 7:5). The terse rendering of this verse implies that Paul's time with James was quite brief. The point again is that Paul wanted to get to know these men but did not come to solicit their imprimatur to authenticate his ministry.

There is some question whether James is designated an apostle here. It is possible to read this as, "I didn't see any other apostle; but I did see James, the Lord's brother." This would differentiate James from the apostles. However, this is not the more natural reading, which connects James with the others as one of them. The incident recorded here is probably the meeting of Acts 9:27–28, when Barnabas introduced Paul to "the apostles" (Luke there would have had Peter and James in mind). Paul told the story of the vision and his conversion and then spent time with them.

Oath regarding the truth of Paul's claims (1:20)

Paul begins verse 20 with a sacred oath, which strongly emphasizes the truthfulness of his story and serves as significant evidence that the Judaizers were disputing his connection to the apostles. An oath "before God" was often used in trials to anchor an official testimony, and it had a semi-technical air about it. Paul begins with *idou* ("behold, look," translated as "I assure you" in the NIV) to emphasize the solemnity of his oath formula here. He is saying that his anecdotes in verses 13–24 are not simple asides but official evidence against the accusations of his adversaries. His authority and the gospel he preaches stem absolutely from God and not from teaching he imbibed from the apostles.

Does this oath contradict Jesus' command "Do not swear an oath at all" (Matt 5:33–37)? At first glance it would seem so, but Jesus' context was frivolous oaths used to support empty promises. He was demanding that people abide by their word rather than make shallow pledges to do things about which they cared nothing. God himself makes an oath in Hebrews 7:20–22, 28, and Paul does so here and in Romans 1:9 and 2 Corinthians 1:23. Jesus did not condemn oaths uttered seriously with regard to important issues.

TIME IN JUDEA AND SYRIA: UNKNOWN TO THESE PEOPLE (1:21–24)

The next stage in Paul's original itinerary was ministry time in the neighboring region of Syria and Cilicia, which together constituted a Roman province north of Galilee. Damascus was in Syria, and Paul's hometown of Tarsus was in Cilicia. This time period is corroborated in Acts 9:30, where the believers in Judea sent Paul to Caesarea and then to Tarsus. What he did during this time is difficult to determine, for all we know from Galatians is that Paul remained in Tarsus until Barnabas came and persuaded him to accompany him fourteen years later (see 2:1). For a great deal of that time Paul must have engaged in missionary outreach and church planting, for in Acts 15:40–41 he and Silas go through these regions "strengthening the churches" he must have established in this earlier time.

This would mean that Paul spent eight to ten years in that region, until about AD 46/47, when he traveled to Jerusalem for the meeting described in Galatians 2:1–10, concurrent with the famine visit of Acts 11:27–30. His headquarters during that time was evidently his former home in Tarsus. The emphasis here is regional rather than political, for Syria and Cilicia are listed separately here and in the apostolic letter of Acts 15:23.

Not recognized in either region (1:21–22)

Paul "was personally unknown" (v. 22) to believers in Judea and (by implication) in Syria and Cilicia as well. The point is that he could not have gone to a region where no one knew him to secure official confirmation of his ministry. Paul cannot mean that he was unknown in those very places where his persecution of Christians had been rampant. Rather, he specifically means that after he had gone into Syria and Cilicia few had gotten to know him "personally." He cannot mean that no one in Judea knew of him, for Acts 9:26 tells of many who were afraid of him, and the next verse will say that people had heard reports of him. Paul surely means the majority could not recognize him by face, though they knew of his reputation.

There is a question as to whether "Judea" refers to the area that includes Samaria and Galilee or only to the specific region south of Samaria. The former is slightly more likely, for Paul is making sweeping statements. These churches were "in Christ," stressing their union with the Lord. Once more, the point is that Paul did not return to Jerusalem for official validation of his ministry.

Known only by report (1:23–24)

The Judean believers did not know Paul by sight, but they "kept hearing" the reports (the stress is on continuous news regarding him). The grapevine was filled with stories of how their former chief persecutor had been met by Christ and converted through the vision on the Damascus road (as in vv. 15–16). Paul did not return to Jerusalem for confirmation, but virtually everyone was doing just that as they circulated the news far and wide. Luke brings out the same point in Acts 9:21, where he relates the synagogue attenders asking rhetorically, "Isn't he the man who raised havoc in Jerusalem among those who call on this name?"

This former enemy "is now preaching the faith he once tried to destroy." "The faith" here is not subjective (believing in God) but objective (a specific reference to the Christian faith). The old Paul never considered it a faith but a danger to true faith. This is the new Paul speaking, and the religion he once sought to destroy is now the true set of beliefs to which one should adhere. Instead of denigrating and ostracizing its adherents, he is now preaching this faith as the true gospel.

The last point is important. Unlike the Judaizers, who had turned Paul's gospel into a false religion, the true believers "praised God because of [him]" (v. 24), echoing Isaiah 49:3 in the **Septuagint** (the Greek Old Testament), where God says of the Servant, "because of you I will be praised." Paul saw himself as a current servant of the Lord, similar to the figure in Isaiah 40-54. When the believers came to realize that God's hand was in Paul's ministry, they broke out in praise. Once again, the complaints of these false teachers have been proven baseless. Those whose eyes were opened to the truths of God not only agreed with Paul but praised the Lord for what he had accomplished and for his gospel message.

Note that they did not praise Paul himself, rightly acknowledging that the new message and movement were the work of God, not of any one person. They praised God on account of all that he had done in bringing Paul to conversion and designating him the apostle to the Gentiles, both of which were directly involved in the ministry in Galatia. The Greek reads "in me," but in this context it is best to construe this causally rather than as a reference to spiritual work in Paul himself.

———

Paul wrote this narrative as a rejoinder disproving his opponents' charge that he was preaching a human gospel copied from the Jerusalem apostles. But this is also important historical material that traces his early years in ministry and adds critical data not found in the account in Acts. It is clear that Paul's was a life well lived, and this passage constitutes a remarkable testimony to what happens when a person surrenders to God's will and allows him to dictate the ongoing details of their life.

The human versus the divine element of calling is a critical issue for all of us. We all must make sure that both the beginning and the end of our ministries is entirely centered on God rather than on our reputation or status among people. Too many Christian leaders are motivated more by the acceptance of others than by their desire to please God. The Judaizers accused Paul of this motivation, but the truth was quite the opposite. God alone was behind Paul's call, his office, and his gospel.

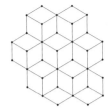

THE PILLARS ACCEPT PAUL
AS AN APOSTLE (2:1–10)

The next important part of the history of Paul's early years as a Christian took place after he had been ministering in Syria and Cilicia for several years (1:21). The "fourteen years" of 2:1 most likely refer to the years after Paul's conversion, meaning that he had spent eight to ten years ministering in Tarsus and the surrounding regions (see comments on 1:21). This means the events of chapter 2 transpired some time after those of chapter 1. There is a slightly different emphasis here as well. In chapter 1 the thrust is somewhat negative, centering on Paul's independence from the apostles and emphasizing that his gospel had not been derived from them. Here it is positive, on their approval of him: They recognized the validity of what he preached and taught. Paul's Gentile mission was erected on the foundation of the same gospel that underlay their Jewish mission.

PAUL TRAVELS WITH BARNABAS
TO JERUSALEM (2:1-5)

Acts 9:19-30 might give the impression that Paul didn't begin his ministry in earnest until he got to Antioch (Acts 11:25), for Luke is silent regarding his time in Arabia and then in Syria and Cilicia. But there is more background information in Galatians 1, where we learn that Paul spent two-plus years ministering in Arabia, followed by eight-plus years in Syria and Cilicia. This means Paul was an experienced leader by the time of this Jerusalem visit.

There is debate over which Jerusalem visit is indicated here—the famine visit of Acts 11:27–30 or the Jerusalem Council visit of Acts 15. This is closely tied to the question of whether this letter was written to South Galatia (before the Jerusalem Council, meaning that this would refer to the famine visit) or to North Galatia (during the third missionary journey, meaning that this would refer to the Council visit). The issue was discussed in the introduction, and here I will presuppose my conclusion there, in which I expressed my preference for the South Galatian hypothesis.[1] This would mean that Galatians was written before the Jerusalem Council, so the famine visit was the most recent visit Paul had made.

The fourteen years Paul mentions, then, evidently measured the time from his conversion to the famine visit, from AD 32/33 to 46/47.[2] It is doubtful that Paul would have failed to mention an important Jerusalem visit and gone straight to the Jerusalem Council, for he has been fairly chronologically complete in Galatians 1–2, and the famine visit makes a great deal of sense here. There were two purposes for that trip: (1) Acts 11 makes clear that, based on Agabus' prophetic prediction of a coming famine, the saints in Antioch had collected money and sent aid with Barnabas and Saul to relieve the poor. (2) Galatians 2 shows that Paul and the three pillars (vv. 8–9) took this opportunity to meet, with the result that they recognized and accepted Paul's Gentile ministry.

We first meet Barnabas in Acts 4:36, where he is reported to have sold a piece of property and given the money to the apostles

---

1.   See "Recipients and Date" in the introduction.

2.   Many date Paul's conversion in 31/32 and the famine relief visit in 44/45. There is no consensus on this issue. My dates are approximate.

to aid the poor. He somehow befriended Paul from the outset and introduced him in Acts 9:27 to the apostles and the church. After Paul's eight-plus years of ministry in Cilicia, Barnabas brought him to Antioch (Acts 11:25-26). While there, Barnabas and Paul led the famine relief collection and delivered the gifts to Jerusalem, accompanied by Paul's assistant Titus. The following year Barnabas led the first missionary journey with Paul (Acts 13-14). The two split before the second missionary journey, however, over Paul's decision not to allow John Mark to accompany them (Acts 15:36-41), and Barnabas was later shown to have been correct about Mark's potential (though Paul may have been right not to bring him along at that earlier time).

Titus was an important coworker, prominent later in Corinth (2 Cor 2:13; 7:6-14; 8:6, 16-23), and the recipient of one of Paul's letters. He is noted here because of the issue of his circumcision (v. 3), a major topic of debate with the **Judaizers**. Titus, a Greek, had never been circumcised, so there were complaints from some Jewish Christians. Paul uses him here as a case in point to verify that God no longer required the covenant rite of circumcision—something the true church already recognized.

The Purpose: Presentation of the Gospel
He Preaches to the Gentiles (2:1-2)

In verse 2 Paul explains the reason for his visit. He does not want to give ammunition to the Judaizers by saying that he needed the approval of the Twelve, so he explains carefully that he "went in response to a revelation"—God had directed him to go in another vision, and he was obeying God rather than seeking to win the favor of people or responding to a demand from the apostles to present his gospel to them for validation. Another revelation, Agabus' prophecy about the famine, led to the Antiochian church sending the team with aid for the Palestinian churches, and Paul's revelation was likely a second directive from the Lord.[3] Perhaps this second revelation was responsible for the Antiochian church's choice of Barnabas and Saul (Paul) to take the gift to Jerusalem.

News of Paul's lengthy and successful ministry to Gentiles in Syria and Cilicia would likely have reached Jerusalem. The leaders of the church there would naturally have been interested in talking to him about this, so a private meeting "with those esteemed as leaders" makes sense. This group of leaders would have consisted of the apostles and elders of the churches, of whom the three "pillars" (2:9)—James, Cephas (Peter), and John—were central. The NIV indicates a single meeting, but some think a public gathering was followed by a private meeting with the leaders. A literal translation would be, "I presented to them the gospel that I preached among the Gentiles, and I did so privately to those esteemed as leaders." This does not necessarily indicate two meetings, so the NIV captures the language well. At any rate, Paul wants the leaders on his side in this critical controversy.

"Those esteemed" means those "of high reputation" among the Jerusalem Christians, and Paul uses this language to stress the high regard these pillars enjoyed among all the churches. This emphasis is critical for convincing the Galatian Christians that the true Jewish Christians of renown were not the Judaizers but the apostles and elders who were on Paul's side.

So Paul brought before them for their careful consideration "the gospel that [he] preached among the Gentiles." His purpose was to make certain that in his gospel preaching he "was not running and had not been running [his] race in vain." This analogy of a race depicts the ongoing Christian struggle for an effective

---

3. Some think that there was only one vision and that Agabus was responsible for both revelations. The issue cannot be proven either way. To me it seems more likely that Paul received his own separate vision.

Christian life, in this case Paul's own ministry to the Gentiles (Gal 5:7; 1 Cor 9:26; Phil 2:16; Heb 12:1-3). It is likely that they would also have discussed in this meeting Paul's apostolic office, as he had never himself walked with the Lord or fulfilled the criteria for an apostle listed in Acts 1:21-22. His Damascus road vision and call would have been essential for proving the validity of his calling.

It is surprising that Paul says he "wanted to be sure," since this could be understood to suggest that Paul doubted his own preaching and was afraid that his form of the gospel might be mistaken. That, however, is impossible, for his entire argument throughout Galatians 1-2 is that God gave him his gospel. It had divine authority behind it. It is not only absolutely correct; any other form of the gospel is under "God's curse" (1:8-9). So in his request Paul is not thinking of the validity of his gospel but of the implications for the church.

If the apostles had sided with the Judaizers against the gospel God had revealed to Paul, a rift would have developed between Gentile and Jewish Christians that would invariably have split the church. "In vain" signifies being emptied of true significance and divine blessing. In Philippians 2:14-16 Paul states that the effects of his ministry in Philippi will be nullified if dissension ripped apart the Philippian church. Here it is the unity of the church and the power of the gospel to hold the church together that would be nullified. It is not the gospel itself that is endangered but the work of Paul among the Gentiles and the relationships among Gentile and Jewish Christians.

CIRCUMCISION NOT REQUIRED (2:3-5)

Paul likely mentioned Titus in verse 1 as part of the famine relief team specifically to prepare his readers for the point discussed here. Since Titus had grown up "Greek," that is, a Gentile, he had never been circumcised. And when he was in Jerusalem in the midst of this controversy over the Judaizers and the place of the law in the church, none of the apostles or leaders required him to be circumcised. His situation thus became a practical example of the debate with the Judaizers. After the Jerusalem leaders had heard Paul's arguments and understood his gospel, they agreed that Titus should not be compelled to undergo circumcision, the Old Testament covenant rite that was required to convert to Judaism. This is Paul's roundabout way of pointing out the Jerusalem leaders' agreement that he was right and his gospel correct.

The Titus determination was one of those landmark decisions in the history of a movement that helps define its future. This situation became a **proleptic** preparation for the Jerusalem Council and helped to prepare the way for its sweeping decision. Precedent had been set: The gospel existed apart from the law and its regulations, proven by the fact that the Gentile Titus did not have to be circumcised to be a Christian.

Later Paul would have Timothy circumcised (Acts 16:3). At first glance this seems contradictory, but there are significant differences from the Titus incident. Timothy was Jewish (he had a Jewish mother and a Gentile father), and Paul's decision was motivated not by issues of salvation but for the purpose of ministry: Paul wanted Timothy to be accepted by the Jews with and to whom he ministered. The issue with Titus was quite different. Paul refused to circumcise Titus because this would have contradicted the law-free nature of the gospel, but he did circumcise Timothy because doing so enhanced his gospel ministry in that context.

In verse 4 Paul proceeds to tell the story behind the Titus incident of verse 3, and this serves to illustrate the recognition of the validity of Paul's gospel to the Gentiles. Some "false believers" had snuck in and "infiltrated [their] ranks" to disrupt the proceedings. It is difficult to ascertain exactly who they were, whether Pharisaic Jews or Judaizers. Jewish opponents of Jesus and his followers in the Gospels and Acts tended to act more directly, so it is probable they were the latter; Galatians 1:8–9 clearly labels them not just as false teachers but as false Christians, under the curse of God. It is clear that we are dealing with heresy, and throughout the New Testament such people are satanic in origin and non-believers (Phil 3:18–19; 1 Tim 4:1–3; 2 Tim 2:14–3:9).[4]

"This matter" refers to the circumcision of Gentile believers like Titus. These interlopers somehow stole into the meeting during Paul's famine relief visit and disrupted it by demanding that Gentiles like Titus be circumcised. This is similar to what would later happen in Antioch (Acts 15:1), when members of this same group infiltrated the church there with the same demands. Here we can see three stages in the Judaizers' attack on the new mission to the Gentiles: challenging Paul at this meeting with the pillars in Jerusalem, sending teams to the Gentile churches established on the first missionary journey and denying Paul's gospel, and arguing against Paul's Gentile mission leading up to and during the Jerusalem Council. At all three stages the false teachers demanded that Gentile converts be circumcised and trained to keep the Mosaic law as Christians.

Paul describes their strategy as twofold: to "spy on the freedom we have in Christ Jesus" and to "make us slaves" to the law. Paul has nothing good to say about these charlatans who masquerade as children of light. They are like soldiers sent into hostile territory to "spy out" their enemy (see Num 21:32; 2 Sam 10:3). In other words, they were looking for information to bolster their accusations and for weaknesses they could exploit. There was no positive motive, only the desire to destroy Paul's ministry. The end result would be to enslave the Gentile believers under the law. In chapters 4 and 5 Paul will explore further the issue of slavery under the law versus

---

4. Heretics by definition are not Christians, for they deny central tenets of the faith on which true Christianity depends (in this case, salvation by grace alone, through the cross). In our day false teachers are not those who differ from us on non-cardinal matters such as eternal security, the rapture of the church, or the charismatic issue, but rather those who reject central doctrines like the Trinity, the deity of Christ, or substitutionary atonement.

freedom in Christ. The law binds us to human regulations and an external system, but Christ has removed us from those constraints and given us an internal relationship with a divine Father. So this demand to return to the old covenant system ran the danger of nullifying all that Christ had accomplished.

Paul wants his Galatian readers to be aware that he saw through their ruse immediately and "did not give in to them for a moment" (2:5). The underlying purpose in their urging that Titus be circumcised was obvious. To "give in" means to "place oneself in subjection to" another, and Paul rightly saw this as an attempt to enslave him as well—Titus as a slave subject to the law, and Paul placed in subjection to his opponents. Interestingly, some ancient manuscripts omit "did not," in effect suggesting that Paul gave in for a time and allowed Titus to be circumcised for the sake of his ministry. However, the manuscript evidence strongly favors the inclusion of the negative, and the context demands that it be present. If Paul had given in, the whole purpose of his argument in 1:6 to 2:21 would have been subverted, giving the Judaizers the ammunition they were looking for.

Paul's point is that "the truth of the gospel might be preserved for you," the Gentile Christians in Galatia. The gospel of Christ must remain pure, and no external means of salvation, like circumcision or adherence to the Mosaic regulations may be added to it. If religious practices or legal observances are made part of the mix, the gospel is robbed of its purity and truth. Only Christ's atoning sacrifice on the cross can suffice, for that alone has redemptive power to forgive our sins and make us right with God. Any other action, whether good works or covenant rite, will destroy that purity and obviate the work of God in salvation. In our own time this threat is carried on in the equally heretical works-righteousness approach to salvation. Salvation comes not through our good deeds but only by belief in Christ and the cross (Eph 2:8–9).

PAUL RECEIVES APPROVAL FROM THE PILLARS (2:6–10)
Nothing Added to Paul's Gospel (2:6)

Paul keeps describing the Jerusalem leaders in terms not of their God-given office but of their reputation in the Christian community, calling them "those who were held in high esteem." This is undoubtedly because the false teachers were elevating the office of these leaders in order to render Paul, in comparison, inferior to them. Far from putting down the other apostles or implying that they didn't deserve their place in the church, he was putting them in their proper place vis-à-vis his own status. The Jerusalem leaders did not deserve the ultra-high position accorded to them by those whose ulterior motive was to diminish Paul. He and the Twelve were equal in authority and proclaiming the same gospel.

So Paul states that such high esteem "makes no difference to me." Status is not his concern. He is completely oriented to God and Jesus, not to the fame of any human servant of God. This is because "God does not show favoritism," that is, never regards one person as more important than or superior to another. The Judaizers elevated the other apostles in an attempt to put Paul down, and Paul refused to allow this attitude in the church.

This point is as important today as it was then. The human tendency is to venerate gifted people. Society is always oriented to the more attractive, charismatic, or popular, resulting too easily in personality worship. Since God shows no partiality for one over another (Deut 10:17; 2 Chr 19:7; 1 Pet 1:17), none of his followers are to do so either.

The important point is the last one in this verse: "They added nothing to my message." While the Judaizers were bent on inserting dangerous additions to the gospel (circumcision and the law), the apostles refused to do so. They accepted Paul's gospel to the Gentiles with no demurral and no additions or amendments. Paul's gospel preaching, they were asserting, was just as "true" (Gal 2:5) as their own. Realizing that the gospel to the Gentiles was the same as the gospel to the Jews, they were on Paul's side, not that of the agitators.

THE VALIDITY OF PAUL'S GENTILE AND PETER'S JEWISH MINISTRIES (2:7–8)

The Jerusalem leaders not only refused to add anything to Paul's "gospel of Christ" (1:7) but completely ratified the validity of his ministry as a whole. The basis is expressed with two causal participles introducing 2:7 and 9, respectively—they did so "because they saw" (*idontes*) that Christ had "entrusted" the message to Paul (v. 8), and "because they knew/recognized" (*gnontes*) the grace shown him by God (v. 9).[5]

Paul's gospel and ministry were no challenge to theirs; in fact, they were a God-ordained extension of their own ministry, the natural outgrowth of the new covenant reality in Christ that God's salvation is intended for Gentiles as well as Jews. The verb phrase "had been entrusted" is a divine passive, meaning God was the One who had acted in giving Paul his commission. So it was not the apostles but God who approved Paul; God had done that. They simply recognized and endorsed what God had already done. They did so because they recognized God's hand on Paul, acknowledging that "the task of preaching the gospel to the uncircumcised" (a common Jewish term for Gentiles) had indeed been given him by divine commission.

To make the point explicit, Paul adds, "Just as Peter had been to the circumcised." He has the same commission as Peter's, and from the same Triune Godhead. Peter had received his appointment directly from Jesus in Mark 3:13–17 ("he appointed twelve, designating them apostles"[6]), as had Paul on the Damascus road.

---

5.   The NIV paraphrases these two participles.

6.   The apostolic aspect is missing in some manuscripts of Mark but should be part of the text.

In 1 Corinthians 2:4 he says, "My message and my preaching were not with wise and persuasive words, but with a demonstration of the Spirit's power." All three members of the Trinity were at work in Paul. Peter and Paul proclaimed the same gospel, such that the two groups, Jews and Gentiles, were being brought together as the new Israel in a new covenant reality. Thus the two men, as apostle to the Jews and apostle to the Gentiles, are coequal, with the same authority to bring together the two ethnic groups in Christ.

This truth is further anchored in terms of God's "work" (v. 8). Not only were Peter and Paul proclaiming the same gospel to the two groups, but the same powerful work of God was evident in both their ministries. The work was not *theirs* but God's in them. God was the active force and Peter and Paul the channels through which his work was being accomplished in the two groups. Both from the standpoint of God's call (v. 7) and his work (v. 8), Peter and Paul had coequal and interdependent ministries.

Interestingly, the word "apostle" appears with Peter in the Greek of verse 8 but not with Paul (the NIV supplies it for completeness). Some believe this is because Paul's apostleship was being debated in Jerusalem at this time. However, the text asserts from the outset that the apostles recognized Paul's gospel and authority. It is more likely that the term "apostle" is meant to cover both, for Paul held the same apostolic office as Peter. The NIV's inclusion of the term, explicitly applied to Paul, is therefore justified.

The Right Hand of Fellowship from the Pillars (2:9)

The leaders of the church "saw" the hand of God on Paul (v. 7) and as a result knew that his ministry was indeed an act of God's "grace," a term Paul often used for the gracious and merciful love of God that had led to his conversion and call (Gal 1:15; see also Rom 1:5; 1 Cor 3:10; Eph 3:2, 7). These leaders did not have to spend much time with Paul to recognize the gracious hand of God in his life, his personality, and his ministry. In an act of divine mercy this grace had been given to him as a gift from the Godhead—a truth recognizable in everything the man said and did.

The inner circle among Jesus' disciples consisted of Peter (Cephas), James, and John (see Mark 9:2), with James and John being brothers. Herod Agrippa martyred this James in Acts 12, and now James, the Lord's brother, had in a sense replaced him at the head of the Jerusalem church. Interestingly, John appears only marginally in Acts and nowhere but here in Paul's writings; Paul had mentioned only Cephas and James when recalling his earlier trip in Galatians 1:18–19. John's writings are usually dated late, in the 80s and 90s. Still, he was a major leader of the church and had a powerful ministry.

These three are "esteemed as pillars" of the church, meaning that the church recognizes them as key leaders on whom it rests. This parallels intertestamental Judaism, in which Abraham, Isaac, and Jacob were seen as pillars. This is most likely a temple metaphor, building on 1 Kings 7:21 and 2 Chronicles 3:16–17, where Solomon placed two pillars in the temple with the names *Jachin* ("he establishes") and *Boaz* ("in him is strength"). In Ephesians 2:20 the church is erected on "the foundation of the apostles and prophets," and the metaphor is even more evident in Revelation 3:12, where the victorious Christians are promised they will be made "a pillar in the temple of my God." The image stresses the security and permanence of the church as God's temple, and these three leaders typify the new **eschatological** temple erected as the sign of the new covenant.

These key figures "gave [Paul] and Barnabas the right hand of fellowship," meaning they accepted them as brothers and recognized their equal ministry in leading the Gentile wing of the church. The right hand was a symbol of power and authority, so this served as an official extension of approval by the Jerusalem church. The term *koinōnia* means not only "fellowship" but also "partnership" (see Phil 1:5), so this may also signify their acceptance as full partners in the work of the Lord. Once again Paul is stressing that both his apostolic authority and the truthfulness of his gospel proclamation are validated by the Jerusalem leadership. The Judaizers are defeated and disproven on both counts.

REQUEST TO REMEMBER THE POOR (2:10)

The request of James, Cephas, and John to "remember the poor" was quite natural, tied in to the famine relief visit of Acts 11:27–30 when Barnabas and Paul brought the collection for the poor to Jerusalem. However, this was a continual emphasis in the church and so would have been noted on every relevant occasion. From the beginning an emphasis on the need to take care of widows and the poor was at the heart of church life. Acts 2:42–47, in recording the practices of the early church, includes the note that "all the believers were together and had everything in common. They sold property and possessions to give to anyone who had need" (Acts 2:44–45), and in 4:32–34 they "shared everything they had," with the goal that "there were no needy persons among them." This became a defining characteristic of the early church.

Paul agrees, and indeed observes that this is "the very thing [he] had been eager to do all along." He has always wanted to alleviate the suffering of the unfortunate. In the Old Testament "the poor" was almost a technical term for the righteous remnant among God's people who were being oppressed by their enemies. The poor are completely dependent on the Lord for justice and help (Pss 9, 10, 35; 74), and they suffered the most in the hostile environment brought about by the apostasy and greed of the nation (see Exod 22:22–27; Isa 3:13–16; Amos 2:7; 4:1). Closer to Paul's time the group at Qumran who wrote the Dead Sea Scrolls called itself the community of the poor. Jesus chose poverty for his own lifestyle (Matt 8:20) and demanded that his followers also gain control over the allure of possessions (Matt 10:1–16; Luke 6:20–26). In connection with the collection for the poor in 1 Corinthians 16:1–4 and 2 Corinthians 8–9, Paul wrote extensively about the church's responsibility in this area. Clearly, concern for the poor was at the top of the church's priority list, and this should continue today. A benevolence ministry is essential for any church that wishes to please God and follow his will.

———

Paul intends this narration of his famine visit to distance him from any thought of dependence on other apostles. Christ, not human authorities, is the ground of his ministry. Both the length of time he spent apart from the other apostles (fourteen years) and the circumstances of his famine visit (he came in response to a revelation, not a request from the Jerusalem leaders) demonstrate this. At this meeting the leaders confirmed his ministry and invalidated his opponents' claims.

There are important principles in this. Meetings to clarify issues of right belief and action are necessary, for there will always be differing interpretations of proper procedure and doctrine. We need conclaves and seminars devoted to examining truth claims and determining proper procedure for the makeup and directions of ministry. We need mature leaders who can study competing claims and guide us. That is the model set before us here and in the Jerusalem Council of Acts 15. When as a result of such meetings we determine that gospel truth is not being subverted, we can acknowledge our deeper unity and live with our differences.

We also need to learn how to proceed when one of the options is deemed wrong or even dangerous, as it was in Paul's day. There are times for tolerance; we may "agree to disagree" when there can be no certainty on an issue and Scripture is not clear. However, there are other situations in which the true church must go to war—when Scripture is clear and we are dealing with heresy or serious sin. Then Christianity itself is at stake, and we cannot sit on the sidelines and hope for the best. We must act as God has acted throughout the pages of Scripture.

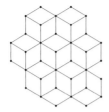

CONFLICT WITH PETER AND THE ESSENCE OF THE GOSPEL (2:11–21)

Galatians 2:11–14 relates the final episode in Paul's narration of the early years of his personal history, as it parallels Acts 9 and 11. As I have said all along in my presentation of Galatians 1–2, Paul's purpose is to defend his apostolic office and his gospel against attacks from the Judaizing false teachers who have traveled through the churches Paul established during his first missionary journey. Paul's overall theme is that he received his apostolic office and authority directly from Christ and not secondhand from the other apostles, and that his gospel is not a fictional hodgepodge he fabricated but something he also received directly by revelation from Jesus Christ. So far in Galatians 2 he has proven that the Jerusalem leaders recognized this and approved his gospel as equal to and interdependent with their own. Thus the Gentile branch of the church, with a completely valid Christian ministry of its own, is now united with the Jewish branch into a new Israel.

In this final part of his defense Paul emphasizes that the gospel he preaches is not only equal to its Jewish-oriented presentation but has absolute authority, both over himself and over the other apostles. When Peter gives in to pressure to depart from it, Paul rebukes and corrects him on the basis of his authority from Christ. This is in keeping with 2 Timothy 3:16–17: "All Scripture is

God-breathed and is useful for ... rebuking [and] correcting." The gospel is at the heart of the God-breathed nature of Scripture, and Paul as a gospel preacher has the authority to use it when Peter falls into error.

Paul concludes this first major section of Galatians by defining the true essence of the gospel (2:15–21). This passage carries on the story of Paul's correction of Peter; in fact, he had probably delivered it first in Antioch as part of his speech to Peter. This both closes chapters 1–2 and prepares the reader for chapters 3–4, introducing key themes about the gospel that will dominate that next section. The gospel is Christ's gospel, not Paul's, and it alone defines the way of salvation. As such, it provides the primary theme of this letter: that we become right with God not by performing the works of the law but only through saving faith in Christ and his atoning sacrifice on the cross.

PAUL REBUKES PETER AND DEFENDS THE GOSPEL AGAINST PETER'S ACTIONS (2:11–14)

Antioch in Paul's day was very cosmopolitan. The capital of Syria, it was the third largest city in the empire (after Rome and Alexandria), with a population of at least 250,000 (some estimate it as high as 500,000). After the death of Stephen the persecution in Jerusalem launched missionaries into the surrounding regions. Some of them reached Antioch, where a hugely successful evangelistic work began (Acts 11:19–21). Word reached Jerusalem, and the church leaders there sent Barnabas to assess the situation. Under his leadership the church there continued to grow. Barnabas, evidently having heard that Saul/Paul was experienced in Gentile mission work based on his years of ministry in Tarsus, proceeded there and recruited his assistance. Because of Paul's deep theological expertise in both Jewish and Christian theology, he was the ideal choice to build a bridge from Jewish to Gentile Christianity in the strategically critical environs of Antioch. Barnabas and Paul worked together there for a year with great success

(Acts 11:26) and then journeyed to Jerusalem for their famine relief visit. Shortly after their return the first missionary journey was launched (Acts 13:1).

THE REBUKE AT ANTIOCH (2:11)

After Peter's deliverance from prison (Acts 12:1-18) he also came to Antioch. The incident narrated here probably took place shortly after Paul's return from Jerusalem. In light of Peter's prior decision to side with Paul (vv. 7-9), some think that this incident didn't actually happen, but it is helpful to bear in mind that Peter was a human being who, like any of us, was subject to the temptation to cave in under peer pressure. It is important to understand that Paul had no personal animosity toward or desire to upstage Peter when he "opposed him to his face." This was strictly a matter of upholding the gospel and maintaining Christian unity.

Paul had to oppose Peter because Peter already "stood condemned," undoubtedly by the Lord, for his actions. Hebrews 3:13 commands that we "admonish [better than the NIV 'encourage' there] one another daily ... so that none of [us] may be hardened by sin's deceitfulness." Paul felt that he had to do this for the sake of both Peter and the church. He would later, in 1 Timothy 5:20, mandate a public confrontation in such a situation, stating that leaders who had fallen into error were to be reproved "before everyone, so that the others may take warning." Public sins demand public correction.

THE SITUATION: WITHDRAWAL FROM THE GENTILES (2:12A)

Two prior events had shaped Peter's initial openness to eating with Gentiles in Antioch. First, while he was staying at Joppa he had received a vision of a sheet holding unclean animals (Jews were not allowed to eat these animals since the meat would have been impure). When he refused to eat some of the meat the Lord directed him, "Do not call anything impure that God has made clean" (Acts 10:9-16). Thereby God had removed the binding nature of the old covenant food laws. Second, after Paul had explained his gospel to the Gentiles (Gal 2:6–8), Peter, along with James and John, had accepted his version as equal to theirs, further anchoring his developing realization that it was no longer forbidden by God for Jews to share meals and fellowship with Gentiles.

On the basis of these developments Peter began having table fellowship with the Gentile believers in Antioch. Some think he still followed the food laws and either ate at a separate, kosher table or expected the Gentiles to avoid unclean food with him. That is highly unlikely, however, for verse 14 indicates that Peter "lived like a Gentile" among them. The verb indicates that this was an ongoing practice that lasted for some time. Peter was partaking of foods the Mosaic law did not allow and was eating freely with Gentiles.

When a group "from James" (the brother of the Lord and the head elder of the Jerusalem church) arrived, however, everything changed. The identification of the groups in this story is quite difficult. Paul mentions two: the delegation from James and "the circumcision group." For many years I believed that this latter group was synonymous with the **Judaizers**, the group whose activities in Galatia Paul condemns throughout this letter. Yet there is no hint here in 2:11–14 that this was happening in Antioch.

There is debate whether the team "from James" was actually sent by him or simply claimed to represent him to add authority to their charges. Paul asserts in verse 9 that James had validated his gospel; the question then becomes why he would have demurred at this point. The answer is that while James accepted Paul's gospel he was still an orthodox follower of the food laws and other Mosaic regulations. He would have resembled the Jewish Christians in Romans 14:2 who "ate only vegetables" to make certain there was no Gentile unclean food among the kosher meat. There is evidence that such pious Jews, based on the perceived danger of impurity, refused to even use the same cooking or eating vessels as Gentiles. In this light James would naturally have been concerned that Paul and Peter were going too far in their accommodation to Gentile ways.

Next there is the "circumcision group." Since Paul often uses this phrase for Jewish people in general (Rom 4:12; Col 4:11; Titus 1:10), the majority of recent commentators have argued that these were unbelieving Jews (it has been estimated that 25,000 Jews lived in Antioch at that time). Thus Peter was "afraid" of them because they could have reacted against his own and others' freedom to eat non-kosher foods with Gentiles by increasing the persecution of the church. Because of increasing anti-Roman sentiment in the first century, there was great demand in Judaism for Jews to stand apart from the pagans surrounding them. There was great pressure on Jewish Christians to be faithful to their heritage.

While all of this makes sense, I think it may better fit the text to think of the circumcision group and the delegation from James as the same group. Paul says simply that the emissaries arrived and that Peter was afraid to go against the demands of (this?) circumcision group (this phrase is used in Acts 10:45; 11:2 of Jewish Christians). This understanding makes sense of the context. These Jewish Christians, expressing concerns from James, strongly challenged Peter's freedom to jettison Torah practices and engage socially with Gentiles. They demanded that he and the other Jewish Christians in Antioch withdraw and stop associating with their Gentile brothers and sisters in Christ. If this were the background, it is reasonable to assume that Peter was afraid of incurring condemnation from James and of disrupting the ministry and message of the church in the process.

THE REASON: PRESSURE FROM THE CIRCUMCISION GROUP (2:12B–13)

The issue of whether Jewish Christians could ignore food laws was a subject of constant debate in the early church. It stemmed from the time just before the Maccabean period of the second century

BC, when many Jews began to live like Gentiles. This caused massive upheavals in Palestine and led to a resurgence of interest in ritual purity among pious Jews. By the time of Christ close to 200 years later, purity laws and Sabbath observance were at the heart of the Pharisees' demands. Here at Antioch this strictly orthodox "circumcision group" of Jewish Christians began castigating those who, like Peter, were relaxing their Jewish ways.

Peter reacted by making a complete turnaround, as he "began to draw back and separate himself from the Gentiles." This does not mean that he rejected them as fellow Christians but only that he started to back away from social contact and to avoid sharing meals with them. He went back to his way of life from before Acts 10, when he saw the vision telling him not to call anything unclean and then visited the home of Cornelius, the Roman centurion (Acts 10:27–28).

He drew back because he was "afraid of those who belonged to the circumcision group." This does not mean he was afraid of James, for the two were obviously close. Rather, he was wary of the charges made by this delegation and the scandal this could cause back in Jerusalem, even to the point of causing a rift in the church. This also does not mean that he changed his theological outlook and joined the ultra-orthodox faction, in effect becoming one with the Judaizers. The alteration was in his practices, not his theology. However, as Paul will show in verse 14, this course of action was mistaken. What we do reflects who we are, and so must at all times flow out of God's truths.

Peter's influence caused the other Jewish Christians of Antioch to follow along, and this included even Barnabas (v. 13): "The other Jews [meaning Jewish believers] joined him in his hypocrisy." There would have been a sizable number of converts from the largely Jewish population in Antioch (nearly half as many Jews lived there as in Jerusalem). Hypocrisy occurs when a person develops external practices that even implicitly contradict internal beliefs, leading to false pretenses. The dichotomy Peter created between practice and theory constituted hypocrisy, since Peter and the others had acted against what they knew to be right.

Peter's actions were so persuasive in the Antiochian church that even Barnabas was fooled into joining his camp. Paul says that he was "led astray," which translates a greek a term used in 2 Peter 3:17 of the deceptive effects of false teachers. This was a crisis that held great danger for the church, one that could have resulted in a serious divide and led to a lengthy battle between the Jewish and Gentile factions. Even worse, it could have derailed the effects of a unified gospel on the evangelistic efforts of the church and disrupted the church's mission for decades to come. The fact that it did not do so resulted from Paul's immediate and Spirit-inspired reaction.

REBUKE AND CORRECTION BY PAUL (2:14)

Paul's correction of Peter relates both to the practical situation at Antioch and to Paul's equal status to the other leaders. Remember that one of Paul's main purposes in Galatians 1–2 is to demonstrate his apostolic authority, to remove all speculation about his being inferior and subordinate to the Jerusalem apostles and elders. But Paul is not tooting his own horn and demanding to be recognized as important. It is the gospel that is at stake, not Paul's pride and desire for status.

Paul may have been away and returned to "see" what had taken place, or he may have watched the events slowly unfold before he suddenly "saw" or recognized their significance. Either way he took decisive action, discerning the true implications of the hypocrisy, which was endangering "the truth of the gospel." The actions of Peter and those following him were not in accord with the true meaning of the gospel, which demands that Gentiles and Jews alike come to Christ by faith rather than through works. The same "truth of the gospel" occurs in 2:5 with respect to the circumcision of Titus, and the issue there as well is gospel versus law. Salvation can only be a free gift of grace, and the gospel message must be unencumbered by any thought of earning it through the works of the law. Food laws and circumcision are connected both to first-century discussions of the works of the law and to early Christian debates on the place of the law in the Christian life. Both involved "the truth of the gospel," and both had to be addressed directly in Antioch.

The issue was so important that it demanded a public rebuke, so Paul had to confront "Cephas in front of them all." His rebuke was also a rebuke of everyone there, since they were engaged in the same hypocritical conduct. The language is direct: This conduct was not "in line with truth"; the verb denotes walking a straight line on an issue. God demands a straightforward Christianity, one that refuses to deviate from the path he has chosen. Peter and the others were doing just that, and they had to correct their hypocrisy before it caused irreparable harm.

There is some question about the extent of Paul's rebuke. Some think that only verse 14 is addressed to Peter, with verses 15–21 an excursus to the Galatians on the nature of the gospel. Yet it makes more sense (and is favored by the style of vv. 15–21) to construe the whole passage as delivered to Peter. Still, the last seven verses do set forth the central theme of the letter—the essence of the true gospel.

Paul began by pointing out to Peter the inconsistency of his actions. Peter's background was Jewish, and he had spent his prior life living like a Jew, including obeying the Torah. But now as a result of his encounter with Cornelius and the recognition by the church pillars in verses 8–9 that the gospel no longer required submitting to the law, he had begun "living like a Gentile and not like a Jew." It is difficult to know how far to take this. I doubt it means that in every area of his life Peter had stopped being Jewish. In keeping with the larger context of verses 11–14, Paul likely means that Peter had stopped practicing the food laws and perhaps participating in Jewish festivals, such as attending synagogue services on the Sabbath. These would have been completely viable implications of the new covenant reality in Christ and would have been in accord with the actions of the "strong" in Romans 14.

Peter's error comes in the last sentence of verse 14. The Gentile believers would have considered Peter to have been one of themselves, so when Peter returned to his Jewish legalism many of the Gentiles felt "forced" or compelled (the same word used of Titus in v. 3) to follow his lead and begin to "follow Jewish customs"— to live like a Jew. The verb is *ioudaïzein*, signifying that Peter had in effect "Judaized" these Gentile believers and joined the enemy. This would have contravened the very gospel Peter had recognized in verses 8–9.

Did Paul's correction work, and how long did the healing process take? Some interpreters have thought Peter and Paul remained opponents, that the rift between Jewish and Gentile Christianity was never resolved. This is extremely unlikely, for Paul speaks positively about Peter in 1 Corinthians (1:12; 3:22; 9:5; 15:5). In a later New Testament letter, this one from the hand of Peter, the two are shown to be close associates (2 Pet 3:15–16). In the Jerusalem Council that followed shortly after this letter (Acts 15) both James and Peter sided entirely with Paul. There was no war between them.

PAUL SETS FORTH THE TRUE ESSENCE
OF THE GOSPEL (2:15–21)

This passage has two purposes. First, as part of Paul's response to Peter it tells why Peter was guilty of hypocrisy against the gospel in his turnaround with regard to his Gentile brothers and sisters. Second and more importantly, it is a message to help the Galatian believers come to understand the true meaning and implications of the gospel. The more I reflect on it, the more I believe this to be one of the most important passages in Scripture on the law-gospel debate. I don't see how the issue could be summed up better than it is here.

DEFINITION: JUSTIFICATION BY FAITH AND NOT
BY THE WORKS OF THE LAW (2:15–16)

Verse 15 is a brilliantly conceived, single-sentence description of the advantage the Jew had over the Gentile during the old covenant period. Paul begins, "We who are Jews by birth [literally, 'by nature'] and not sinful Gentiles [literally, 'sinners from the Gentiles']." "By birth" means a lot more than just being a natural-born Jew. It refers to the covenant privileges Jews possessed by virtue of their being descended from Abraham. As God's chosen people they were automatically "in," while the Gentiles were by the same token automatically "out."

Paul did not mean that only Gentiles were sinners. The Old Testament is as clear as the New that all human beings are inherently sinful. Paul is here using "sinner" from a Jewish standpoint to refer to people who did not follow the Mosaic regulations and keep themselves pure before God. Gentiles were sinners in a way that did not apply to Jews: They were not just morally sinful but guilty of cultic sin by disregarding God's laws.

Paul was reminding Peter of the special privileges all Jews enjoyed and of their reasons for feeling superior to the Gentiles. But Paul was setting up Peter for a serious correction; all of this would change with verse 16, with Paul's making clear that these covenant privileges had been in effect for the old covenant period but that everything had changed with the coming of Christ. Several scholars place a concessive here ("*Even though* we are Jews by birth, … *yet* we know …") in order to clarify that Paul is correcting the old perspective. The new covenant follows a vastly different trajectory, and the gospel of the cross has radically altered the situation.

In the old system Jews maintained a relationship with God by right of birth and by keeping the Mosaic law. That could never be a permanent situation, for the law could only point out transgressions, not solve their sin problem (3:19a). Its purpose was to prepare for the coming of Christ, when the answer to sin would arrive (vv. 19b–20). Paul here in 2:16 details the true essence of the gospel, declaring that it superseded the old covenant to the extent that "Christ is the culmination [literally, 'end'] of the law" (Rom 10:4).

Verse 16 is all the more important because it is here in Paul's first letter that we are introduced to the language that will dominate Christian soteriology (the doctrine of salvation) for the rest of human history. The two key phrases are found in the antithesis between "justified by faith" (which occurs three times) and "the works of the law" (also three times). These would become the primary concepts for Paul's understanding of salvation by faith in Christ alone, with "justify" appearing twenty-seven times in his writings.

The term for "justify" (*dikaioō*) belongs to the word group meaning "righteous" (*dikaios*), and the form for justifying is in the passive (*dikaiōthē*). This is a divine passive, meaning that God is implied as the One doing the justifying. It carries a forensic or law-court emphasis, meaning "to be declared right with God" or innocent at his judgment seat. There is also strong **eschatology** here, since it is at the *bēma* or judgment seat (with eternal consequences) that the decision is made.

There are three levels at which this justification takes place: Because of the atoning sacrifice of Christ when he takes our place and bears our sins, we are (1) declared righteous by God and forgiven. Our sanctification process begins as we are (2) made righteous by the Spirit, and the ethical side occurs when we (3) live rightly ("in righteousness") before him. All three elements are indicated in the "righteous" word group.

We are justified entirely by faith in the saving blood of Christ—in no way by "the works of the law" (*erga nomou*). This phrase is found eight times in Romans and Galatians, always in connection with the issue of justification. While obeying the law could never bring salvation, it had been enough to maintain a right relationship with God in the Old Testament. Now that Christ has come, both salvation and relationship with God result from the cross.

The works of the law cannot justify a sinner, cannot produce forgiveness of sins, and cannot make a person right with God.

It is clear that the works of the law are inadequate, but there is debate among interpreters over *why* this is so. We need to understand the exact nuance of "works of the law" in this context, and there have been three stages of understanding it since the Reformation:

1. The understanding from Luther until recent times involved seeing "works of the law" in terms of Jewish legalism. These works, actions performed before God to gain favor with him, could never be enough because fallible human beings could never perform them completely and consistently enough to be justified.

   The problem with this view is that the Jewish emphasis was not on merit but on covenantal relationship. These works centered on obedience to divine actions specified in the law rather than on attaining favor.

2. Under the "new perspective on Paul" (see "Occasion and Opponents" in the introduction) these works are viewed as "boundary markers" used to keep Judaism distinct from the Greek world. The Mosaic law was intended to protect God's people from pagan ways and to preserve the covenant for Israel. Paul's purpose here, then, was to remove those distinctions and unite Jew and Gentile under Christ. These works—signs of the old separation between these people groups—could never have brought them together. They belonged to the age of Torah, and Christ has established a new paradigm.

   The problem with this approach is that it takes a salvation-historical tack and sees the entire difference in the coming of Christ. More likely Paul is teaching a combination of this option and option 1. The Jewish people were dependent on obeying the law to remain right with God, and the coming of Christ brought about a new era of salvation. The concept of works as human achievement was very much a part of this, and while Judaism was not a legalistic religion there were elements of legalistic merit in the practical observance of the people.

3. So the best option is a combination of the first two. The central issue is the actual deeds stipulated in the Mosaic law—like the rite of circumcision, the food laws, and the Sabbath laws. Both the legalistic and the salvation-historical elements play a part. Since Christ came and died on the cross for our sins, the enslaving power of sin has been broken, and salvation by faith is a free gift. Performing the works of the old covenant law cannot suffice to solve the sin problem, which has been resolved in Christ. Neither Peter nor anyone else may dare to depend on works. Faith, and faith alone, is necessary and sufficient. Salvation is a free gift attained through faith in Jesus and his sacrificial death for us.

Paul's answer to the insufficiency of the works of the law is simple and at the same time incredibly profound: Justification is "by faith in Jesus Christ." Like "works of the law," this phrase has also been the subject of significant debate. The Greek literally reads "faith *of* Jesus Christ," and this can be interpreted in two ways: as an objective genitive ("*faith in* Jesus Christ," speaking of human belief in Christ) or as a subjective genitive ("*the faithfulness of* Jesus Christ," emphasizing his work in salvation history). More and more interpreters have opted for the latter. This would make a great deal of sense, since Paul adds, "so we too have put our faith in Jesus Christ," and it could seem redundant to include this twice. According to this understanding Paul would be emphasizing Christ's faithful work as the basis for our faith. Still, I prefer the traditional translation (as in the NIV). Paul in this view is stating our faith generally and then unpacking it in the following sentence, making it absolutely clear that our faith, not our works, leads to justification.

His emphatic conclusion makes the point crystal clear: "that we may be justified by faith in Christ Jesus and not by the works of the law, because by the works of the law no one will be justified." The repetition is almost tedious, but it is critical because the point is so essential to a true understanding of the "gospel of Christ" (1:7). The point is that Jews as well as Gentiles can be declared right with God only by personal faith in Christ—never by works (of the law). No Jew could attain salvation by observing the commands of the Mosaic law, and no person can ever be justified by good works. "No one" in the Greek here is "no flesh," stressing the finite nature of all human beings. Paul is alluding to Psalm 143:2, "Do not bring your servant into judgment, for no one living is righteous before you." Paul is in agreement with the psalmist that all of us are immersed in sin and can never attain righteousness on our own. Only divine mercy and grace can make it possible.

Our trust cannot be in the law or in our inherent goodness and good deeds, for they can never be kept well enough or performed consistently and often enough to overcome sin and purchase salvation. We are like the rich young ruler who had observed the law from childhood and hoped that his record would be sufficient, only to go away crestfallen because he couldn't overcome his lust for wealth (Mark 10:17-22). It would take a morally perfect person to earn salvation, and there is no such person apart from Christ.

The Problem of Sin: From the Law, not from Christ (2:17-18)

Paul now further clarifies his point, using what is called a condition of fact (an "if" saying that assumes the truth of the statement to follow): "If, in seeking to be justified in Christ, we Jews [inserted by the NIV for clarification] find ourselves to be sinners [which is indeed the case]." Some think this refers back to Paul's and Peter's conversions, when both realized that they, like the Gentiles, were sinners who could find forgiveness only in Christ. Others see this as a post-conversion experience when they fully realized that the law could not solve their sin problem and turned unequivocally to faith in Jesus. This would not, however, imply a second conversion. Paul was not referring to a conversion experience but to a later, fuller realization regarding their relationship to the law as Christians. Both views can make sense of the sentence, but I prefer the post-conversion interpretation because it fits the whole setting and argument of verses 15–21.

Either way, however, Paul's emphasis is on the reality of sin. As he worked through the implications of the gospel and his own salvation, Paul realized that the law could not have removed the reality that he was a sinner in need of grace. The presence of "in Christ" with "justified" indicates the mystical union with Christ that ensues in the experience of justification. In realizing that justification takes place apart from keeping the law, Peter and Paul in the eyes of the Jews had become "sinners," just like the Gentiles who did not follow the law.

At this point Paul points out a possible false conclusion ("Does this mean that Christ promotes sin?"), responding to his own rhetorical question with that strong negation made famous in his diatribes of Romans 3:4, 6 and others: "Absolutely not" (KJV: "God forbid")! If faith in Christ means abandoning the law, these Judaizers charged Paul, then following him means turning Jewish Christians into sinners like the Gentiles. Paul unequivocally rejects such a charge. Far from promoting sin, Christ resolves and negates its.

Paul gives a full answer to this charge in verse 18. The language is somewhat enigmatic: "What I destroyed" refers to the Jewish demand to keep the Mosaic law. The same term (*katelysa*, "destroyed"), is found also in Matthew 5:17, where it is rendered as "abolishing" the law. Paul is destroying that requirement by arguing that the gospel is based on the free gift of salvation through faith in Christ. Neither Jew nor Gentile has to keep the law any longer, so Paul has set forth the gospel in a way that has destroyed or abolished the centrality of the law in the process of salvation.

Yet this introduces a seeming contradiction. Jesus says in Matthew that he has *not* come to abolish the Law or the Prophets, yet Paul says here that he has done just that. This question is at the heart of the gospel-law debate. The key appears in the second half of Matthew 5:17: "I have not come to abolish them but to fulfill them." Paul means Christ culminates or brings to completion the true purpose of the law. The Torah is intact in Jesus. Far from having been destroyed, it has been fulfilled—"ended" or "culminated" (Rom 10:4), in that in Jesus it has finished its work. Paul likewise has not destroyed the law but he has abolished its binding power over God's people. The law, while intact in Christ, has been replaced by the cross as the basis for salvation.

By "rebuilding" the law here Paul means reinstating it as the mandatory requirement for being Christian, as the Judaizers have done. If Paul were to allow Peter and the other Jewish Christians to renege on the gospel of Christ, and thereby on the centrality of faith and the cross, then he would join the Judaizers as true "law-breakers" or "transgressors." The critical point is that it would not be the Mosaic law they were breaking but the eternal laws of God. That would be a far more serious transgression and would have eternal consequences. To go back to the law would break the new covenant reality and destroy the true essence of the gospel.

While the issue in this passage may seem to have more historical than contemporary significance, the implications are just as important for our day. It is the gospel that is at stake. There is a continuing tendency in all religions to develop a salvation system based on works-righteousness: the belief that if we are only good enough and can follow the demands of our religious system well enough, we can achieve our own salvation. This is inherent in every non-Christian religion and, sadly, is followed by too many Christians as well. The basic error is that the whole process centers on the "I," on the hope that I can through my own efforts somehow earn my salvation. The heart of sin is the worship of self, and "I"—egotistical as I am—do not want to depend for my salvation on God and what he has done. Paul will respond to this tendency in the following two verses.

THE SOLUTION: DIED TO THE LAW, CRUCIFIED WITH CHRIST (2:19–20)

Paul now solves the classic problem of the "I" and the desire to control my own salvation, either by keeping the law (for these Jewish Christians) or by being a morally upright person (for most of us). He says, "For through the law I died to the law so that I might live for God." In the new era that has come with Christ, the prevalent transgression is not removing the law as a required instrument of salvation but reinstating it. This observation should not be restricted to Jewish Christians, for the Judaizers were also making the Gentiles feel that obedience to the law was required of them to qualify as Christians. All human beings are included in Paul's words here.

In the period before Christ, the age of the law, God's people lived for the law and according to it. They remained in covenant relationship with God by keeping its mandates. But when Christ came and fulfilled the law, that old system was no longer sufficient. The free gift of grace replaced the requirements of the law with faith in Christ. In light of this new development, two things had to happen: The centrality of obedience to the law had to be abolished (2:18), and God's people had to "die to the law," in effect making it the instrument of its own death.

As a Jewish follower of the law, Paul was faithful to its demands. Yet when Christ came the divine purpose of the law, as well as of Paul's obedience to it, was fulfilled. When the usefulness of the law ended, Paul in a sense died to it. Beyond making a personal, religious comment here, he is declaring a salvation-historical principle. In the new covenant era of Christ and the Spirit, Paul's old life is over. Likewise for us, when we die in Christ we die not only to the law but also to sin. We are united with Christ and thus freed from the law. Paul will explore this further in the next verse in his comment on being "crucified with Christ."

The result of this death is that we then can truly and finally "live for God." There is no legal intermediary and no set of obligations that must be fulfilled in order to belong to God. This (now) is the time of salvation, and Christ is the only mediator. Our covenant relationship with God is direct and final. This new life in Christ enables his followers to live for God in a new way, without restrictions. There is here a redemptive antinomy: In Christ life comes through death.

One of the more famous verses in the Bible (v. 20) develops this metaphor in a wonderfully rich way. This was my favorite verse as a teenager, and it remains one of my favorites to this day. Carrying on from verse 19, Paul states that he died to the law when he was "crucified with Christ." The perfect tense of the verb is stative; Paul is saying that while he used to live in a state of submission to the law, he now lives as united with Christ in his crucifixion. To be crucified with Christ is to be united with him in his death—to have died to sin, this world, and the law. We cannot ultimately begin to live until we have died to that which will keep us from God and Christ. We do that by uniting with Christ in his death.

The results of dying with Christ are essential to the Christian life: "I no longer live, but Christ lives in me." The first clause could be translated "the I [the ego] no longer lives." This "I" is linked with the "old self" (KJV: "old man"), and there is a double meaning in the concept. First, the old self is humankind in Adam (Eph 4:22; Col 3:9), enslaved by sin and controlled by the flesh. That old self was crucified with Christ and the "body of flesh" nullified (Rom 6:6), so that each of us has become a new self in Christ, "created to be like God" (Eph 4:24). At the same time the "I" (the sinful, egotistical control of the self) has been done away with in Christ. Sin is no longer an internal force controlling us but an external power that tempts and tries to regain control through the "flesh"—or sinful tendency—in each of us. The key to victory is surrendering totally to the "Christ who lives in" us and drawing strength from the Spirit to defeat the flesh (Rom 8:5-13).

We are a "new self" through our union with Christ. However, we continue to "live in the body" (that is, "the flesh") and to struggle regularly with our sinful tendencies. This earthly life in all its frailty therefore demands that we live this life "by faith in the Son of God." Sin remains a reality in the Christian life, and temptation can seem overwhelming. When faced with temptation we do well to remember 1 Corinthians 10:13: "No temptation has overtaken you except what is common to mankind. And God is faithful; he will not let you be tempted beyond what you can bear. But when you are tempted, he will also provide a way out so you can endure it." We find that way out only "by faith in the Son of God." As we depend and trust solely in him, we become "more than conquerors" (Rom 8:37). Paul's "Son of God" language stresses the deity and power of that unique Son who has won the victory for us.

Paul describes this Son of God in two interconnected ways to show how his victory is transferred to us: as the One "who loved me and gave himself for me." This is reminiscent of Romans 5:8: "But God demonstrates his own love for us in this: While we were still sinners Christ died for us." The love of the Godhead transcends time and redemptive history. When God decided to create this world, and us in it, he knew that we would fall into sin, so from eternity past God's love demanded that Christ "give himself" for us (see also Eph 5:2, 25). In this way substitutionary atonement (Christ dying as our substitute to reconcile us to God) is grounded in his universal, salvific love. Note also the centrality of "me ... for me." Christ's self-sacrificial love is intensely personal for each one of us.

GRACE THROUGH CHRIST, NOT THE LAW (2:21)
Paul concludes this portion of his argument with a brief meditation on the grace of God as it bears on the issue of gospel and law

He declares that we cannot experience the grace of God through the law, "for if righteousness could be gained through the law, Christ died for nothing." There cannot be two equal avenues to justification—the way of Christ and the cross, on the one hand, and the way of obedience to the law on the other. The second cancels out the first, since salvation attained through works would render the free gift of grace unnecessary. If by keeping the law we could on our own have gained righteousness (become right with God and capable of living morally upright lives), Christ's death would have been pointless—just one more sad ending to the life of an innocent (and in this case misguided) man. It is grace alone, not law, that leads to justification. God can give his justifying law-court verdict only because Christ has paid for our sins. His grace is not only uppermost but exclusive and absolute.

———

In the first half of this section (2:11–14) we learn three practical things. First, this is a wonderful example of conflict management over a very serious issue in the church. The danger was immense, for the very gospel was at stake. The key is that Paul met the threat head-on and did not shrink from his difficult duty. Many churches today are leery of discipline situations, afraid of the dissension they may cause. Yet Scripture is clear. We are to "admonish daily" (see Heb 3:13) and "gently instruct" opponents to bring them to repentance (2 Tim 2:25). Discipline is a critical component of discipleship, and we all, like Peter, need it from time to time.

Second, any of us could cause this sort of problem. If we were to choose the two most important leaders in the history of the church, they would undoubtedly be Peter and Paul, and yet these two were the participants in this drama. We are all finite, fallible human beings, subject to mistakes in judgment, and discipline should become a positive factor in our churches. There is no hint that Peter resented Paul's insistence that he follow through on what he had to do. We must all admit that we need correction and must want to grow, as well as realize the importance of loving admonition in our lives.

Third, we must all be prepared for attack (referring to negative, demonic attack, not constructive rebuke) at any time. This happens to all of us at one time or another. Paul was being assaulted from three directions at once—by the Judaizers in Galatia, by the emissaries sent from James, and by Jewish Christians in general.[1] Satan is continually at work against us when we are in ministry, and one of his most effective strategies is to turn us against each other. When criticism comes we must first ask whether it is valid. If so, we should change course accordingly. When it is unfounded we find ourselves in union with the prophets and the apostles, continuously under barrage.

The second half of this section (vv. 11–15) is at the heart of this letter, for it emphasizes the centrality of the gospel for everything we think and do. It is behind every aspect of our life and ministry. We are all sinners saved by grace, and sin has to be dealt with before any lasting growth can take place in our lives. Adherents of every religion, including some Christians, tend to think that their goodness and their works can (in the case of Christians, either alone or in concert with Christ's atonement) make them right with God. Yet our own goodness can never solve our sin problem. God in his grace and love sent his Son to give himself for us—a no-strings-attached gift we do not earn but receive wholly by faith. If we want to be justified we must unite with Christ crucified and accept his atoning work as wholly instrumental in our salvation. The law-gospel debate with which Paul grapples here is not a mere historical anachronism but essential to being a Christian. The works of the law are antithetical to the gospel of grace, and we must come to Christ in faith to have life.

---

1. A fourth possibility is unbelieving Jews; see the comments on 2:12.

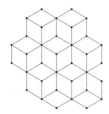

DEFENSE OF FAITH OVER THE WORKS OF THE LAW (3:1–18)

We now move into the central section of the letter, which contains Paul's primary defense against the false teaching of the **Judaizers**. He defended his apostolic office and authority in 1:11–2:21, and now he turns to proving the truth of his gospel (3:1–4:11). He provided the basic themes in the last paragraph (2:15-21) and here moves into a detailed exposition of his position.

In 3:1–5 he asks a series of rhetorical questions about the Galatians' reception and experience of the Spirit as the sign of the new age of salvation. Paul's point is that the presence of the Spirit in the Galatian believers is definitive proof of the change from the era of the law and obedience to the era of grace and salvation. They no longer need circumcision or the Mosaic regulations to be the covenant people because in the new covenant age they have the grace-gift of the Spirit. Since they have the Spirit by means of faith, not by following the law, grace rather than works is the clear basis of their justification.

Then in verses 6–14 Paul turns from the experience of the Spirit to the witness of Scripture. He quotes a series of Old Testament passages interpreted in light of the gospel, namely the righteousness of Abraham attained by faith and passed on to the Gentiles. Paul wants to prove that the gospel of justification by faith has Old Testament support, and he uses Genesis 15:6 and 12:3 to make his point. In Genesis 15:6 righteousness was credited to Abraham on the basis of faith, and in Genesis 12:3 that grace became universal when it was passed along to the nations through the Abrahamic covenant (Gal 2:8). The result is that the works of the law produced a divine curse (v. 10), for the righteous were required to live by faith (v. 11). There was only one solution to this problem: Christ became the curse for us so that the Abrahamic blessing could come to the Gentiles (vv. 13-14).

Finally, in verses 15-18 Paul addresses the issue of faith versus works from the standpoint of the relationship between the Abrahamic and Mosaic covenants. His point is that salvation history makes Abraham and his covenant primary, since they came first. So the Mosaic law and works cannot void the Abrahamic covenant and faith. God gave that covenant to Abraham on the basis of the divine promise, and it remains primary.

PAUL DEFENDS THE GOSPEL BY EXPERIENCE: THE RECEPTION OF THE SPIRIT (3:1-5)

THEY MUST HAVE BEEN BEWITCHED (3:1)

Paul is incredulous that the Galatian Christians could have been so easily duped by these false and dangerous teachings that claimed the law to be central for salvation. Therefore he begins, "You foolish Galatians!" This is unusual because Paul rarely names a group like this in his letters (typically using "brothers and sisters"). The specificity shows how deeply disturbed he is. "Foolish" (anoētoi) refers to an inability to think clearly or understand. He is accusing these Christians of not using their brains to figure out something that should have been clear to any thinking individual.

The accusation is also unusual: "Who has bewitched you?" The term "bewitch" literally means to cast an evil eye on a person. It is used in ancient magical texts to talk about gaining control over people (as in the NLT, "Who has cast an evil spell on you?"). Paul is using the term here not literally of magic or demon possession but rhetorically, in an attempt to jolt the Galatians into acknowledging their foolishness by showing the dire implications of having fallen into such error. Still, he does see satanic influence in this. There are evil forces at work behind the Judaizers, and their pernicious teaching is an attempt by the dark powers to subvert the gospel. The Galatians, by allowing themselves to be swayed, have fallen into "the devil's trap" (1 Tim 3:7).

The reason the Galatians' actions are so foolish is that Paul's teaching of the gospel was so unmistakably evident: "Before your very eyes Jesus Christ was clearly portrayed as crucified." The truth was openly proclaimed and publicly understood ("before your very eyes"). Note the play on words: The Galatians' opponents used an "evil eye" to bewitch them, but they had earlier seen the truth with their own eyes and should never have been taken in by that satanic logic. There is no way they could have missed that truth, and yet these heretics had managed to pull the wool over their eyes. Paul is in effect asking "How could you be so gullible?" Jesus Christ crucified is the heart and soul of the gospel, and to replace the cross with the works of the law is unimaginable.

They Received the Spirit by Faith (3:2)

Paul continues, "I would like to learn just one thing from you." It is not that he is uninterested in anything else but that this one issue is of supreme importance, crowding out all other considerations. His second rhetorical question that follows provides the key evidence for the truth of the gospel: "Did you receive the Spirit by the works of the law, or by believing what you heard?" The Holy Spirit is the central sign of the new covenant reality in this age of the Spirit. In his farewell discourse of John 13–17 Jesus' message to his disciples, preparing them for the cross, was, "I must depart so the Spirit might come."

The Old Testament predicted the coming of the Spirit to usher in the messianic age. Isaiah 32:15 speaks of the Spirit being "poured out from on high," and in the valley of dry bones passage in Ezekiel 37:14 God stated through his prophet, "I will put my Spirit in you and you will live." The best-known Old Testament passage on the Spirit is Joel 2:28–32, which portrays the Spirit being poured out as a signal of the last days. In Romans 8:14–17 the gift of salvation is accompanied by the receiving of the Spirit, just as we will see below in Galatians 4:6. So the Galatians' experience of the Spirit in fulfillment of prophecy, as the sign that the final era of salvation history has arrived, is proof positive that God has moved decisively in establishing his final kingdom in this world. This means that the gospel of Christ is real and that the Judaizers are contravening God's will in trying to make the Galatians revert to the principles of the old era.

So Paul's question is already answered, and the Galatians know it. It is not the works of the law but faith in Christ alone that is adequate for receiving the Spirit and entering the kingdom of God. As we have seen throughout Galatians, human achievement can never produce true righteousness. The law, given to point out transgression (3:19), can never solve our sin problem. It was only during the old dispensation that becoming a Jewish convert and obeying the Torah requirements could keep the Galatians in right covenant relationship with God. This could never be enough in the new covenant age, for Christ has come and everything has changed. In the messianic age only faith in the free gift of God's grace in Christ is adequate for salvation.

It is interesting that Paul calls for "believing what you heard" (literally, "from the hearing of faith"). Some have asked whether "hearing" refers here to the act of hearing or to the gospel message that is heard, and whether "faith" is the act of believing or the gospel content that is believed. This is a false debate, for in actuality there is a both/and dynamic at work. Paul means that the Galatians have heard the gospel of Christ and believed, and this (not obeying the works of the law) has enabled them to find salvation and receive the Spirit. It is hearing that leads to faith, and faith alone justifies.

The Spirit Is Antithetical to the Flesh (3:3)

Here again Paul is shocked by the Galatians' "foolish" (v. 1) acquiescence to this dangerous, false retreat from the truth of the gospel back to the old realities of an age that ended when Christ came. The Galatians could not be thinking clearly; their minds have become clouded by the empty, worthless concepts being spoon-fed to them by the Judaizers, who themselves were filled with demonically inspired falsehood.

The central concept in this verse is the beginning and end of the Christian life. The Galatians began the Christian life and received the Spirit, referring to their conversion under Paul. But then when they embraced the Judaizers and the demand for performance of the works of the law, they went back to the old ways of the law. They are moving in a direction that, if unchecked, would negate their salvation in Christ and the life in the Spirit they enjoyed.[1]

To "finish by means of the flesh" means that the Judaizers had developed a fleshly religion, a this-worldly "gospel" that turned backward toward works and away from the life of the Spirit and the heavenly kingdom of which Christians are already citizens (Phil 3:20). Paul calls those who do this "evildoers, those mutilators of the flesh" (Phil 3:2). When righteousness by faith in Christ is replaced by the works of the law, circumcision ceases to be about covenant and is reduced to mutilation.

In Christ there is movement forward to finishing in God's eternal kingdom, while in the law there is movement backward to the beginning that is no beginning, for the works of the law have lost their significance and been replaced by faith. Beginning the Christian life and growing in the Spirit must not be replaced by a digression into works. The sanctifying work of the Spirit must

---

1.   For a brief discussion of whether it is possible to lose one's salvation, see my comments at the end of 5:1–12.

ever progress in the Christian walk, not be repudiated in favor of an obsolete philosophy of works-righteousness.

THE QUESTION OF AN EMPTY RELIGIOUS EXPERIENCE (3:4)

There is a serious warning in Paul's next rhetorical question. To take the path the Galatians are now on will empty the Christian life of all value, in effect nullifying it and destroying its future. Everything they have received will be "in vain," devoid of worth. There is some question about the Greek *epathete*, which the NIV translates as "experience." This can at times mean to "experience" something, but its consistent meaning in the New Testament is to "suffer," and that makes great sense here. This means it should read, "Have you suffered so much in vain?" In 4:29, the suffering of the Galatian Christians is implicit, and in the first missionary journey to this area in Acts 13–14 there is a great deal of opposition to the gospel. In Pisidian Antioch the Jews "stirred up persecution" and forced Paul and Barnabas to flee (Acts 13:50); in Iconium there was a plot to stone them and they were forced to leave (14:5–6); and at Lystra Paul was stoned and left for dead (14:19–20).

The point is that all they had suffered and went through would be meaningless if they surrendered their life in the Spirit and returned to a religion based on the works of the law. Many interpreters see in this a warning of the dangers of apostasy. To have so much, and to throw it all away on a lie—that is the quintessential tragedy!

Happily, however, all is not lost just yet. There is some basis for hope, for the Galatians have not gone all the way into the Judaizer camp. So Paul adds the qualifying clause, "if it really was in vain." There is time for them to renounce these pernicious views and return to Christ and his gospel truth. Paul prays that this letter will convince his readers of the danger of the Judaizers' error and bring about revival in their midst, enabling them to return to their earlier experience of the Spirit and once again enjoy the fullness of Christ in their churches.

The Spirit and Miracles Come by Faith, Not Works (3:5)

Paul now brings together and summarizes the issues of this paragraph with a question about how God supplies the Spirit to his children. The Galatians have received the Spirit and experienced his presence and power, as evidenced by miracles. In Iconium the Lord "confirmed the message of his grace by enabling them to perform signs and wonders" (Acts 14:3), and in Lystra Paul healed a man lame from birth (14:8-10). When Paul was stoned in Lystra, the ones who perpetrated the act thought him dead and dragged him outside the city. He had to have been in a coma, most likely with broken bones and other injuries. Does a person after an experience like that simply "get up and go back into the city" (14:20)? Paul did. How can that be anything but a stupendous miracle?

So Paul asks them once again, with virtually the same wording as in verse 2: Did they receive the Spirit and experience miracles "by the works of the law, or by ... believing what [they] heard?" In verse 2 the emphasis was on the act of receiving the Spirit; here it is on the continued work of the Spirit in their midst. The Spirit is always working in their midst, and they know it. As a church and as individual believers, they have the Spirit guiding and empowering their lives. Paul's point is that this could not take place on the basis of their works. It is not that they are paid wages for living in righteousness, with the Spirit the currency of the payment. The Spirit's working of miracles comes by faith, not works.

PAUL DEFENDS THE GOSPEL USING SCRIPTURE: ABRAHAM AND FAITH (3:6-14)

Thesis: Faith Credited as Righteousness (3:6)

This is a transition verse, connected to verses 1-5 with "so also." It functions as a conclusion to the earlier material and at the same time the introduction to the paragraph on Abraham and faith (vv. 7-14). Since it includes the quote from Genesis 15:6 that functions as the thesis for the next section, I think it better to place it thematically with the following paragraph. This paragraph contains six Old Testament quotations, two in verses 6–9 and four in verses 10–14. Paul uses these passages to counter the law-based salvation of the false teachers and to establish the true gospel. He does this by showing that the arch-example of Abraham points to faith—not to the works of the law—as what determines who Abraham's children are. Through the law there can be no justification—only a curse, and Christ alone has the power to redeem us from the curse of the law by *becoming* the curse for us.

Paul's opponents undoubtedly used Abraham as a mainstay in their argument for the continuing validity of the law as the effectual instrument of salvation. They would have said that since Abraham instituted circumcision it remained a necessary rite of qualification for membership within God's people. The Judaizers pointed to Abraham's obedience, but Paul turns that thinking on its head by emphasizing Abraham's faith. His use of Genesis here proves his point. Abraham was the first central figure in salvation history through whom the world changed. He prepared for that central historical moment of the Christ, and both moments centered on faith. Abraham was more than an example; he represented the changing of the eons.

The context of the quote is God's second presentation of the covenant to Abraham (after Gen 12:1–3). God had promised that Abraham's offspring would become a great nation, but Abraham had expressed misgivings, since he has not produced an heir. God went on to promise innumerable offspring, and Genesis 15:6 reminds us that "Abram believed the LORD, and he credited it to him as righteousness." Paul here presents Abraham as the model for the patriarchs and for the nation that would emerge from his loins. Faith is the natural response of God's people to his promises.

The word rendered here "credited" or "counted" is a legal term in Genesis in the same way it is in Paul. Forensic righteousness—what God credits to our account in his own ledger—is the meaning in Genesis too. Obedience does not produce righteousness but results from the righteous status that accrues to us only by faith.

Finally, righteousness in the Genesis passage is right standing before God rather than righteous conduct. Paul is completely faithful here to the original context of the Abraham account. The Judaizers are wrong not only about the gospel of Christ but also about the Old Testament teaching on faith. None of us can ever be made right with God through works. For Abraham, as well as for us in the new covenant era, justification was and is always and exclusively a matter of faith.

The Children of Abraham Come by Faith (3:7-9)
Faith the requirement (3:7)

This verse ties together the emphasis on faith from verses 1-6 and the emphasis on the children of Abraham in verses 8-14. "Know" (NIV: "Understand") always points to a truth that readers should have realized but somehow have missed. Paul is saying it is evident from the Genesis account that only those who come by faith can be the children of Abraham. The Galatians' failure to understand that obvious truth is appalling to him.

Membership in Abraham's family cannot be tied to observing the Mosaic law or to works. Only "those who have faith" are Abraham's children. It is the Galatian Gentiles rather than these Jewish Christian heretics who belong to Abraham. These Gentiles do not have to be circumcised or to follow Jewish dietary laws to be children of Abraham; they simply have to believe in Jesus the Christ. Their relationship to God is determined by their being people of faith, not people of works.

The gospel announced to Abraham and the nations (3:8)

For Paul the Abrahamic covenant is the final arbiter in the debate. The primary covenants of the Old Testament—those with Abraham, Moses, and David—are in a line of continuity, and many agree that they virtually form one covenant. If this is correct—and I believe it is—Abraham's covenant provides the basic premise upon which the others build.

Here Paul introduces his point by saying that "Scripture foresaw that God would justify the Gentiles by faith." Saving faith is a matter of divine foreknowledge. God had already determined that the Gentiles would join the Jews as part of his covenant people and had pointed to this later reality already in a Genesis prophecy, the Abrahamic covenant, which the Jewish people understood to launch Israel, the seed of Abraham, as God's people. Paul is saying that another purpose of this covenant was to indicate the manner in which Gentiles would join the Jews among the covenant people. The Jewish people were part of the family of God through the covenant rite of circumcision, while the Gentiles would join the family of God through the means of justification: faith.

A covenant can be defined as a treaty between two parties that binds them together by a promissory oath. There is both obligation and promise. This is seen in the initial form of the Abrahamic covenant in Genesis 12:1–3, where Abraham is told to go to the land God would show him and then is given promises centering on a twofold divine "blessing." The first blessing is the one God's people would *receive*, that they would become a "great nation," and the second the one they would *bestow*, that "in you all the families of the earth will be blessed." Apart from exceptions like Isaiah's theme of the procession of the nations to Zion (Isa 60:1–14), Israel embraced the first and ignored the second.

For Paul the salvation of the Gentiles was part of the reason God had chosen Israel in the first place. From the beginning God had wanted the offspring of the one faithful man to become the channel through which the nations would come back to him, so he chose Israel as his covenant community with the intent of using them to draw the Gentiles to himself. The divine intention all along had been the justification of the nations, and God prepared the children of Abraham for this by proclaiming it prophetically at the very beginning. Thus the gospel of Christ was the subject of the Old Testament from the start, foreseen by God and "announced in advance" to Abraham.

The form of the quote, "All nations will be blessed through you," combines Genesis 12:3 and 18:18, both iterations of the covenant, declaring that from the beginning the nations were called to join Abraham in faith. It is true that Genesis 12:1–3 itself emphasizes Abraham's obedience in traveling to the promised land (see also 22:18, "because you have obeyed me"), but Paul sees Genesis 15:6 as having priority. Abraham's faith both preceded his obedience and provided the basis for it. Like him, the Gentiles are justified entirely "by faith" and not by works. Obedience does not produce faith but is the byproduct of faith.

The means: with Abraham the Gentiles rely on faith (3:9)

The logical consequence of the Abrahamic covenant, Paul argues, is to recognize that "those who rely on faith are blessed along with Abraham, the man of faith." Literally in the Greek it says, "those of faith are blessed with believing Abraham." It is important to translate the adjective *pistos* here as "believing" rather than as "faithful." It was not the faithfulness of Abraham in obeying God but his faith in God's promises that was credited to him by God as righteousness. Again, Paul's emphasis is on faith rather than works.

Since all nations are blessed in Abraham (Gen 12:3), and since faith is the ground for that blessing (Gal 3:8), the natural inference is that all believing people will be blessed along with that man of faith, Abraham. This point is absolutely critical. The blessing of justification comes neither through circumcision nor through obeying the law but only through faith, with "believing Abraham" the archetype and faith-pioneer. This is equally important for our day, with many so-called Christians counting on works-righteousness to get them to heaven. We join Abraham only when we come to Christ in faith.

THE REMOVAL OF THE CURSE (3:10–14)

Paul now introduces another level of argumentation as he turns from blessing to its opposite: cursing. The point is that the works of the law cannot bless; to the contrary, they bring a curse. This leads to an obvious question: Since the works of the law can never lead to divine blessing but instead will always end in divine curse, what hope is there? That is the subject of verses 10–14. This paragraph will move step-by-step to its denouement in verse 14, where Paul declares that redemption and the promise of the Spirit come in Christ. Note the contrast between verse 9 ("those who are of faith") and verse 10 ("as many as are of the works of the law"). This juxtaposition has dominated Galatians thus far and has beleaguered the Galatian believers on account of the false claims of the Judaizers. To be under the law is to be under a curse—under condemnation and judgment from God.

The curse on those who rely on the law (3:10)

This basic truth is now anchored in a quote from Deuteronomy 27:26 (also 28:58). Found at the end of Moses' second address on the grace of God in his law, it warns of the divine curse on those who failed to keep Torah regulations. The chapter rehearses the blessings and curses of the law, commanding the people to exercise faithfulness, and warning in no uncertain terms about failure to keep the whole law. This means that all who rely on their obedience to Torah cannot help but be under a curse because they cannot possibly "continue to do everything written in the Book of the Law." That inability to keep the law perfectly is the basis of the curse. Sin always intervenes.

Paul is saying that since it is impossible to "do everything" in the law, anyone who comes to God on the basis of the works of the law is doomed to be under the curse. It is inadequate to simply desire and strive to be perfectly faithful. The point of the Deuteronomy text, according to Paul, is not striving to obey, and the problem is the inevitable human failure to succeed.

The righteous must live by faith (3:11-12)

Paul now proceeds to the next part of his argument. In verse 10 he declared the works of the law inadequate based on the lack of human capacity to keep the law perfectly. Now in verses 11-12 he reinforces the point of their inadequacy, this time arguing that they were never meant to be the basis for justification before God. The point is not doing but being, not obeying but living, not works but faith. Far from justifying a person, the works of the law bring about the divine curse (v. 10).

There are two reasons the works of the law cannot justify (that is, produce acquittal at God's tribunal). The first is that though they can keep a person in covenant relationship, they are unable to solve the sin problem. The second is salvation-historical: When Christ came the law had completed its purpose and was fulfilled or consummated in Christ and the cross. Both aspects are present in verses 11-12.

In verse 11 Paul anchors his point in Habakkuk 2:4, "The righteous will live by faith," made famous by his use of the same quote in Romans 1:17. Habakkuk prophesied to Judah at the end of the seventh century BC. He predicted judgment on the evil kingdom of Judah at the hands of the Babylonians—a prediction that would be fulfilled a few decades later. In chapters 1-2 the prophet complains, asking why God is not acting on behalf of the righteous remnant and punishing the wicked. God's answer in Habakkuk 2:4 centers on the righteous in Judah, calling on them to be faithful and to put their trust in him. Still, the exact meaning of these words, both in Habakkuk and in Galatians (as well as in Rom 1:17), is debated.

There is an interesting movement, first from the original Hebrew to the Greek Old Testament (the **Septuagint**) and then on to Paul's quotation of it. The Hebrew contains a pronoun that centers the action in God's people ("The righteous will live by *his* faith") while the Septuagint centers on God ("The righteous will live by *my* faithfulness"). Paul is closer to the original thrust of Habakkuk in the Hebrew, omitting only the pronoun:

"The righteous will live by faith." God's people must live in faith that the covenant God will fulfill his promises. The emphasis, both in Habakkuk and in Galatians, is on faith rather than on faithfulness, on belief rather than on works. Some have suggested that the emphasis is on Christ's faithfulness, but the context here, as well as Paul's use of *pistis* (faith) throughout Galatians, favors the view that this denotes faith (as opposed to works). Also, the "righteous" are those who have been justified (declared righteous at the throne of God) on the basis of Christ's atoning sacrifice.

Another issue is what term "by faith" modifies. Are we to translate Paul's words as "The one who is righteous by faith will live" or as "The one who is righteous will live by faith"? Is the emphasis on the internal faith of the righteous or on the external faith by which they live? The end result is much the same, but it is slightly better to see the emphasis on the life of faith (option two), as most versions have recognized. Also, "live" here refers not to one's life on earth but to eternal life, for Paul is talking about eternal salvation throughout this passage. Our final home in heaven can be secured not by our faithful actions but only by our faith in Christ.

The reason the law cannot justify is expressed in verse 12: "The law is not based on faith," for it centers on faithfulness in obeying the commands rather than on faith in God. By "law" Paul means the Mosaic law, and by "faith" he refers to belief in Christ for salvation. The Mosaic law centers on works and obedience, on doing rather than on believing. Thus it is not "based on faith" but on works. The contrast is clear: Justification is "by faith" (v. 11), while the law is "not of faith" (v. 12). So no one can turn to the law to be right with God.

By way of clarification, the law *did* function to restore covenant relationship with God, but that was under the old covenant, and for those who were already the covenant people, the Jews. We live in an entirely different era, the new covenant period under Christ, and the old situation no longer applies. The NLT expresses this well: "This way of faith is very different from the way of law."

Law is the old covenant mode for being right with God, and the way of faith cannot cohere with it.

To anchor this Paul quotes Leviticus 18:5, "The person who does these things will live by them." This is part of the Holiness Code of Leviticus 17–26. Leviticus 18 centers on sexuality, exhorting the Israelites to live differently from their pagan neighbors by faithfully following, by living according to, God's decrees. The passage delineates blessings and curses, with the implication that God's blessing rests on those who keep his commandments. There is a double meaning in "live by them." When God's Old Testament people lived their lives on the basis of his decrees, he in turn poured out on them a life of blessing and happiness.

How exactly is Paul using this quote? Most likely he intends it as a description of the old covenant situation before Christ arrived. Now that God's final salvation has come in Christ and is realized by faith, living according to the law can no longer suffice because no one can "do these things" perfectly. The Mosaic period is over, and we neither can nor should revert back to it. Our life now is in Christ, a status attained through justification by faith.

So there is a development of thought from verse 11 to verse 12, centering on two quotes, with the conclusion that the works of the law are the antithesis of justification by faith. In verse 11 the law cannot justify because faith is the only basis (from Hab 2:4). In verse 12 the law can have no part with faith because its injunctions have to be lived out in works (from Lev 18:5). Taken together, these verses declare that the law cannot justify because only faith can do so; the law, existing apart from faith, consists of works.

Christ redeemed us by becoming the curse (3:13)

We now return to the issue that dominates verses 10–14. Those who depend on the law for salvation are under God's curse and face eternal judgment (v. 10), for the law can never justify a person before God (v. 11). Depending on the law can never be based on faith, the only thing that can justify and lead to salvation (v. 12).

The solution lies in the salvation-historical event of the coming of Christ.

Only Christ can nullify the curse brought about by the law, and he has come for that express purpose. The "one and only Son, who is himself God" (John 1:18) has "redeemed us from the curse of the law." This is the major sentence here, and the rest of verses 13–14 consists of a series of subordinate clauses, all of them harking back to the redemptive work of Christ.

Several interpreters think that by "us" Paul has just the Jews in mind since the Gentiles were not under the law, yet this is unlikely because every human who is enslaved by sin is under the curse. Redemption covers all peoples, not just the Jews, and certainly Paul intended the Galatians to be included in this critical point. To be "redeemed" (*exagorazō*) means to be "bought up" or "purchased"; the term was used of the setting free of a slave. The imagery is that Christ on the cross freed us from the enslaving power of sin and purchased us for God. This has become a "new exodus"; Israel was redeemed from slavery in Egypt, and now those enslaved by sin are liberated by the cross of Christ. This deliverance can take place only on the basis of faith in the atoning sacrifice of Christ. We could never purchase our own freedom by our works, for we are imperfect beings whose sin invariably renders even our best works null and void. We cannot save ourselves, so Christ took it upon himself to bear our sins and purchase our salvation for us.

Paul then tells us how this redemption was secured: Christ did it "by becoming a curse for us." This is a critically important statement, since "for us" (*hyper hēmōn*) has a substitutionary sense and can almost be translated "in place of us" (see John 11:50; 2 Cor 5:14),[2] echoing the vicarious sacrifice of the Servant of the Lord in Isaiah 53:5–12. No finite human being could ever have lifted the curse, and here we see in a nutshell the reason for the incarnation

---

2. The primary meaning is still "on our behalf," but the substitutionary sense is included in its meaning.

of Christ. Jesus came entirely to pay the price to redeem us. The only way that could have been accomplished was for him to take our curse upon himself and die in our stead.

The substitutionary act of Christ as the "curse for us" is grounded in a quote from Deuteronomy 21:23: "Cursed is everyone who is hung on a pole." In Deuteronomy and in ancient practice this referred to the exposure of a criminal's body on a pole following execution as a warning to others, but by the time of Paul it was applied specifically to crucifixion. The point here is that Christ embraced on our behalf not only execution but the curse entailed specifically by crucifixion. He took our place and came under the curse by allowing himself to be hung on a cross to remove the curse from us and redeem us. He "bore our sins in his body on the cross" (1 Pet 2:24) and was "made to be sin for us" (2 Cor 5:21) so that we could be redeemed. This the law could never have done; only Christ could accomplish this.

Abraham's blessing comes to the Gentiles (3:14)

Here Paul explains two purposes of Christ's redeeming work, with the first acting as a summary of verses 10-14 and the second summarizing verses 1-5. The divine curse that dominates the lives of fallen human beings has been lifted by the redemptive work of Christ, and as a result not only Jews but Gentiles as well can now experience the promise given to Abraham. In this new era of salvation history faith in Christ enables Jew and Gentile alike to live under "the blessing given to Abraham," the promise that his seed would bring their blessing to the nations, as stated in 3:8 above. The Gentiles join in this blessing not by the works of the law but by believing in Christ.

The second purpose is "that by faith we might receive the promise of the Spirit." The topic again is the salvation-historical switch from the old covenant to the new. This is determined by two prophetic fulfillments: the coming of Christ and the arrival of the age of the Spirit. As Paul argued in 3:1-5, the fact that the

Galatians are living in the new age is proven by their experience of the Spirit. Paul further defines the Abrahamic blessing, in that the redemptive work of Christ brought both salvation and the Spirit to those who believe. Both justification and the gift of the Spirit come by faith.

The "promise of the Spirit" refers especially to the promise of the Abrahamic covenant, and the coming of the Spirit is seen as the inheritance promised to Abraham and his offspring but intended by God from the outset to be shared with the Gentiles. Paul's emphasis is twofold: The Spirit both comes by faith and is experienced in Christ. All peoples, Jew and Gentile, inherit the blessing, but it can be experienced not by keeping the works of the law but only through faith. Paul may have had in mind especially Isaiah 44:3, proclaiming the blessing of the Spirit: "I will pour out my Spirit on your offspring, and my blessing on your descendants."

PAUL PROCLAIMS THE SUBSIDIARY NATURE OF THE MOSAIC LAW (3:15–18)

In this section Paul continues his case regarding the serious problem of positing a law-based salvation. In the last section he focused on the functional side, showing what the law could not do: remove the curse from us. Here he turns to the ontological side, to what the law in its essence actually entails. In other words, he turns from what the law does to what the law is. There are two parts to his argument here: First, the Mosaic covenant is subordinate to the Abrahamic, serving to further draw out aspects of that first covenant. Second, the "promise" is given with the Abrahamic rather than with the Mosaic covenant, further establishing its primacy. The promise comes to us not through the works of the law but through the faith that was central to the Abrahamic covenant.

THE PERMANENT NATURE OF A HUMAN COVENANT (3:15)
Paul begins by calling the Galatians "brothers and sisters," showing that his comments stem from love. Jew and Gentile alike are

all part of the family of God, and it is brotherly concern that lies behind what he says. He then introduces "an example from everyday life" (literally, "from a human perspective"). When human treaties or covenants are ratified and finalized, no one can "set aside or add" any stipulations. In other words, they are binding and irrevocable. Some have surmised that Paul is referring to a last will and testament rather than to a treaty, but wills were no more irrevocable in the ancient world than they are now, so it is more likely that he does indeed have a covenant in view. In short, Paul begins this paragraph with the example of the binding nature of covenants.

The Promise Given to Christ as the Seed of Abraham (3:16)

The emphasis in this verse is the seed of Abraham. The phrase "Abraham and his seed" stems from Genesis 13:15; 15:18; and 17:8, where the land promises are found. In Genesis the "seed" is a collective singular noun referring to Abraham's innumerable offspring, but Paul uses rabbinic logic to argue that "seed" is a singular noun. Such an argument was fairly common in Jewish exegesis. This prepares Paul's readers for 3:29 ("If you belong to Christ, then you are Abraham's seed"). It was common in Judaism to refer to the Messiah as "the seed of David" (2 Sam 7:12), so Paul is using common Jewish forms of exegesis to make his point that all of the Abrahamic promises are fulfilled in Christ.

Paul has more than once spoken of the promises given with the Abrahamic covenant. But in verses 2–5, 14 it was the Spirit who was the promise of the Abrahamic covenant; his point here focuses on the primary promissory fulfillment, namely the gift of Christ. Multiple promises flowed from the Abrahamic covenant: innumerable descendants that would become a great nation, the inheritance of the land, and the blessing of the Gentiles. All the nations were intended to share in those blessings, but they were especially given to "Abraham's seed." When linked with verse 15, the emphasis is on the irrevocable nature of these promises. The covenant God is guaranteeing these blessings, and they will not be revoked. The one both making and fulfilling the promise is God, and so the promise is connected to faith in God rather than to human works.

The thrust of this verse is that all of these promises to Abraham have been fulfilled in Jesus Christ and channeled through him to those who by faith are united "in Christ" and have thus become the new seed of Abraham, the church. Several interpreters have noted that this sums up the basic narrative of Scripture itself: The promises to Abraham reverberate throughout the history of Israel, from the patriarchs to Moses to David and to the prophets, as the successive stages of the people of God remain in corporate solidarity with Abraham and the divine promises for his seed. These narrow to the messianic promises in the seed of David, as fulfilled in the son of David. Jesus is both the son of Abraham and the son of David, the "seed" in whom all the promises are realized, and the church, composed of both believing Jews and believing Gentiles, is united with Christ and thereby becomes the heir of these promises.

THE PRIORITY OF THE ABRAHAMIC COVENANT (3:17)

Paul's Jewish Christian opponents had so elevated the Mosaic law that it had virtually supplanted the Abrahamic covenant. For them the law took absolute precedence, and Abraham had merely prepared the way for it. Some rabbis even went so far as to say that Abraham himself had obeyed the Torah, and Jews commonly held that the Mosaic laws were eternal in effect. Paul's counterargument in this verse works from the weightier to the lighter, with timing the major factor in determining which is weightier or more important. Paul says that the law was "introduced 430 years later"; it did not come into existence until hundreds of years after the covenant with Abraham. While Genesis 15:13 claims that there were 400 years between the two events—the giving of the covenant and the giving of the Ten Commandments at Sinai—Exodus 12:40 specifies 430 years. The rabbis thought the lower number represented the time in Egypt and the higher number the period from the Abrahamic covenant to the giving of the Sinai Law. Paul is arguing here that the Abrahamic covenant takes priority over the Mosaic covenant because it came first.

Since the Abrahamic covenant both came earlier and is weightier in importance, the Mosaic law could not "set aside" or nullify its force and its promises. Moreover, the Abrahamic centers on faith and promise, while the Mosaic centers on legal obedience and transgression. God was central in the first and his people in the second. Paul's point is that the lesser cannot have precedence over the greater. Yet the Judaizers and their system are doing just that—replacing the primacy of the faith and the promise of the Abrahamic covenant with the works-righteousness of the Mosaic covenant.[3]

The Inheritance Given via an Eternal Promise (3:18)

Paul now turns from the salvation-historical view in verse 17 back to the essential attributes of each covenant. Not only is the Abrahamic covenant prior to the Mosaic covenant, it has at its heart divine promise and the fulfillment of that promise in inheritance. The Mosaic covenant centers on temporary obedience and present faithfulness, the Abrahamic on eternal promise and future hope. So "if the inheritance depends on the law, then it no longer depends on promise." Under this misguided paradigm works would have gained ascendancy over future hope. The works of the law could not, Paul argued, be the basis of the future inheritance, for the promise had come through grace, as "God in his grace gave it to Abraham through a promise."

---

3. Again, in the old covenant the law did not constitute works righteousness, for it was an act of God's grace. However, after Christ came and brought salvation by faith the law became works righteousness in the Judaizer system, as it replaced the cross.

In Genesis this inheritance referred to the promised land (17:8; 21:10; 22:17; see Josh 11:23; 12:6; 13:1), but in the prophetic period it increasingly came to symbolize the people of God inheriting the world at some future time. In the New Testament the inheritance is Christ and the life he has brought. Paul uses *kecharistai* for God "giving" the inheritance to Abraham, constituting a "grace-gift." The Abrahamic promise is a special gift of grace, but if it is made subservient to the works of the law, God's grace is obviated and rendered ineffectual. Works are opposed to grace, as in Romans 1:6: "And if by grace, then it cannot be based on works; if it were, grace would no longer be grace." This means that the Judaizer system, with works taking precedence over grace and faith, nullifies the very basis of God's salvation. When God graciously gave the promised inheritance to Abraham, there were no works involved. Abraham did not have to produce anything to earn the gift. It was free grace, accepted by faith.

———

This important passage is not just a historical study about an early set of false teachings that at one point endangered the church. It is about the true meaning of the gospel and the critical centrality of salvation by faith rather than by works. Paul, who had taught the Galatians well about the true gospel and the basis of salvation, was shocked and dismayed that any of them could have been so easily led astray by the Judaizers.

I cannot help but wonder whether we have the right to be shocked if the people in our own churches don't know their theology. We are living in an age of shallowness, when any desire for truth is too often replaced by a preference for passive entertainment. Those of us in Christian leadership positions need to teach our people well and develop an atmosphere in our churches in which people are eager for Bible study and theological discussion.

There are many churches in which this is happening, but far too many in which it is not.

For Paul the Spirit was the sign of the new age of Christ and proof positive of the reality of justification by faith in the new age of salvation. Moreover, our experience of the Spirit comes via faith rather than works. This turns us from a narcissistic works-righteousness, in which we view ourselves as virtually saving ourselves by our works, to a Christ-centered salvation in which faith enables us to accept what God has done for us. The law cannot save; it can only bring a curse because it points to transgression. Christ alone has solved our sin problem by becoming our substitute and taking our curse on himself. That is the gospel, the good news of Christ!

The point of this section is that the Abrahamic covenant takes priority over the Mosaic, with faith taking precedence over works. The promised inheritance belongs to Christians, in Christ and in the Spirit, not in the works of the law. This is equally true and important in our day. Every believer must be Christ-centered and faith-based. We must remember that our walk with Christ is what matters, not our basic goodness or worthwhile activities. Our merit is Christ and the experience of the Spirit, and we live wholly by faith—not by works.

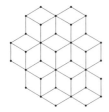

THE LAW'S TEMPORARY PURPOSE (3:19–29)

G alatians 3 answers the false teachers by proving that the Galatians, not the Judaizing heretics, are indeed the children of Abraham and heirs of the Abrahamic blessings. They had experienced the Spirit (vv. 1-5) and received the promises by faith rather than by the works of the law (vv. 6-9). Christ had removed their curse by becoming a curse for them (vv. 10-14), proving that the Abrahamic covenant (intended to bless the Gentiles) had priority over the Mosaic covenant (intended for the Jews; vv. 15-18). The current passage (vv. 19-29) builds on what has come before by describing the divinely intended purpose of the law and its place in redemptive history as a temporary instrument meant to prepare for the coming of Christ.

There are two parts to this section. In verses 19-25 Paul addresses the question "Why was the law given?" He answers that its divinely intended purpose was to point out transgressions, making clear that human sin transgressed God's law and was punishable. The law is not antithetical to the promises, but it could not solve the problem of sin and give life. Rather, by pointing out the reality of sin it imprisoned people under sin. As the "custodian" of the future reality, it pointed the way forward to Christ and to salvation by faith. Now that the new era had come, the law was no longer needed.

The second part of the passage (vv. 26–29) identifies believers as the offspring of Abraham and sons of God based on their union with Christ. The Mosaic era no longer has a hold on them because they belong to Christ by faith.

PAUL STATES THE LAW'S PURPOSE AS A TEMPORARY INSTRUMENT (3:19–25)

The Purpose behind Its Interim Status (3:19–21)

Now that Paul has proved in verses 15–18 that the law was subordinate to the Abrahamic covenant, he asks the natural question: "Why, then, was the law given at all?" If salvation comes by faith and the promises come through the Abrahamic rather than the Mosaic covenant, what purpose could there be for the law?

Paul says that the Mosaic law was "added" to its more important predecessor "because of transgressions." The preposition (*charin*, "because") may point to purpose more than to cause—the law was added "in order to" deal with transgressions. This means two things. First, the law's purpose was to highlight the true nature of sin as transgressing God's law. As Paul points out elsewhere in Romans 5:13, "sin was in the world before the law was given, but sin is not charged against anyone's account when there is no law." In Romans 4:15 he adds, "The law brings wrath. And where there is no law, there is no transgression." This is the forensic or legal purpose: to condemn sin in God's law court as transgression. Second, the law was given to "increase" transgression (Rom 5:20)—not to cause more sinning but to make everyone aware of the many sins of which they were already guilty. Before the law people would not have been able to recognize their own sin, but with its standards in place they know they have committed many sins and are indeed sinners. Moreover, by showing sin to be transgression, the law made it more attractive to the fleshly mind. The law could not restrain sin; in fact, it had the opposite effect, for the depraved mind is attracted to what it knows is wrong.

So the law can point out sin, but it cannot solve our sin problem. For that, we need Christ, which is the point of the next
clause: "until the Seed to whom the promise referred had come."
In Galatians 3:16 Paul presented Christ as the "seed" of Abraham,
meaning that the law was intended to prepare for the coming of
the Messiah (Greek: *Christos*). When the Messiah arrived and died
on the cross, effecting redemption and the justification of sinners, the law's purpose came to an end and the interim period was
over. In this new dispensation sinners confront their transgressions in Christ rather than in the law, so its purpose had become
obsolete. Furthermore, the "promise" of the Abrahamic covenant
has through Christ's atoning sacrifice been fully realized. Since
the promise came 430 years before the law and pointed directly
to Christ, it bypassed the law and further highlighted its temporary nature.

Paul's next argument for the lesser status of the law is the fact
that it was mediated through angels and Moses rather than coming
directly from God like the Abrahamic covenant. The terse nature
of this verse has led to multiple theories about its meaning, and it
has jokingly been observed that there is a different interpretation
for every one of the 430 years mentioned in 3:17.

Interestingly, the presence of angels at Sinai is not found in
the biblical account. The closest approximation is Deuteronomy
33:2: "The LORD came from Sinai. ... He came with myriads of
holy ones." The **Septuagint** (Greek) of the end of this verse also
includes "angels with him." Even though the Old Testament evidence is inconclusive, the tradition of the presence of angels at
Sinai was clear in extrabiblical Jewish literature (Jubilees 1:27-
2:1; Josephus, *Antiquities of the Jews*, 15.136) and accepted by New
Testament writers (Acts 7:53; Heb 2:2). We can accordingly accept
it as fact that angels were with God at Sinai.

The law was "entrusted to a mediator" (literally, "ordained by
the hand of a mediator"). This is likely a reference to Moses, and the
"hand" an image of the bringing down of the Ten Commandments

from the mountain in the hands of Moses (Exod 32:15). Some see Moses mediating the law to the angels, but that doesn't make sense in this context. Almost certainly it refers to Moses bringing the law down the mountain to the people of Israel. Moses also was the interpreter of Torah for the people, as seen in his sermons in Deuteronomy. The picture is of two mediators, God giving the Torah to the angels, who in effect gave it to Moses, who took it to the people. The people of Israel, not Moses, were the recipients of the law, with Moses acting as the mediator through whom God gave it.

The point (v. 20) is that while the Abrahamic covenant went directly to Abraham, the Torah had to be doubly mediated: "A mediator, however, implies more than one party." The fact that the transmission of the law required two parties (three, if one counts the angels) places it in contrast to the Abrahamic covenant, which needed no mediator and so is more closely aligned with God, for "God is one." The oneness of God is the heart of the **Shema** (Deut 6:4), and this oneness is better reflected in the faith promises to Abraham than in the works stipulations of the Mosaic law. The Mosaic covenant, then, brought together two opposing parties and thus needed a mediator, while the Abrahamic covenant was propounded in One-ness through direct divine initiative and needed none. The promises came directly to Abraham, but the law came indirectly to the Israelites.

Now, Paul has argued that the law came later than the promises, and that the Mosaic covenant is subordinate to the Abrahamic. Since the law was mediated and indirect as opposed to the direct promises, Paul anticipates a possible conclusion by asking rhetorically whether it was then "opposed to the promises of God" (v. 21). That suggestion takes the conclusion too far, and he answers with his patented "Absolutely not!" It is true that the law's purpose was always to prepare for Christ's coming, and that when that day arrived it had fulfilled its purpose and "ended" (Rom 10:4 ESV). But that does not mean that it was opposed to the promises.

As in Romans 7:12–13, Paul affirms the basic goodness of the law in God's plan. The law and the promises have different functions, but the law plays its proper role in God's economy.

One of the primary areas of difference lies in their respective purposes. The law cannot impart life. Paul uses a device known as a contrary-to-fact conditional to say this: "If a law had been given that could impart life [which could not have happened], then righteousness would certainly have come by the law [which didn't happen]." Even though many Jewish writings between the Old and New Testaments claimed the law to have been the source of life (for example, Sirach 17:11; 45:5), the atoning work of Christ shows that notion to be wrong. In the old covenant the law did bring life, but that life was defined by a right covenant relationship with God. When Christ came, life, embracing final salvation, meant much more. The law could not produce that kind of life. "Righteousness" in Galatians means being declared forgiven and right with God, and it is the result of the promise realized in Christ and attained by faith. The purpose of the law was to point out the need; only Christ could meet that need.

Two Analogies behind the Law's Purpose (3:22–25)

In these verses Paul uses two analogies, presenting the law as being like imprisonment and like a custodian. There is a syllogism behind them, and it brings us to the heart of Paul's argument against the **Judaizers** and their system. These analogies tell why God instituted the law under the old covenant reality:

> MAJOR PREMISE: Imprisonment and the
> custodian are temporary instruments.
> MINOR PREMISE: The law imprisons
> and serves as a custodian.
> CONCLUSION: Therefore, the law
> is a temporary instrument.

The law as a prison (3:22-23)

The "but" (*alla*) that begins the analogies sets them in contrast to what the law cannot do, according to verse 21: give life. There are various views on the meaning of "Scripture" here. Some think Paul uses the term as a synonym for "law," but that seems unlikely. Others think it refers to a particular verse, Deuteronomy 27:26, quoted above in Galatians 3:10 and singled out here because of its importance to Paul's argument. Yet one would have expected him to be clearer if that were the case, since there are several other quotes in the intervening verses. Most likely Paul means Scripture as a whole, conveying that the entire Old Testament supports the law in locking everything up under the power of sin.

The verb for "lock up" is *synekleisen*, meaning to imprison, confine, or enclose. This creates a picture of people in a prison cage confined under the control of the jailer, as in Romans 11:32, "God has bound everyone over to disobedience." It is interesting that here it is not "everyone" but "everything" (*ta panta*) that is confined. Some think the neuter here refers to people, but more likely it includes all of creation. In Romans 8:20-22, for example, all creation is said to be "subject to frustration" and "groaning" under the sin situation ("bondage to decay") that humankind has foisted upon it. The enslavement of people to sin is part of a larger drama involving the whole of God's creation. Every human being is "under the control of sin," and the law not only cannot help but is itself part of the problem. In Romans 6 sin is portrayed as an invading army seeking to conquer and enslave humankind, and here that invasion is shown to have been successful.

Yet there is a divine purpose behind this imprisonment. God and Scripture have locked everything under sin "so that [*hina*] what was promised, being given through faith in Jesus Christ, might be given to those who believe." The imprisonment is intended to force sinners to turn to the promises. The law cannot solve the problem of sin, but it can make people turn to what does: the promises of God in Christ. "What was promised" looks not to the covenant itself but to the blessings promised in the covenant, namely the promise of righteousness and life in verse 21.

The gift is attained "through faith in Jesus Christ." Here we are back in the debate of 2:16, 20 as to whether we are to translate this as a subjective genitive—"the faithfulness of Jesus Christ"—or as objective—"faith in Jesus Christ." Is it Christ's faithful fulfillment of his divine destiny or our faith in him that is the subject here? For the same reasons I noted in the commentary on 2:16, 20, I think that Paul is emphasizing the centrality of our faith response by using the noun and the verb ("those who believe") to highlight it. It is faith, not works, that liberates people from the imprisoning power of sin. Yet it is God, not our own strength, that supplies this faith: "given through faith … given to those who believe." We do not find faith in ourselves; we are given it by God.

In verse 23 Paul emphasizes the temporary nature of the law's confinement "before the coming of this faith." Once again, the law is an interim measure meant to prepare for the era of faith. God never intended for the Mosaic system to be in effect after Christ came. One could almost change BC and AD to BF and AF—"before faith" and "after faith." During that earlier period "we were held in custody," with the law as the warden for those imprisoned under sin. The "we" could be the Jewish people living under the law, held in bondage by its regulations that could not solve their sin problem (see 2:15). However, it is generally agreed that Paul also sees the Gentiles as part of the old era and included in the "we." "Faith" in verse 23 is not the general placing of one's trust in God but specifically that "faith in Christ" noted in verse 22. The coming of this faith is the arrival of the new age, the new order that Christ inaugurated.

There is some debate whether "held in custody" should be viewed positively, as a protective shield guarding God's people from the sins of the world around them. While possible, that is unlikely in this context of their being "confined under sin" (v. 22). To be under the law means to be under sin, and the law, given to make sin visible and highlight the need for liberation, could only point forward to Christ. Several times Paul reinforces the dilemma—we are "under sin" (3:22) = "under the law" (3:23) = "under a guardian" (3:25) = "in slavery" (4:3) = "under the elemental spiritual forces of the world" (4:3). The imprisoning forces held all humanity in bondage, and the Mosaic era saw everyone enslaved under sin, with little hope for liberation until Christ came.

Still, as desperate as the situation was, it was a temporary phenomenon, for humankind was "locked up [*only*] until the faith that was to come would be revealed." The law cannot redeem people from sin, but its salvation-historical purpose is to reveal the nature of sin and point to the need for rescue from sin. The law was an interim measure that prepared for its own climax and removal in Christ. Paul's point is clear: Why would anyone want to remain in imprisonment when their freedom from captivity and emancipation from slavery has arrived? When the prison doors have been opened, no one in their right mind would want to continue stagnating in a cell!

The law as a guardian (3:24–25)

The result ("So," Greek: *hōste*) is that the law functioned during that interim period as "our guardian until Christ came." The term for "guardian" (*paidagōgos*) signifies a "pedagogue" or "custodian." Often these were household slaves trained to watch over a child and guide their development until they reached adulthood. These slaves were not really teachers but primarily supervisors and custodians, dealing with moral and ethical standards and generally guiding the children and disciplining them appropriately. Many interpreters have cited a positive function for the law here, seeing in it a teacher and guide preparing Israel for the coming of the Messiah and thus serving as a protector and a restraining force against sin.

This interpretation is indeed quite possible, but the context of Galatians makes it unlikely. In verse 22, remember, everything was "locked up under the control of sin," and it is doubtful Paul would have veered from that focus. The law supervised the people temporarily, guiding them "until Christ came that we might be justified by faith." The Judaizers had rejected this interim function of the law and wanted to make it permanent, exactly opposite God's intention. At the turning point of the ages Christ completed the law and faith replaced its works. Israel had been redeemed from Egypt, and in fulfillment of that the saints are now justified by faith. Paul emphasizes here that Christ came in order that we might be declared right with God as we turn to Christ in faith.

Verse 25 acts as a summary of both analogies: "Now that this faith has come, we are no longer under a guardian." "Faith" is a symbol for the new age of salvation history that has been instituted in Christ. He has arrived and has died on the cross as our atoning sacrifice, and his substitutionary atonement has been credited to our account in God's courtroom. We participate in God's salvation by faith, so this is not only the age of the Spirit (3:1–5, 14) but the age of faith. As in verse 23, the "we" refers especially to the Jews but also includes the Gentiles who have joined believing Jews in the new Israel. The interim status of the law as the custodian of God's people has ended, and it is no longer needed. God's people have reached adulthood. We are a "mature" people, in the process of "attaining to the whole measure of the fullness of Christ" (Eph 4:13).

PAUL IDENTIFIES BELIEVERS AS THE CHILDREN OF GOD (3:26–29)

The message of this chapter is that the law was a temporary instrument meant to point out the need for sinful people to get right with God, but never able to make them right with God. Rather, it served a custodial function, imprisoning people under the law and preparing the world for the new messianic age that was to come.

When Christ came and brought with him the new era of salvation, he fulfilled the law and completed its purpose in himself. In the old economy Israel had maintained their covenant relationship with God by performing the works of the law. Now all peoples, Jews and Gentiles alike, are declared right with God by faith in Christ. This passage specifies the results—that those who believe become the children of God and join his new family.

FAITH AS THE BASIS OF SONSHIP (3:26)

The best-known passage on sonship[1] is Romans 8:14–17. This passage details how those who come to God by faith are given the Spirit of sonship who brings about their adoption as the children of God. "All" (emphatic here to denote both Jews and Gentiles) who come will join Jesus as the seed of Abraham and inherit the promises, becoming "children of God through faith." No longer under the custodial power of the law, they have entered adulthood as the body of Christ. The emphasis, as throughout Galatians, is on the centrality of "faith,"[2] as opposed to the works of the law. The gift of salvation is just that, a gift from God, in no way something we earn by our works.

As throughout Paul's writings, this all takes place "in Christ Jesus." Here we are at the heart of the "in Christ" theme in Paul's theology, referring to union with Christ and the resulting incorporation into his body. This theme is especially dominant in the Prison Letters (Colossians, Philemon, Ephesians, and Philippians). The faith that brings us to Christ and leads to our justification at

---

1. I use "sonship" rather than the more general "adoption" because underlying this term are Roman inheritance laws that gave sons very particular rights. While those who are made children of God include men and women, it is still best to use "sonship" in this context. This was also true in the Old Testament world, where inheritance was always passed from father to son.

2. Those who argue for the "faithfulness of Jesus" in 2:16, 20; 3:22 also see this as teaching Jesus' faithfulness. As I argued in my comments on those verses, this does not make as much sense here as saving faith in Christ on our part.

the same time unites us with Christ and through that union with each other in him.

The Results of Sonship (3:27–29)
Clothed with Christ (3:27)

This verse builds on the "in Christ" theme of verse 26, explaining that union with Christ means "putting on" or "being clothed with" Christ. There are two stages here. Those who are sons of God are first "baptized into Christ" and then "clothed with Christ." It is difficult to know why Paul chose to describe the new believer as having been "baptized into Christ." The language fits closely with Jesus' resurrection command in Matthew 28:19, "Baptizing them *into* the name of the Father and of the Son and of the Holy Spirit" (my translation). This means that we are baptized "into union with" the Triune Godhead. Paul may have been borrowing this phrase from early church catechesis, the oral instruction of new converts. This became a major source of the material used by Paul for ethical and spiritual exhortation in his letters.

Paul uses baptism here as a symbol of our conversion. This is seen also in Romans 6:3 and Colossians 2:12, where the word picture of baptism as immersion (the meaning of *baptizō*) is used to describe conversion as union with Christ's death (being immersed in the water) and resurrection (coming out of the water). Baptism is not the instrument of salvation (a view that is called "baptismal regeneration") but "the pledge of a clear conscience toward God" (1 Pet 3:21). This means that baptism is in a sense the final step of the salvation experience, the point at which we in effect sign the salvation contract (my view of the meaning of "pledge") with God.

This leads naturally into the image of being "clothed with Christ," as "baptized into Christ" is linked with the "in Christ" theme when we are united with Christ and incorporated into him and his body, the church. The idea of "putting on" (being clothed with) Christ is another major metaphor in Paul's writings, used in Romans 6:4, Ephesians 4:24, and Colossians 3:10 for "putting on the new self." The old self is Adam's nature, and the new self is Christ as the Last Adam who has triumphed over the sinful realm Adam brought into the world (Rom 5:12–21). The image here is of the new life that begins with sonship. To put on Christ is to unite with him and enter his victory over the dark forces. As in Isaiah 61:10, we put on "the garments of salvation" and become new persons in Christ. The law could not bring us into relationship with Christ; only faith can do that. This faith brings sonship, immersion into Christ, and a new depth of union symbolized as a new set of clothes.

Oneness in Christ (3:28)

Having established our sonship and union with Christ, Paul now turns in a well-known passage to discuss the removal of social barriers in Christ, probably again using catechetical material developed in the early church. There are other passages like this in Paul; 1 Corinthians 12:13 and Colossians 3:11 carry the same message that our union in Christ and with one another brings about the eradication of social and religious distinctions. The point here is that by faith we are enabled to become the children of Abraham and of God, and that this union has brought together all humankind.

This means there is "neither Jew nor Gentile." The Abrahamic covenant marked the beginning of the idea of Abraham's descendants as a distinct people chosen by God, and the Jewish people always appealed to that covenant when emphasizing their distinctiveness and national destiny. Yet at the same time that covenant also stipulated that their destiny included being a blessing to the Gentiles. That blessing, Paul is pointing out here, was eventually to lead to the Gentile mission and the removal of distinctions in Christ. In other words, God did not choose Abraham's descendants as a matter of preference but to reach out and bring the Gentiles to himself. This had been his intention all along, meaning that the Judaizers were completely wrong.

Similarly, there is now "neither slave nor free." There were many slaves and former slaves in the early Christian house churches, as seen by the numerous slave names in lists like the one in Romans 16. There is no call in the New Testament for the end of slavery as an institution; notice that Paul in his letter to Philemon did not call for him to free his slave Onesimus.[3] Most of the people of the first century could not have conceived of a world without slavery, since the institution had existed throughout human history. However, the teaching of the New Testament, with its emphasis on the essential brotherhood between slaves and masters and the equality of slave and free in Christ, pointed inevitably to the eventual disappearance of slavery from the world scene. In the church typified by oneness there is no room for slave and free. While Paul probably had no reference point from which to understand the full implications of this, God certainly did!

Finally, there is in God's economy no "male and female." Interestingly, the grammar changes here. The first two juxtapositions are "neither/nor," while this third one reads literally as "no male *and* female." This is likely a quote from Genesis 1:27: "Male and female he created them." Paul is quite emphatic, but it is difficult to know the precise implications within his context. This comment has spawned considerable debate between two camps that have come to be known as egalitarian (stressing equality between genders) and complementarian (stressing distinct gender roles). Both agree that men and women are equal before God, "joint-heirs of the grace of life" (1 Pet 3:7), but the camps strongly differ regarding their respective roles in the home and church.

How do we reconcile this verse with Ephesians 5:22–23, "Wives, submit yourselves to your own husbands as you do to the Lord. For the husband is the head of the wife as Christ is head of the

---

3. He may have hinted that he would like him to be set free, but for ministry's sake and not based on ideology.

church"? Galatians was written about AD 48–49 and Ephesians about 61–62, around fourteen years later. This tells us that "nor is there male and female" for Paul did not mean the removal of submission from marriage, since he continued to teach it. Therefore equality for Paul did not indicate removal of marital roles (or the complete removal of master-slave distinctions). The thrust is that in Christ there is equality, though social roles in this world still continue. As several have noted, this likely reflects the new creation theme found elsewhere in Paul (2 Cor 5:17; Gal 6:15). God's creation has entered its final stage in preparation for eternity; the old distinctions brought about by human sin have been overcome in Christ.

The conclusion is that "you are all one in Christ Jesus." That is a major result of the salvation-historical switch that occurred when Christ came, and this kind of equality had no place in the Judaizers' system. Moreover, such unity can be a reality only in the church, for the world and its evil system are based entirely on the dynamics of the strong trampling the weak and the rich taking from the poor. We will not experience complete oneness until Christ has returned and evil has once for all time been removed from God's creation. Sin is focused on the centrality of the self, and so long as we exist in the flesh we will be unable to enjoy perfect unity. Still, as we mature in Christ and learn to live as God's children in this world we will continue to grow and improve in this area. The goal of every church is to live as a community of God's children—to live and love together as one people.

Heirs of Abraham (3:29)

Chapter 3 focuses on the Abrahamic covenant and its twofold promise for the multiplication of Abraham's seed and the blessing of the Gentiles. These promises coalesce in Paul's emphasis on believing Gentiles joining believing Jews as the children of Abraham (3:7, 14, 16). Paul sums this up with his conclusion, "If you belong to Christ, then you are Abraham's seed, and heirs according to the promise." Abraham's offspring, those who inherit the promises, are not the Jewish people per se but the new Israel, those who "belong to Christ" (= are in Christ) on the basis of faith, consisting of believing Jews and Gentiles. Christ was the "seed" of Abraham (v. 16), and the rest of the offspring are those who belong to him through faith.

Paul in verses 19–21 clarified the reason God had given the Torah to Israel. Its purpose was to show that sin transgresses God's laws and that sinful humankind desperately needed a solution to its sin problem. But the law could not provide resolution and in fact needed to be mediated to God's people by both angels and Moses. That solution entered this world in Christ, ushering in a new era in salvation history, for the new life that has entered the world is attained exclusively by faith. The two analogies of verses 22–25 expand this image, for Paul presents the law as a temporary instrument intended by God to prepare for the coming of Christ and of the age of faith, both by imprisoning Israel under sin and by serving as their custodian until his people reached maturity under Christ.

Note the piling up of metaphors in verses 19–29 to describe the true people of God—children of Abraham, the redeemed, receivers of the Spirit, inheritors of the promise, those who believe, children of God, those baptized into Christ, those clothed with Christ, and those who belong to Christ. Paul wants his readers to realize the riches of being a Christ follower and also the empty reality awaiting those who had fallen into the Judaizers' heresy. The Galatians had to decide whether they wanted the treasures of heaven or the emptiness of an earth-centered religion. That is our choice as well: Are we seeking a life of false works, in which we try to earn our own salvation but inherit an eternity of nothingness, or are we willing to come to Christ by faith and inherit an eternity of joy and God's rich salvation?

———

There is only one path to life, and we, like the Galatians, must make certain we are not misled by false teachers into taking another path than that of faith. Only those who have come to Christ in faith are the children of God and the children of Abraham. The law and its works offer only empty promises. Justification by faith has made us the seed of Abraham and the children of God, and life under Christ is characterized by newness, by the putting on of the garments of salvation, meaning Christ. With this newness came the removal of social and gender barriers, so that God's people enjoy unity both with Christ and with each other.

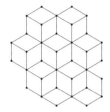

SPIRITUAL LIBERATION FROM SLAVERY (4:1–11)

S o far in this letter we have seen that Paul's Jewish Christian opponents, the **Judaizers**, had visited the churches he had established on the first missionary journey and attacked two aspects of his ministry: the validity of his apostleship and the truthfulness of his gospel preaching. They had argued that he was merely a self-appointed leader subordinate to the Twelve, and that his gospel was in error because he rejected the law. They demanded that the Gentiles become Jewish converts and embrace the law before they could become Christians. Their arguments seemed convincing to many Galatian Christians, who began to follow that creed and observe the Mosaic regulations.

Paul responds to the first charge in the first two chapters, countering that he had received his apostolic commission directly from Christ and that he was not subordinate but equal to the Twelve. Moreover, the Twelve had themselves embraced his gospel, not that of the Judaizers. He responds to the second charge in chapters 3–4, proving that when Christ came he initiated a new period of salvation history. The period of the law has ended, replaced by the new era of justification by faith and the age of the Spirit. Moreover, even before Christ came the Mosaic covenant had not been central. The Abrahamic covenant was the core of the Old Testament, in that faith was already present with it and the blessing of the

Gentiles was the express purpose of God in choosing the Jews as his special people.

THERE IS A SALVATION-HISTORICAL SWITCH FROM SLAVERY TO SONSHIP (4:1-7)

This passage builds especially on 3:15-29, which showed that the promises to Abraham were fulfilled in the conversion of the Galatian Gentiles. Negatively, the law with its works had not set aside the promises, nor had it solved the sin problem. Positively, however, the law had been given to point out the nature of sin as transgression. From the start it had functioned both to imprison people in sin and to serve as a custodian, preparing this world for the coming of Christ (3:22-25). This passage adds a third metaphor, slavery, to the two of 3:22-25, depicting the temporary nature and purpose of the law. The law enslaved humankind under "the elements of the world" (4:1-3) and prepared for the coming of the Son to redeem sinful humanity (vv. 4-5), as well as for the coming of the Spirit to proclaim redeemed humanity to be the children and heirs of God (vv. 6-7). In light of this reality it is pure insanity (and worse, apostasy) to return to the law (vv. 8-11).

THE ANALOGY OF SLAVERY (4:1-3)

In context, this is the third analogy about the law as an interim measure preparing for the coming of Christ, following the first two, those of imprisonment and guardianship (3:22-25). Paul returns to the analogy from 3:24-25 of the law as custodian but takes it in a different direction, focusing here on the subservience of the child to the custodian, even when the child is the heir of the entire estate and the custodian merely one of the slaves owned by the estate.

The submission of an heir, while a child, to custodians (4:1-2)

The first verse is framed with a statement of the child's actual status: As "heir" to the estate, he is in reality "lord of all" (*kyrios pantōn*, translated "owns the whole estate" in the NIV). There is emphasis on the "all," with the implication that the child owns the custodian/slave as well.

Paul's point, however, appears in the middle of the verse, where we are told that so long as he is "underage" (*nēpios*, "an infant" or "a minor"), the child is, in practical reality, "no different from a slave." That assertion would have garnered everyone's attention, prompting the question "In what way?"

The child in this analogy is likely the oldest child of a wealthy Roman, the one who will inherit both the estate and the exalted place in society the father possesses. In spite of the child's exalted future, as a minor he is placed under overseers. They have absolute control, and the child has to obey their every command. The typical practice, discussed in 3:23–24, entailed the appointment of a servant or slave to function much like a full-time babysitter, watching over the child and controlling his movements and development to adulthood, the "time set by his father" for him to receive his inheritance.

But here the analogy shifts. The "guardians and trustees" (v. 2) are not really the custodians or pedagogues of 3:23–24 but probably the managers of the estate. Paul seems to have moved beyond the image of the maturation of a child in verse 2 to illustrate his point. The "time set" for the onset of adulthood was determined not by the father but by custom; a fourteen-year-old child was officially deemed an adult. Many expositors think that the appointed time to which Paul refers, along with the mention of "guardians and trustees," points back to the exodus of Israel from Egypt (see v. 3), when God's people were awaiting their inheritance in the promised land. This fits Paul's emphasis on redemption and adoption as God's children. Paul's point is that the Galatians have experienced a second exodus and dare not throw it away by returning to the law. God has established the time—the "fullness of time" in verse 4—and they have entered their maturity and received their inheritance: Christ and the gospel.

Application to the enslavement of Jews and Gentiles (4:3)

Paul goes on to apply to his readers the exodus illustration behind the imagery in verse 2. However, its actual connection and meaning are fiercely debated, for Paul identifies the enslaving power in verse 3 not as the law but as "the elemental forces [Greek: *stoicheia*] of the world." The term "spiritual" in the NIV does not appear in the Greek but is an interpretive addition showing that the NIV translators preferred the third option explained below.

To interpret this verse, we must first determine the meaning of the "elemental forces" and then consider them in the context of the larger metaphor discussing the status of Paul's readers when they were "underage" and virtual slaves under the control of custodians. Does verse 3 continue the imagery from verse 2 of the Jewish Christians who were formerly under the control of the law, or does it alter that image? There are four options for understanding *stoicheia* here:

1. It could refer to the basic elements of the universe: earth, air, fire, and water. This was the primary meaning of "elements" in **Hellenism** and the one used in 2 Peter 3:10, 12 ("the elements destroyed by fire"). This is the preferred choice of a majority of recent commentators. Here it would be used metaphorically to depict the law as a set of concrete regulations involving the elemental forces of this world, seen especially in the Jewish food laws and purity regulations. It would be even more true of the Gentiles whose gods represented the various natural forces in this world. So both Jews and Gentiles were people of this world, controlled by the laws of this world in their pre-Christian situation.

2. It could refer to the basic or elemental principles, the ABCs of truth, as in Hebrews 5:12: "the elementary truths [*stoicheia*] of God's word." Here it would mean Paul is speaking of the law as a basic set of truths in God's plan, revealed

to his people when they were still underage, before Christ
came as their inheritance and they reached maturity in him.
In this view circumcision and the laws of Moses would be
the elementary principles that were enough when God's
people were young but have now been set aside since they
have reached maturity in Christ.

3. In Colossians 2:8, 20 Paul refers to the "elemental spiri-
tual forces of this world," meaning the demonic powers.
Here it would speak of both Jewish and Gentile groups as
under the control of satanic powers before they came to
Christ. This interpretation would fit Romans 6–7, in which
Paul views sin as an invading army gaining control and
then enslaving the people of this world. Here in Galatians
this is the point of 4:8–9, below: "When you did not know
God, you were slaves to those who by nature are not gods.
... How is it that you are turning back to those weak and
miserable elemental forces [*stoicheia*]?" As in Galatians
3:1 ("bewitched"), this would then be stating that demonic
forces are in control of the world and trying to gain control of the Galatian Christians.

4. The last option is similar to option three. The "we" here
could be the Galatians in particular, whose situation par-
alleled the slavery of Israel under Egypt in light of their
own enslavement to "the elemental spiritual forces of this
world." They had been "underage" before they had become
believers, so the elemental forces here would have been
the Greco-Roman gods, with the demonic powers behind
them. Paul's words would have reminded them that before
they had heard and believed the gospel of Christ they had
been in their spiritual infancy, under the control of the evil
powers posing as the Roman gods.

As always, context must help us make the decision. Verse 3 both
provides the primary illustration of the enslavement metaphor of
verses 1–2 and concludes that emphasis, leading into God's solution

for the enslaving power of sin in the sending of his Son in verses 4-5. Which of these options best fits this scenario?

The least likely would be the fourth, which does not fit as well as the others in this context of the Mosaic law. The others are all viable and make good sense of the context, making the interpretation difficult. The second appears to be the weakest of the three in that it seems a little narrow, centering more on the teaching side of the issue. Of the other two, though the first would make great sense as a theme, the language Paul uses makes the third more likely. It fits the immediate context, in conjunction with verses 8-9, as well as Paul's use of *stoicheia* in Colossians 2:8, 20. Paul is saying that all of his readers, both Jew and Gentile, had been under the control of sin and the demonic powers before they had met Christ. Without Christ they had been equally bereft of hope.

THE SOLUTION FOR THIS SLAVERY (4:4-7)

Paul has just expanded the imagery of verse 2, in which the people of God were depicted as young and under the law, to embrace both his Gentile and his Jewish readers. Whether Jews under the law or Gentiles under the pagan gods, they were enslaved and under the control of sin and the demonic gods of this world before they found Christ and became mature children of God. This leads well into verse 4, which presents the sending of Christ in the fullness of time.

In the sending of the Son (4:4-5)

Christ came "when the set time had fully come." In him the final stage of salvation history—the messianic age, the age of the Spirit—has arrived. This important statement demonstrates the extent to which God has superintended time and the events of world history. He carefully planned the moment of the incarnation, and he guided all of history to that moment of fullness. Here *plērōma* (NIV: "fully"), as in Colossians 1:19 ("to have all his fullness dwell in him"), connotes the attainment of God's perfect time when "the culmination of the ages has come" (1 Cor 10:11). This culminating moment is the "time set by" the father in verse 2, that moment when adulthood begins and the promises are realized. Christ's coming has brought God's final kingdom (Mark 1:15). It is the central moment of human history, for God's salvation is now here.

The state of immaturity, of enslavement under the elemental forces and the law, is over. The young man (in the Roman world this was always a son) has reached maturity and received his inheritance. As a result of the Galatian believers' faith, they have received Christ and been adopted into God's family. This all occurred because at the perfect moment "God sent his Son, born of a woman, born under the law." Again, the language describes the salvation-historical switch from the time of preparation to the time of fulfillment. The sending of Christ echoes Romans 8:3—God's "sending his own Son in the likeness of sinful flesh to be a sin offering."

The emphasis here is on Christ's common humanity with us, as he was born into this world and took on its finite life. He who was "very God of very God," as the Nicene Creed describes him, became human to provide salvation for humanity (see Phil 2:6-7). The first phrase used to describe Jesus in verse 4 ("born of a woman") indicates the incarnation, in which "the Word became flesh" (John 1:14). The second ("born under the law") means that Christ entered this world under the old covenant reality of the Mosaic law.

All of the teaching of 3:1-4:3 underlies this. Christ entered a world into which God had placed the law in preparation for that very "fullness of time" that was realized by his birth. The fullness of his coming awaited the cross, however, so Jesus too was under the law and its regulations. Yet though he was under the law and the finite elements of the world, he was the lone human being not enslaved by sin. He was the true seed of Abraham, fulfilling the Abrahamic promises and providing redemption, the subject of verse 5.

The twofold purpose of God's sending the Son, redemption and sonship, sums up themes found earlier in this letter (see 3:13–14). Again, the law could not solve the problem of sin or provide life. In God's economy that was why the law looked forward to its fulfillment in the Son. In verses 4–5 there is a **chiasm**, a stylistic device used often in the Bible to provide emphasis:

A   born of a woman
   B   born under the law
   B′   to redeem those under the law
A′   that we might receive adoption to sonship

This fits Paul's emphasis in Romans 8:14–17, where he teaches that God sends the Spirit of adoption at our conversion, as we become God's children and joint-heirs with Christ. Jesus joins us in our common humanity to allow us to share with himself our new humanity under God.

There is some question as to whether "those under the law" should be understood as referring to all believers or be restricted to Jewish Christians. The language could indicate Jews who were actually "under the law," but the context favors including the Galatian Gentiles (and all of us) under those who are redeemed by Christ. This was an issue earlier in the letter (see my comments on 3:23), and there too the conclusion was that Paul at times uses "under the law" as a term to describe the time before Christ, and that the Gentiles should thereby be included.

As in 3:14, "redeem" here means that Christ by his blood sacrifice paid for our sins and purchased us for God, leading to the forgiveness of our sins and freeing us from the enslaving power of sin. The stages are delineated in Romans 3:24–25: Christ on the cross became our atoning sacrifice by substituting himself for us and paying for our sins with his blood sacrifice. This became the ransom payment that redeemed us and led to the forgiveness of our sins. God the Father then took this ransom payment and credited it to our account from his *bēma* or judgment

seat, declaring us to be justified, or right with himself, and adopt-
ing us as his children.

Thus Jesus purchased us for God so that "we might receive
adoption to sonship." "We" again refers to Jewish and Gentile
believers who have joined the family of God. There were rules
regarding adoption in the Roman world that granted particular rights and privileges to adopted children. Only Christ is the
natural-born Son, and he has paid the adoption price that has
enabled us to become part of God's family and to belong to him.
This means that every member of the Triune Godhead is involved
in our adoption as sons. Christ paid the price, the Father accepted
us into his family, and the Spirit was sent to indwell us at the
moment we became God's children, causing us to cry in acknowledgment "Abba, Father" (v. 6). We as believers in Christ are now
the new Israel, continuing the Old Testament emphasis on Israel
as the son of God (Exod 4:22).

In the sending of the Spirit (4:6-7)

Following the emphasis on our "adoption to sonship" in verse 5,
Paul now turns to the other emphasis that he also later places
in Romans 8:14-17: the sending of the Spirit. He introduced this
topic in 3:1-5 when he reflected on the reception of the Spirit as
proof of salvation. Now he returns to that topic at this key point
in his argument. This is all conversion language, detailing what
happens when we are born again. Note the steps in verses 5-6—
redemption, adoption into sonship, and the reception of the Spirit.
Note also the two "sendings" in verses 4, 6—the sending of the
Son, and the sending of the Spirit. The first set takes place in that
moment when we turn over our lives to Jesus by faith. The second
set is salvation-historical, referring to the work of the Godhead in
inaugurating the new age. Those who read chronology into this,
suggesting that we first become God's children and then receive
the Spirit, are mistaken. All of this takes place at the moment
of conversion.

The sending of the Spirit builds on several Old Testament passages, such as Ezekiel 36:26-27 ("I will give you a new heart … and put my Spirit in you"); Isaiah 48:16-17 ("And now the Sovereign LORD has sent me, endowed with his Spirit"); and, of course, Joel 2:28-32 ("I will pour out my Spirit on all people"). Here, as often in Paul (Rom 8:9; Phil 1:19; see also Acts 16:7; 1 Pet 1:11), the Spirit is described as "the Spirit of his Son" to emphasize his connection with Christ, as well as with God the Father. Each member of the Trinity is involved in our salvation. When we speak of the Spirit as "Jesus in our heart" it is actually the Spirit of Jesus who has entered believers. He represents Christ in this world. He empowers and guides us as we engage in the Christian walk, enabling us to live according to the will of God.

As the Spirit enters our lives, it is he who "calls out, 'Abba, Father.'" The language indicates a loud cry, undoubtedly a cry of exultation. Interestingly, here the Spirit cries "Abba, Father," while in Romans 8:15 we are identified as the ones who make this cry as the Spirit "testifies with our Spirit." Combining the two, we have an antiphonal act of worship, as we respond to the Spirit by echoing his cry of victory that God has now become our Abba.

Abba was a term of deep intimacy for the father-child relationship, and its use here speaks of that intimacy between us and our heavenly Father. This cry of worship in the early church builds on Jesus' prayer life, as every prayer of his, with the exception of only one, was delivered to his "Father" (that one being his cry of dereliction on the cross, "My God, my God, why have you forsaken me?" in Mark 15:34 and its parallels). Our God is that same Father who holds us in his arms and loves us completely.

Paul presents the result (hōste, "so") of the Spirit's work in our hearts in verse 7: "You are no longer a slave, but God's child; and since you are God's child, God has made you also an heir." Christ has redeemed or purchased our freedom from slavery to the "guardians and trustees" of verse 2, the "elemental spiritual forces of the world" of verse 3, and sin and the law in verse 5a.

Moreover, our liberation means that we have been adopted as
God's own children (v. 5b). Even beyond that, we have been made
"heirs" (3:29; 4:1), who as the children of Abraham will receive an
inheritance. Paul states in Romans 8:17 that we are "co-heirs with
Christ." Roman law stipulated that an adopted child had a right
of inheritance only if the natural child (a non-adopted sibling)
allowed it, so our inheritance comes by the agreement of both the
Father and the Son.

PAUL POINTS OUT THE FOLLY OF
RETURNING TO THE LAW (4:8-11)

This is a transition paragraph that closes the previous large section (3:1-4:7) and introduces the section that will follow (4:12-5:12).
In my opinion it is more closely related to what precedes, so I see
this as the conclusion of Paul's defense (3:1-4:11). In it he addresses
the Galatians directly and applies the points to their situation,
noting their past liberation from false gods (v. 8) and their present
reality of being known by the one true God and then asking how
they could go back to similar weak powers and be enslaved now
to the works of the law (vv. 9-10). Their folly runs the danger of
emptying Paul's ministry of value (v. 11).

THE PAST: ENSLAVED TO FALSE GODS (4:8)

This verse reminds the Galatians of what they escaped when they
came to Christ. Note the movement: In the past, they did not know
God (v. 8), but now in the present, God knows them (v. 9). That
is hardly a reality one would want to throw away! Moreover, the
false gods they did know had enslaved them. Slavery has been
the primary theme of chapter 4: to the guardians in verse 2, the
elementary spiritual forces in verse 3, and sin and the law in
verse 5. Now Paul presents a fourth enslaving force—the false
gods of the Gentiles. In reality these are identical to the elemental
forces of verse 3, for the satanic powers lay behind the pagan gods
(Deut 32:17; 1 Cor 10:20). When Paul speaks of "those who are not

gods by nature," he is referring to real spiritual beings, not just to idols fashioned of wood or stone.

THE PRESENT: KNOWN BY GOD (4:9–10)

When the Galatians were converted they had finally come to know God with all the richness of true knowledge. This meant that they had gotten to know him both intellectually and experientially. All of their senses were involved, including their spiritual senses. More importantly, Paul clarifies, God knows them. All the marks of conversion from verses 1–7 are part of this. Their name came up in God's courtroom, with him on his *bēma* (judgment seat). He applied Christ's sacrifice to their personal account, accepted Christ's payment for their sin, declared them forgiven and right with himself, and sent his Spirit to take up residence in their lives. By this means he adopted them as his children and welcomed them into his family, making them citizens of heaven. That was infinitely more than any of them could have dared dream. And it was the result of grace, not works!

Known by God, yet tempted to turn back (4:9)

In verse 3 Paul labeled the false gods "elementary spiritual forces." Now he calls them "those weak and miserable forces" (*stoicheia*, as in v. 3). This is in one sense a surprising twist. On what grounds does he label these satanic powers "weak and miserable" (literally *ptōchos*, "poor") and even "powerless"? We ordinarily picture the demonic hordes as something out of *Lord of the Rings*: incredibly strong, with an army of orcs at their beck and call!

A brief biography of Satan and his fallen angels will help to explain Paul's characterization. Satan had probably been one of the archangels, and before creating this world God had given the angels the same choice he would give Adam and Eve. Satan fell, and Revelation 12:4, 7–9 records that he seduced one-third of the angelic realm into falling with him. As a result they were defeated and cast out of heaven to earth, which became their prison house

(2 Pet 2:4; Jude 6). The authority of Satan, "the god of this world" (2 Cor 4:4) and the "prince of this world" (John 14:30), has been restricted to this world, his prison. He has no power over God's people; indeed, they wield authority over him (Mark 3:15; 6:7). When we are surrendered and dependent on Christ we are indeed "more than conquerors" (Rom 8:37). This means that *in comparison with God and his people* he and the powers he commands are "weak and powerless." Satan "knows his time is short" (Rev 12:12); indeed, his doom is certain.

So Paul finds it incomprehensible, as he had stated in 3:1–4, that the Galatian Christians are in process of giving in to the blandishments of the Judaizers and "turning back" to those impotent powers (an oxymoron!). Many interpreters have rightly called this the language of apostasy—having the truth but abandoning it for a lie. The Galatians are about to throw away their hard-fought liberation and return not just to slavery but to slavery under weak and evil powers—a double failure with eternal ramifications. They are not returning to their pagan gods but turning to the god of the Judaizers, a "weak and miserable god" that is just as insidious.

Demonic powers are behind this "god" as much as they are behind the gods of the Romans. Remember that since Christ had come and the new age of salvation had been initiated with the sending of the Spirit, the law had been "culminated" in Christ (Rom 10:4). This means that reinstating the law as a salvation mechanism is heresy—a false religion with a false god forged by Satan to resemble the God of the Old Testament. It is important to emphasize the Judaizers saw the law *as a salvation mechanism*, for Paul had no problem with those who wanted to obey the food laws or the calendar laws as a means of worship. To follow the Mosaic regulations is wrong if it is a matter of salvation but all right if it is a part of worship that one did not force on others (for this distinction, see Rom 14:1–15:13).

The error: observing the Jewish calendar (4:10)

As would have been expected from people who had been deceived by the Judaizers into obeying the Mosaic regulations, these Galatians had started to follow the Jewish calendar and observe the Jewish feasts and the Sabbath laws—"special days and months and seasons and years." As the list here seems to parallel the tendency in most ancient religions to follow the movements of the stars and the heavenly bodies in devising the religious calendar, many interpreters think that Paul is referring to pagan rather than to Jewish calendars. However, that does not make much sense in this context. It is more likely that Paul is continuing his emphasis from verse 9 on the Judaizers' heresy having turned the observance of the law into just another false religion, tantamount to the Roman religions from which the Galatians had been converted.

It is possible that these terms refer to various aspects of the Jewish festivals, with "days" denoting the Sabbath, "months" the new moon festival observed on the first of every month (Col 2:16), "seasons" perhaps signifying the weeklong festivals like Passover and Tabernacles, and "years" possibly referring to the Jubilee cycle of sevens. Paul may also be echoing the creation story of Genesis 1:14: "Let there be lights in the sky to separate the day from the night, and let them serve as signs to mark sacred times, and days and years." In this sense the calendar reflects the order of creation. The point of this verse, as also verse 9, is that falling into the Judaizers' trap means a reversion to the same enslavement by false god(s) that had been the Galatians' tragic lot before they had come to Christ.

THE DANGER: EMPTYING PAUL'S MINISTRY OF VALUE (4:11)

Paul's fear is twofold. These Christians are about to commit apostasy and lose all that they had gained in Christ (the emphasis of v. 9), in the process nullifying Paul's ministry among them up to the writing of this letter. This danger frames the section, since in 3:4 he asked with regard to their own walk with Christ "Have you experienced so much in vain?" and now at the end of the section he voices a similar concern over squandered effort with respect to the effects of his ministry among them: "somehow I have wasted my efforts on you" (literally, "I have labored for you in vain"). Both their walk with Christ and Paul's own labor on their behalf would be emptied of value and meaning if they indeed opted to "turn back" to the false god of the Judaizers.

———

In this section (4:1–11) Paul has continued his emphasis on the temporary role of the law in salvation history, now adding the metaphor of slavery to signify that the law has not only imprisoned people under sin (3:22–23) but has enslaved them. This metaphor is relevant for our day, in that all attempts to develop a path of salvation that doesn't center on Christ end up enslaving those who settle for a works-centered set of lies. All human beings yearn to be free, not owing anything to anyone—including God. However, apart from Christ none of us will ever be free, for we could never do enough to earn our salvation. We will end up enslaved by the very system we have embraced in our quest for freedom!

The next major section (4:12–6:10) will turn from enslavement to our freedom in Christ. We are first liberated from the enslaving power of sin when we are redeemed by the blood of Christ and given the Holy Spirit. Only this will effect our freedom to join the new Israel (vv. 4–7). Once we have received true freedom in Christ, how could we be so foolish as to throw it all away and believe the false promises of motivational speakers like the Judaizers? When we make such an exchange we are forfeiting our eternity and voiding the ministry efforts we have received from true Christian leaders. May we never give in to the temptation to replace Christ with a "self-help" system of works!

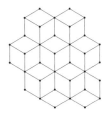

PAUL'S RELATIONSHIP WITH
THE GALATIANS (4:12–20)

Paul began the letter's first major section (1:11–2:21) by conveying his shock that the Galatians were deserting Christ and turning to the false gospel of the **Judaizers** (1:6–10), after which he reminded them of the true gospel of Christ he had preached to them (1:11–12). He began the second section (3:1–4:11) by restating his dismay that they had allowed these false teachers to "bewitch" them, reminding them once again of their conversion and receipt of the Spirit (3:1–5). Now at the start of the third section (4:12–6:10), for the third time Paul takes them back to the founding of their church when he had brought them the gospel.

The Galatian Christians understood that salvation comes by faith and knew that their conversion had entailed the forgiveness of their sins and their receiving of the gift of the Spirit. That should have made it easy for them to realize that the "works of the law" religion of the Judaizers had nothing of benefit to offer them, yet many were being led astray by it. Wanting these believers to experience the freedom of the gospel of Christ, Paul appeals to the relationship he has established with them and asks them to follow his example. His is a model of Christian liberation, exemplifying freedom from the law and from sin. He wants only what is good for them, in contrast to the motivations of the Judaizing heretics.

PAUL REMINDS THE GALATIANS OF
THEIR RELATIONSHIP (4:12-16)

Paul begins on a note of deep friendship in the Lord, addressing the Galatians as "brothers and sisters." The following plea is
strong: He asks them to "become like me," challenging his readers to imitate him just as he himself imitates Christ (1 Cor 4:16;
Phil 3:17; 2 Thess 3:7, 9). Paul provides no specifics regarding just
what they are to imitate, expecting his readers to infer the specifics from the letter thus far, as well as from what they already
knew of him. Implicitly, this imitation would have entailed acting
in accordance with everything he had already stated: They needed
to realize that they were free from the works of the law, having
been saved by the grace of God through faith in Christ's finished
work on the cross.

THESIS: IMITATE PAUL (4:12A-B)

Paul's request for the Galatian believers to "become like me" is
based on the reality that he "became like [them]" when they first
met. Most likely he means that he forsook his "previous way of life
in Judaism" (1:13) and became in practice like a Gentile, turning
to Christ entirely by faith. The startling truth about the Galatians
was that many of them were reversing this pattern and abandoning Christ in favor of the obsolete Old Testament law, reverting
from living faith back to lifeless works. Paul here appeals to them
to reciprocate by following his model and fully embracing Christ
by faith, with no element of works-righteousness.

THEIR TREATMENT OF PAUL (4:12C-16)

The last part of verse 12, "You did me no wrong," belongs with
what follows. The context was the first missionary journey,
when Paul had initially preached the gospel to them and won
them over to Christ. At that time the converts had welcomed Paul
with real warmth; of infinitely greater importance was that they
had welcomed Christ into their hearts. They had done him no

"wrong"—had not persecuted him for his witness to them.[1] In contrast, now many of them were turning from Christ to follow the Judaizers. So when Paul asked them to become like him in verse 12a, his plea included a call to return to the good relations they had previously enjoyed. Paul was implying that the Galatians had deeply wronged him, as will become clear in verses 15-16.

The past: warm welcome when he was ill (4:12c-14)

When Paul had arrived in the Galatian cities of Pisidian Antioch, Iconium, Lystra, and Derbe (Acts 13-14), he was quite ill (Gal 4:13). The Greek of this verse literally says that he had been suffering from a "weakness of the flesh." Some interpreters think this refers to the persecution Paul had been experiencing at that time: being expelled from Antioch and Iconium (Acts 13:50; 14:6) and stoned and left for dead at Lystra and Derbe (Acts 14:19-20). While this is possible, it is more likely that Paul is referring to a physical ailment. The two most frequent speculations are poor eyesight, hinted at in the letters where he mentions signing his own name (1 Cor 16:21; Col 4:18), and malaria from the marshlands of southern Galatia. There is no way to know for certain, though Galatians 4:15 appears to suggest poor eyesight as the more likely. At any rate, we can probably link this to the "thorn in the flesh" of 2 Corinthians 12:7-9.

It is difficult to know whether the Greek *peirasmon* in verse 14 should be translated "though my illness was a *trial* to you" (NIV) or "though my condition *tempted* you to reject me" (NLT). The word can mean either. Is Paul saying that his illness was a trial because they had to take care of him or because it was a temptation to reject him? The latter is slightly more likely in that most Gentiles would have construed a fleshly "weakness" (v. 12) as a sign of the gods' displeasure. The Galatians refused to take that approach and

---

1.   The persecution came later in these cities and was instigated mainly by the Jews there (Acts 13:50; 14:5, 19).

instead welcomed Paul with open arms. The Greek of this verse is interesting in that it speaks of "despising" Paul and "spitting" (NIV: "scorn"). It is possible that this does refer to scorn, but it might be preferable to take it in the sense of trying to avoid exposure to the same evil spirits that had been plaguing him. Many today spit to protect themselves against evil spirits; think of the scene in *My Big Fat Greek Wedding* where spitting is said to "keep the devil away."

The Galatians had welcomed Paul "as if [he had been] an angel of God, as if [he had been] Christ himself." Some think this a reference to Acts 14:11–14, where the Lycaonians mistook Barnabas for Zeus and Paul for Hermes, but Paul was horrified at that blasphemy he had inadvertently caused and would never have referred to it positively. Most likely he has in mind their recognition that he had come as God's envoy, like an angel or even like Jesus himself. They saw God at work in his preaching and heard God's (and Jesus') voice in his words. Paul had been profoundly touched by their openness to him and to the gospel, and that made their current rejection all the more difficult to take.

The Galatians' welcoming attitude refers both to their friendly reception of Paul and to their openness to the Christ he was proclaiming. They recognized that God had sent Paul in spite of his compromised physical condition. The gospel he proclaimed had been so powerful and the evidence of God in him so strong that their hearts had been opened and they had been led by God to accept both Paul and his Lord and to turn to Christ in faith and to Paul in friendship.

The present: displeasure when being told the truth (4:15–16)

All of this had changed because of the Galatians' openness to the Judaizers. Paul transitions to the present with a rhetorical question, "Where, then, is your blessing?" He could be speaking in a general way about a sense of peace and contentment in their churches ("Where is that grateful and joyful spirit you felt then?"

NLT, also NASB, LEB, ESV, NET), or perhaps about their experience of the new Abrahamic blessings: their reception of the Spirit (as in 3:1–5) and their sense of justification and forgiveness in Christ. Several recent commentators have opted for the latter, since in 3:14 "blessing" refers to the Abrahamic blessings. However, in light of the context of this verse (see below), it is best to construe "blessing" as a reference to their initial reception of Paul as they blessed him with their welcome. So the NIV translation is correct: "Where, then, is your blessing of me now?" (see also NRSV). They had reversed their earlier acceptance of Paul and turned against him by embracing the Judaizers' heresy.

Paul spells out the extent of the Galatians' earlier "blessing" of him in the second half of verse 15: "If you could have done so, you would have torn out your eyes and given them to me." While this could be seen as a metaphor for the depth of their love for Paul, it seems more probable that Paul meant it literally, indicating his poor eyesight that may have been a factor in his "illness" in verse 14. While we don't know how bad his vision was, we might imagine that the Galatians' love and concern were demonstrated in their willingness to switch places with him so that his poor vision would not hamper his ministry.

There is now a complete reversal of this former good relationship (v. 16). As the Galatians embraced the false gospel of the Judaizers, they turned against Paul and his gospel and did not want to hear more. They reject his gospel first and then reject him afterward. When Paul is "telling [them] the truth" that they are embracing heresy, they treat him as an "enemy." If this is the case, it is implicit that the God behind Paul's gospel will also become their enemy. It does not get more serious than being God's enemy (Jas 4:4)! However, Paul is not saying things have gotten this far, but the situation is moving in this direction. By asking this rhetorical question, Paul wants them to think seriously about the repercussions of continuing on the path they have chosen.

FALSE TEACHERS HIDE THEIR INTENTIONS (4:17-18)

Paul's speaking of the Galatians considering him their enemy was probably in response to the accusations being leveled against him by the Judaizers. They desired to alienate the Galatians from Paul and his team, and in a certain sense they were right: Paul was indeed the enemy of all that stood opposed to God and to the gospel. Since these opponents were false teachers, Paul was indeed their adversary, as we all should be. When people teach what goes against God and the truth of his word, we must be unalterably opposed to them. To the extent that the Galatians had turned away from God to these heretical ideas, Paul (and all true believers) had indeed "become their enemy." But God had become their enemy as well!

THEIR PLAN TO ALIENATE THE GALATIANS FROM PAUL (4:17)

The heretics were truly "zealous," but their zeal was "for no good." They had an evangelistic zeal to win converts, but tragically it was not for a good cause. They wanted to convert the Galatians to their own false gospel, to turn them away from the God of the Bible to their false god (vv. 8–10). Note the contrast with 2 Corinthians 11:2: "I am zealous for you with a godly zeal."[2] Paul had a godly zeal to win people for God, while the Judaizers exercised a self-centered zeal that was focused on two goals. They first wanted to "alienate" Paul from the Galatians and then to win over the Galatians to themselves, so that the Galatians in their turn would have "zeal for them." Unlike Paul, they were not as concerned about the

---

2. Many versions read "I am jealous for you with a godly jealousy" (2 Cor 11:2 NIV). The Greek *zēloō* means both to be zealous and to be jealous, and both meanings are likely in view here. Paul's zeal to see the Corinthians repent has led to his jealous concern for them.

Galatians' spiritual needs as they were about their own honor and status in the community.

THE NEED FOR PROPER ZEAL (4:18)

Paul then clarifies the meaning of proper zeal. The Greek of the first part of this verse is literally translated "good to be zealous for the good." Many see behind this a proverb similar to the rendering in the NIV: "It is fine to be zealous, provided the purpose is good." The good is that which pleases God and is in accordance with his will, here especially related to the gospel. Therein was the rub, since the opponents had a terrible purpose behind their ardor. Zeal for evil will only make people God's enemies and bring down his wrath upon their heads.

Paul wants the Galatians to maintain their zeal for God and for the good "always, not just when I am with you." He had been in their midst on his first missionary journey when they had been converted to the gospel of Christ and become eager to know God better. But because of the false teaching that had taken them in they were no longer zealous for the good. So by enjoining them to be "always zealous," Paul is pleading with them to return to their former enthusiasm for the gospel, to turn their lives around and get back to being right with God.

PAUL IS ANGUISHED AND PERPLEXED
ABOUT THE GALATIANS (4:19–20)

HIS ANGUISH OVER THEM (4:19)

Paul appeals to the Galatians as his "dear children" to show them how deeply he cares as he asks them to redirect their zeal toward the God of the Bible rather than the god of his opponents. He then uses the powerful metaphor of an expectant mother on the verge of giving birth, "for whom I am again in the pains of childbirth until Christ is formed in you." The critical term is "again." Paul had already in a sense given birth to the Galatians when they had turned to Christ on his first missionary journey. Implicit here is that they had committed apostasy and were longer Christ-followers. They needed once again to be reborn.[3]

Because of his anguish Paul is re-experiencing "the pains of childbirth," an image used by the prophets (Isa 13:8; Jer 4:31, 50:43) and by Jesus (Mark 13:8) to describe the coming of the messianic age. Likely the metaphor refers here both to the anguish Paul feels as he seeks their conversion and to the suffering he has already endured in the process of bringing them the gospel. It is debated whether he is thinking of them individually or corporately (as a church). I think it likely that he has both in mind, with the emphasis on individual rebirth and spiritual formation.

At the end of the verse Paul reverses the imagery, shifting from the Galatians' rebirth to the picture of Christ being "formed in them." In other words, he moves from their birth in Christ to Christ being born in them, a reference both to their conversion and to their process of growth in Christlikeness. The idea of Christ being formed in them probably includes the Spirit entering them anew.

HIS PERPLEXITY WITH THEM (4:20)

Paul's concluding note for this section is difficult to interpret, for he says, "How I wish I could be with you and change my voice [NIV: 'tone']." Paul wishes he could address the Galatians face-to-face, but it is hard to determine exactly why. The verb for "change" can also mean "exchange," and three options have been presented for what he means here: (1) The simplest is that he would like to exchange his written voice in the letter for speaking directly to them, to be able to express face-to-face the anguish and anger that he feels. (2) Positively, it might mean he wishes he could change his tone to express the earnestness and friendship he feels for

---

3. For a brief discussion of whether it is possible to lose one's salvation, see my comments at the end of 5:1–12.

these "dear children" (v. 19). (3) Negatively, he wishes he could change his tone to reflect the chagrin and deep-seated frustration he feels regarding them.

My feeling is that the first is the primary meaning, with the third also intended. I rule out the second option because, while many have called this section (4:12–20) a "friendship letter," the emphasis here on friendship reflects the past situation more than the present, in which they have turned against Paul. He is now filled with anxiety and frustration, as seen three times already in this letter (1:6; 3:1–5; 4:11), and he wishes he could get this across to them more forcefully than he can in writing.

So for a fourth time he states his shock at their spiritual failure, "because I am perplexed about you!" He is confused and puzzled as to how they could abandon Christ for the works of the law. They clearly understood the gospel and accepted it when they had been converted on his first missionary journey. They had come to Christ in faith and experienced the Holy Spirit, thereby receiving the Abrahamic blessings. They had enjoyed it all, but now they are in process of throwing all this away because of the false and shallow arguments of one group of Jewish Christians. How could they do this?

———

Paul's purpose in this section has been to awaken the Galatians from their spiritual doldrums and make them aware of the serious error into which they have fallen. He rehearsed the wonderful results of his first missionary journey, when they had warmed up to him so fully and so readily accepted his gospel and the Christ he proclaimed. Those had been fantastic times, and the friendship they had developed with Paul had been deeply satisfying to him. This backdrop to the current situation made Paul doubly chagrined as he witnessed from afar the results of the Judaizers' foray into the Galatian churches. It was as though he had never truly known these believers. This heresy in which they had become embroiled had caused them to turn away, both from God and his truth and from Paul as Christ's emissary. How could they have given up all they had received from God and been so easily deceived?

This is the same question we often ask today as we see people whom we thought had a close walk with Christ abandoning the faith with all its benefits, then turning back to the world's shallow and meaningless lifestyle. Paul's plea to the Galatians to wake up to the apostasy that was about to ruin them for eternity should be our response to similar tragedies in ministry. We do not fight the same Judaizing heresy, but we do combat temptations and teachings that are just as pernicious—the pressures of the world and the insidious attraction of works-righteousness for believers. Many who have been serious followers of Christ have abandoned the faith, often trying to live for the attractions of the world and still be right with God on the basis of the "goodness" they perceive in themselves. Paul's arguments in this section for turning back to Christ, and the love he showed for these sadly deluded brothers and sisters, are both models we need to embrace in ministry to the fallen among our churches.

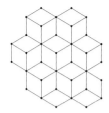

FREEDOM OVER SLAVERY: AN ALLEGORICAL ARGUMENT (4:21–31)

P aul is in his third major section (4:12-6:10), centering on the
freedom that is to characterize the Christian who is liberated
from sin and the law. To make his argument he turns once again to
Abraham (see 3:6-18). This time he uses an allegory, which treats
individuals as symbols of general truths. This allegory focuses on
Abraham's two wives, Sarah and Hagar. The free woman, Sarah,
represents freedom through salvation by faith, while the slave
woman, Hagar, represents the enslaving power of the law. Their
respective sons, Isaac and Ishmael, form a spiritual line of succession leading to Paul's gospel, on the one hand, and the **Judaizers'**
"gospel" on the other. Sarah/Isaac represent the line of freedom
made up of those who relate to God via faith, and Hagar/Ishmael
the line of slavery made up of those who attempt to relate to God
via the works of the law. Paul believes that literal descent from
Abraham (referring to the Jews as the old covenant people) is not
nearly as important as spiritual descent (referring to believing
Gentiles and believing Jews as the new covenant people).

Paul uses this allegory to demand that the Galatians choose
which path to pursue. The Judaizers argued that salvation comes
by the law, and had probably themselves used the Abraham-Isaac
story (especially the incident of Abraham's obedience in the binding of Isaac) to illustrate for the Galatians the purported belief that

they must obey the law to be saved. Paul turns that argument on its head here, showing that this is in reality the path of slavery. Only by faith can one find freedom in Christ and become part of the true Abrahamic line.

PAUL PRESENTS AN ALLEGORY
FROM SCRIPTURE (4:21-23)

The Command to Listen to the Law (4:21)

The Galatians want to be "under the law," but they don't realize the true significance of this. Paul had shown in 3:19-4:7 that the law actually imprisons people under its decrees (3:23-24) and enslaves them under the power of sin (4:1-7). These foolish Galatians (3:1) need to "listen" (Greek: *akouō*; NIV: "be aware of") to what the law says. If they did they would see how dangerous it is to place themselves under its decrees. To be "under" something is to be in complete subjection to it, and that constitutes slavery. In Scripture, to "listen" means to obey, so Paul is accusing them of subjecting themselves to something they fail to understand and therefore cannot obey. If they truly understood the law, they would know the danger of placing themselves under it.

The Two Sons of Abraham (4:22-23)

Paul introduces this important section with *gegraptai*, "it is written," stating clearly that through taking this allegory seriously the Galatians will fulfill the challenge of verse 21: letting the law speak with its own voice.[1] The story stems from Genesis 16-21, which narrates the early lives of the two sons of Abraham: Ishmael (the son of the slave woman, Hagar) and Isaac (the son of the free woman, Sarah). Note that the "law" here includes Genesis. Paul is using the term as a reference to the Pentateuch, the first five books of the Bible, known to Jews as the Torah (Hebrew for "law" or

---

1. Many interpreters think that Paul's switch to allegory here may constitute the "changed voice" of v. 20. That is possible.

"instruction"). The Jews used the phrase "the Law and the Prophets" to refer to the Old Testament as a whole.

In verse 22 Paul does not name either the mothers or the sons, expecting his readers to be familiar with the story of Ishmael the son of Hagar, and Isaac the son of Sarah. He wants to center on the message and so calls Hagar and Sarah the "slave woman" and the "free woman," respectively.[2] Slavery and freedom are contrasted in both verses to prepare for the application: that the Galatians need to choose between slavery under the law and freedom in Christ. Those who opt for the law will end up in slavery, while those who put their hope in Christ will experience liberation. For Paul the issue is the two spiritual lines descending from Abraham, which are no longer determined by biological succession but by spiritual choice.

In verse 23 the oppositions are further developed as Paul contrasts the manner in which each child was born. Sarah was unable to bear an heir and so suggested that Abraham, at the age of eighty-six, arrange to have a surrogate heir by bearing a son through her Egyptian slave and handmaiden, Hagar. This method of bearing an heir when the main wife was barren was completely accepted in the ancient world, but here it was Sarah, and not God, who suggested it. Thus Paul describes Ishmael as having been "born according to the flesh" because the impetus behind his conception was human rather than divine. Sarah and Abraham did not in this incident exhibit faith in God but took matters into their own (fleshly) hands.

Isaac, on the other hand, had been "born as a result of a divine promise," becuase in Genesis 17:16; 18:14 God had already promised that Sarah herself would bear a son. In fact, when God promised the aging couple an heir, Abraham laughed at the very suggestion (17:17), as did Sarah (18:12). How could they not have responded

---

2. Sarah, in fact, is never named at all in this narrative and is called throughout "the free woman."

sardonically, when according to Genesis 17:17 Abraham was a hundred years old and Sarah ninety? Yet God was completely faithful to his promise, and in Galatians 4:29 Paul calls Isaac "the son born by the power of the Spirit." On the earthly plane the contrast is flesh versus promise, but on the heavenly plane it is flesh versus Spirit. Moreover, the covenant itself was at stake (see v. 24, below); in Genesis 17:19-21 Ishmael was declared by God to be destined to become the father of a "great nation," while God pledged to "establish my covenant with [Isaac] as an everlasting covenant for his descendants after him." The Galatians are choosing not just between works and faith but between a fleshly destiny and an eternal covenant.

THE TWO WIVES REPRESENT TWO COVENANTS (4:24-27)

For the readers' sake Paul explains, "These things are being taken allegorically" (NIV: "figuratively"). He is using the story of Sarah and Hagar to point figuratively to another reality, the Galatians' choice between seeking freedom in Christ and placing themselves under the enslaving power of the law. He combines his allegory with typology, a technique in which an Old Testament passage or story (the type) points forward to its spiritual fulfillment in a New Testament truth (the antitype). Sarah and Hagar are the types, or the promise, looking forward to the antitypes, the two opposing groups behind this letter. The faith group has found freedom in Christ, and the works group has been enslaved by the law. Here the births of Ishmael and Isaac represent a contrast between the enslaving force of the law and the liberating force of faith in Christ.

THE OLD COVENANT: HAGAR / JERUSALEM BELOW REPRESENTING SLAVERY (4:24-25)

Paul further expands the allegory of Hagar and Sarah, stating that "the two women represent two covenants." In light of Galatians thus far these would be the Mosaic covenant and the Abrahamic covenant (= the new covenant of Christ). Paul makes this explicit in what follows: "One covenant is from Mount Sinai and bears children who are to be slaves." Hagar as a slave woman is a natural image for the enslaving power of the Mosaic covenant and the law. The children of a slave woman are themselves slaves. Some have identified the referents here as the Jews in general, based on verse 25, but it is more likely that Paul is here speaking about the Judaizers and their followers,[3] including those Galatians who have joined their movement. They are leading the gullible Galatians directly into slavery!

In one sense it seems strange to link the slave woman with Sinai, for the Old Testament connects Sinai with freedom—with liberation from Egypt. But Paul isn't thinking here of redemption imagery but of his earlier arguments that the people of Israel were "held in custody under the law" (3:23) and "in slavery under the elemental spiritual forces of the world" (4:3). There has been a salvation-historical switch: The law has culminated in Christ and is no longer a part of the new realm of redemption by his blood. Far from being a liberating provision, it can now bring only bondage.

In verse 25 Paul uses some strange wording that can be translated literally, "Now the Hagar Sinai mountain is in Arabia." This further expands the allegory and provides an additional link, as Hagar is connected directly with Sinai and then to the Jerusalem of Paul's own day. There are two steps in the progression: Hagar to Sinai, and Sinai to Jerusalem. Paul's point is that the Jewish people of the first century are enslaved under the law and that the Judaizers in particular have joined them. Those Galatians who are joining the Judaizers could only be considered Jewish proselytes and no longer Christians. They voluntarily joined the Jews, and especially the Judaizers, in bondage to the law.

---

3. He goes on to expand this in verse 25 to the Jews in general.

The mention of Arabia has puzzled many commentators, and some have thought it almost a throwaway comment with no significance. But Paul does not do such things; he is always meticulous about his wording. It is likely best to see this as heightening the comparison geographically—as saying in effect, "Mount Sinai is in Arabia but nevertheless corresponds to Jerusalem [in Judea]." This makes a great deal of sense in the context. As I indicated in the last paragraph, first-century Jerusalem especially describes the Judaizers, who in coercing the Gentile converts of Galatia to join in their folly had become masters imposing a life of slavery on these Galatians. This is reinforced in Paul's added "because she is in slavery with her children." The children are the Judaizers who have left Christ to return to Jerusalem and to Judaism.

THE NEW COVENANT: SARAH/JERUSALEM ABOVE REPRESENTING FREEDOM (4:26–27)

In verse 26 Paul centers on the heavenly Jerusalem and the freedom of the gospel. In contrast to the Jerusalem of Paul's day, characterized by unbelief and the works of the law, is "the Jerusalem that is above," the heavenly Jerusalem. Building on verse 24, where Hagar symbolizes the earthly Jerusalem, Sarah, the free woman, is implicitly identified with the Jerusalem above. Hebrews 12:22 contrasts Sinai (Heb 12:18–21) with the "heavenly Jerusalem," and both that passage and this section of Galatians refer to the "new Jerusalem" that constitutes the "new heavens and new earth" (Rev 3:12; 21:2, 10). The Jerusalem above is an **eschatological** reality, the future heavenly home that awaits the faithful, the descending city of Revelation 21 that consummates the victory of the saints and will end this present world of evil.

There is a present sense to this as well, for in Christ the "not yet" has entered the "already" of this present age and brought God's kingdom to earth. We are already victors in Christ, and the last days have been inaugurated. Yes, there are many trials and a great deal of suffering for God's people, but these are the "messianic woes" in which we share the suffering of Christ (Phil 3:10; Col 1:24; Rev 6:9–11) and experience a foretaste of "the sufferings of the Messiah and the glories that would follow" (1 Pet 1:11). The new age has begun, and we are part of it.

This heavenly Jerusalem is "free." With regard to the primary issue behind this letter, this refers to freedom from the works of the law (5:1), as well as to the freedom from sin brought about by the atoning sacrifice of Christ. In contrast to those who struggle futilely to earn their salvation by works, we have been liberated and live in the freedom placed at our disposal by Christ. Now that Christ has come, the law can no longer suffice to keep us in right standing with God; the reality is that this temporary stopgap never could solve the human sin problem and bring life. Only the grace of God and faith in Christ can do that, and that is the basis for the freedom Christ offers.

Paul goes on to describe this Jerusalem above as "our mother," for it is she who has given birth to all of us in Christ. Paul in his letters uses two images for our relationship to heaven—the mother-child relationship here and the image of believers as citizens of heaven in Philippians 3:20. Both picture believers as not belonging to the earth (as "foreigners and exiles" here, 1 Pet 1:1, 17; 2:11) but already belonging to heaven. Behind Paul's image here in Galatians lies Isaiah 66:7–11, where Zion is pictured as a mother giving birth to her children and providing abundantly for them as they grow. Paul likely has in mind the abundance God supplies to his children, of which freedom is a major component.

In verse 27 Paul anchors this claim in a quote from Isaiah 54:1, part of a section detailing the future glory awaiting Zion, the "barren woman ... who never bore a child." Underlying both Isaiah and Galatians is the image of Sarah as barren all her life until the point of Isaac's miracle birth. In Isaiah this picture refers to the nation in exile, and the promise of the rest of the verse is of the return from exile and reinstatement in the land. God would bring his people home, and prosperity would return to the nation.

Here in Galatians the barren woman is the church, the community of God, in process of gaining eschatological glory through its suffering. Paul wants the Galatians to realize that this promised glory will never be theirs as long as they follow the Judaizers' heresy. They have to repent and return to the promises engendered by faith. If they do, they too will "shout for joy and cry aloud." Jesus has brought about the final return from exile, and the gospel of Christ (1:7) has reinstated the promises of God to his people.

"The desolate woman" (Sarah) and "her who has a husband" (and is fertile, Hagar) both likely refer to Jerusalem at various times. The desolate woman is Jerusalem in exile, like Sarah forced to depend on God and his promises. "Her who has a husband" would be Jerusalem in times of prosperity but living for itself and estranged from God. The same God who could take a desolate, barren woman like Sarah and produce from her womb a great nation could take a small group of believers like the Galatians and produce a great church.

In short, Hagar represents the Jewish Christian heresy that brings the slavery of the law to its adherents, and Sarah is the gospel proclaimed by Paul that brings freedom and institutes the new age of the Spirit for God's true people. New life and prosperity are the lot of those who in Christ return from exile and inhabit the Jerusalem above. Through the church God is restoring his covenant people as the new Israel, but only *those who come by faith rather than works* can be a part of that group, the Jerusalem above that constitutes the eternal city of God.

PAUL APPLIES THIS TO THE
CURRENT SITUATION (4:28-31)

When Paul says "Now you, brothers and sisters," he begins to apply the allegory to the Galatians. The Judaizers had undoubtedly told them that they as Gentiles belonged to the children of Ishmael who would remain apart from God's covenant people unless they embraced circumcision and the Mosaic law. Paul was demonstrating the fallacy of that claim by retelling the story and revealing its true significance. In reality, as long as they embraced the gospel of Christ, the believing Galatians were fully "children of promise," while these Jewish (and ostensibly Christian) opponents who embraced the law were enslaved by sin.

THE CHILDREN OF THE FLESH PERSECUTING THE CHILDREN OF PROMISE (4:28-29)

Isaac, the son of Abraham, was the one who had inaugurated the Abrahamic covenant, for the offspring of Abraham according to the promise had come from his line. He was "the child of promise," meaning the child who had inherited the promise. The Abrahamic promises pointed to the blessing of the Gentiles as the purpose of the covenant, and Paul emphasizes that this promise was being fulfilled in the Galatians, not in the Judaizers. The covenant promise symbolized by Isaac was being fulfilled in the new Israel, but it is a promise inherited only by faith and never by works. For Paul, Isaac was the type and the Galatians the antitype. The Judaizers and their followers were the ones excluded from the promise.

Paul notes one other point of fulfillment in verse 29: the opposition of Ishmael's offspring to the people of God. As Ishmael persecuted Isaac (Gen 21:9, where he "mocked" Isaac), so "the son born according to the flesh persecuted the son born by the power of the Spirit" (literally, "born according to the Spirit"). Paul sees the heirs of Ishmael as the Judaizers—as "children of the flesh" in that they have developed a fleshly religion centered on works. This insistence on the law as the core of salvation has rendered them heretics and non-Christians. They are not operating not from within but from outside the Christian camp.

Those Galatians who are still followers of Christ are therefore the ones "born by the power of the Spirit," having received the Spirit at their conversion (Rom 8:14-17; Gal 3:2-5, 14). Here we see an example of Paul's typical flesh-Spirit dualism. The flesh operates in opposition to the Spirit (see Rom 8:1-11), and the people of the flesh are totally opposed to the people of the Spirit.[4] These Jewish Christian opponents are reenacting this persecution against those Galatians who have remained faithful to Christ.

Like Ishmael mocking Isaac, the Judaizers were not physically persecuting the Galatians but threatening that God would abandon them unless they embraced the law. This verbal persecution is similar to the persecution in 1 Peter, in which the pagans around the Christians were verbally slandering the Christians (1 Pet 2:15; 3:13–16).

THE INHERITANCE ONLY FOR THE FREE WOMAN'S SON (4:30)

In the first verse of this section (v. 21) Paul challenged the Galatians that if they truly wished to be under the law they first needed to read and understand what that law actually said. He now approaches the conclusion of his allegorical reasoning by asking, "But what does Scripture say?" Paul quotes Genesis 21:10, which comes just after the verse from the preceding passage about Ishmael mocking Isaac. As a result of Ishmael's mockery Sarah concluded that he was a threat to Isaac and demanded that both Ishmael and his mother be sent away. Abraham, who loved Ishmael, was reluctant, but God took Sarah's side and Abraham was obliged to comply with her wishes. Hagar and Ishmael were expelled into the desert.

The verse quoted here consists of Sarah's demand: "Get rid of the slave woman and her son, for the slave woman's son will never share in the inheritance with the free woman's son." In Genesis this inheritance referred to the blessings of the Abrahamic covenant: to be the chosen nation of God and to inherit the land. Here in Galatians Paul identifies these blessings as given to the new

---

4. "Flesh" here, and later in 5:24, refers not to the physical body but to the sin tendency in every human being.

Israel, the people of God, but now inheriting the land is expanded and means inheriting eternal life.[5]

There is debate regarding which group in Paul's day was to be rejected—whether it was the Jewish people in general or the Judaizers in particular, including the Galatian followers of that movement.[6] In the second instance rejection would have resulted in excommunication—both the false teachers and those who had aligned themselves with them would have had to be cast out of the church. It is hard to envision how it would have been possible to remove the Jewish people in this way, however, for they had not been part of the church in the first place. This rejection could conceivably have entailed having nothing to do with Jewish people, but that hardly fits the context; Paul says in Romans 1:16 that the Jewish people remained his top priority for evangelism. The group more likely in view was that of the Judaizers and their followers, who needed to be cast out of the church. Paul has said more than once that those who embrace these false doctrines are no longer believers (Gal 1:6–9; 3:4, 10; 4:9, 11, 19), and as such they can hardly remain part of the church.

PLEA TO REMAIN CHILDREN OF THE FREE WOMAN (4:31)

While the previous two verses are definitely a passage on discipline in the church and a warning to the readers, Paul is overall positive about the spiritual state of most of his readers. In verse 28 he called them "children of promise" (as in 3:29, "heirs according to the promise"), and here he addresses them as "brothers and

---

5.   Many think that "land" in the Bible is always intended literally, as the geographical home of God's people. But this is not the case in the New Testament, where the term is in the majority of cases used spiritually and metaphorically for the heavenly inheritance of God's people.

6.   But not all Jewish Christians in general, needless to say.

sisters," asserting that "we are not children of the slave woman, but of the free woman." Their home is not the earthly Jerusalem but the Jerusalem above, and they belong to Abraham and Sarah, not to Moses. As a result they are people of faith, not works—of Christ, not the law. There was great danger in the Judaizing heresy, and the inroads it had made among the Galatians were alarming, but most of them continued to follow Christ.

———

The allegory in this section is highly relevant for us today. Many Christians want to follow Christ but fail to understand what God's word really says about what this entails (as in v. 21). We want our pastors to tell us in one thirty-minute message a week, but that is hardly sufficient. The teaching office of the church needs to be resurrected in our day, and we need more groups like Bible Study Fellowship to help us properly center on Bible study.

This section also points to the real danger of apostasy, for Paul portrays those in Galatia who were following the heretics as replacing the cross with the works of the law. His language could hardly have been stronger—they were "of the flesh" and "enslaved" to sin, and as those who had left Christ and the church to espouse a false religion they were to be "cast out" or removed from the church (v. 30). The issue is the same as that in Hebrews or 1 John. Did Paul mean that they were believers who had left the faith, or that they had never been true believers in the first place? There is no easy answer to the ongoing debate over eternal security. The conclusion is for each reader to decide for herself. What is clear is that these people were once part of the church but now are not. In this sense apostasy is tragic but real.

It is incredibly important for each of us to reflect carefully on our own choice between freedom and slavery. All too many believers want freedom but choose the wrong kind. We want license to choose sin whenever we desire "pleasure," which we too easily define as fleshly pleasure. We must realize, however, that there is no liberating side of sin. What we think of as freedom is a new form of slavery. There is no lasting satisfaction in sin, but only deeper and deeper addiction until we are robbed of both peace and joy and are destroyed. The only true freedom is that found in Christ and the Spirit.

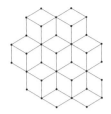

THE LAW'S THREAT TO
FREEDOM (5:1–12)

After presenting the allegory of Sarah and Hagar and arguing that the Galatians needed to take the path of freedom to avoid the slavery the law would have imposed on them, Paul now names the threats to freedom that the law presents for the Christian. He chooses circumcision as his prime example (vv. 2-3), showing his Gentile readers exactly what would happen if they allowed themselves to be circumcised.

To stand firm in the freedom of the gospel, the Galatians needed at all costs to avoid circumcision and the Old Testament Jewish law, for to embrace them and what they represented would have meant alienation from Christ (vv. 2, 4) and enslavement to the demands of obedience (v. 3). Their only hope is in the gospel, in responding in faith to God and receiving the Spirit (vv. 5-6).

Another danger to freedom was the false teachers themselves, who had invaded the Galatian churches and turned many away from following Christ (vv. 7-9). These **Judaizers** would pay for their sins and needed to be opposed, not tolerated or encouraged (vv. 10-12).

TAKE A STAND FOR FREEDOM (5:1)

As is typical for a transitional verse like this one, interpreters disagree whether it concludes 4:21-31 or begins 5:2-11. It fits either way, but I think it is best seen as providing the thesis for chapter 5. Literally, it reads "It is for freedom that Christ has set us free" (as in the NIV), with "for freedom" articulating the purpose: "Christ has set us free so that we might live in freedom." Freedom is the theme of 4:12–6:10, and the freedom/slavery antithesis sums up Paul's teaching about the law. To return to the works of the law would result in a life of slavery to human regulations, and Christ has come to set us free from sin and the law. Redemption in Christ means that he has purchased our freedom and liberated us from slavery. As Israel was redeemed from slavery in Egypt, so we have been liberated and given new life in Christ.

In light of this gift of freedom, Paul exhorts his readers to "stand firm," to anchor themselves in this new life of liberty that must provide a capstone to direct their daily conduct. This point is so critical that he then restates it negatively: "Do not let yourselves be burdened again by a yoke of slavery." As we saw in 4:21–31, the Galatians must choose between freedom in Christ and slavery under the law. Referring to the law a "yoke" or "burden" was frequent in Judaism (Sirach 51:26; Matt 11:29–30, 23:4; Acts 15:10), and Paul's emphasis on this point increases as the sentence goes on—to turn back to the law is to be burdened with a yoke on one's neck (like that on an ox). Such a yoke is more than a heavy weight controlling an individual; it enslaves them. Paul calls the Galatians to take a strong stand in the freedom of Christ and to refuse to allow themselves to be subjected to the yoke of the law, which would mean slavery rather than freedom.

PAUL WARNS ABOUT THE DANGER OF CIRCUMCISION (5:2-6)
THE END RESULTS OF CIRCUMCISION (5:2-4)

Circumcision was the old covenant sign (Gen 17:11–12; Josh 5:2–3), and throughout Jewish history it increasingly became the distinctive sign differentiating God's people from the Gentiles. While Paul mentioned circumcision earlier in the letter (Gal 2:3), it is not a major issue until here. He has saved it until now, for first he wanted to establish the theological center of the gospel (which he did in 3:1–4:11). Now he can demonstrate further the error of the Judaizing heresy. The Judaizers put great stress on circumcision, making the rite as mandatory for Gentile converts to Christianity as it was for Gentile proselytes to Judaism. The problem was that they elevated it to the status of an essential component of salvation, thereby negating the cross as the sole means of salvation. As a result the law, not Christ, was elevated to the status of "savior."

Robs Christ of any value (5:2)

Paul begins strongly: "Behold [NIV: 'mark my words'], I, Paul, tell you" (see also Rom 8:9; Phil 1:19; as well as similar non-Pauline wording in Acts 16:7; 1 Pet 1:11). He emphasizes himself not just as their apostle but also as their friend. He has to do this because the dangers are so great. If the Galatians undergo circumcision, it will destroy their relationship to Christ. The cross will be nullified, and Christ as Lord and as Savior will lose any value for them.

With that in mind, Paul states, "if you let yourselves be circumcised, Christ will be no value to you at all." Their salvation would no longer be anchored in Christ but in circumcision. "No value" (Greek: *ōphelēsei*, "no profit") means that they would be robbing Christ and the cross of any salvific benefit whatsoever. Most likely Paul's focus here is **eschatological**, meaning that at the last judgment all their trust would have been in the old covenant rite of circumcision and in keeping the law. They would have attempted to render Christ unnecessary for their final salvation, with the tragic consequence that they would have been rejected from heaven.

Paul is warning the Galatians that such a mistake would have dire eternal repercussions. If they chose works they would be rejecting faith. If they opted for circumcision they would no longer have Christ, nor would they be able to appeal to him when they faced God. They would be able only to bring up circumcision and the law as evidence that they were believers, and that would not have been enough to save them. Christians could be circumcised if they were doing so for the sake of ministry, as Paul did with Timothy (Acts 16:3), but they are not to put their hope for salvation in circumcision, as was the case with the Judaizers.

Demands perfect obedience (5:3)

At this point Paul shows the relationship of circumcision to the law: "Again I testify [NIV: 'declare'] to every man who lets himself be circumcised that he is obligated to obey the whole law." The verb "testify" pictures God's courtroom, with the Galatians on trial before him. Paul is giving pre-trial testimony, telling the Galatians why they are on trial for embracing circumcision. The word "again"[1] refers to verse 2, making this a second point in Paul's diatribe against the Judaizers' insistence on circumcision as a basis for salvation. There he stated that those who did so reneged on any benefit they had enjoyed in Christ and his redemptive work (v. 2); here he is saying that they follow a works-oriented salvation that demands perfection (v. 3).

At the same time this also refers back to 3:10, where Paul had made the same point: "Cursed is everyone who does not continue to do everything written in the Book of the Law." This is one of Paul's primary arguments against works-righteousness. While circumcision had been initiated before the law came into being, it was still considered to be part of the works of the law because it demanded obedience and was necessary for membership in the covenant people. As such it functioned as an essential part of "the whole law." In the words of James 2:10, "Whoever keeps the whole law and yet stumbles at just one point is guilty of breaking all of it."

---

1. Paul uses "again" frequently in successive verses to draw his points together, as, for example, in Rom 15:10–12; 1 Cor 3:20; 12:21; Gal 1:9.

When one depends on keeping the law to earn salvation, that law has to be kept perfectly and completely. If a person commits a single sin she is a lawbreaker.

Scholars debate Paul's purpose in making this claim. Some suggest that he makes the point because the false teachers had not yet informed the Galatians that they had to observe *all* of the Mosaic obligations. However, it is hard to conceive how they could have accepted circumcision and yet not known about the Mosaic law. Moreover, they were already observing the feasts (4:10) and so must have known about the law.

Rather, Paul is reminding them of something about which they already knew but had not thought through clearly. Like many today, the Galatians assumed that if they put forth a great deal of effort and were generally faithful, that would be enough to keep them in right standing with God. Paul wants to make certain they recognize the true implications of the kind of salvation they are buying in to.

Because the new era of salvation-history has come and the sacrificial system has culminated in Christ and the cross, there are only two conceivable ways to be saved and to enter heaven— the cross of Christ or perfect obedience to the law. Perfect obedience would have to have been mandated at this point because the Old Testament sacrificial system was no longer in place to effect forgiveness. The law had "ended" (Rom 10:4) and been fulfilled in Christ (Matt 5:17-20), meaning that any sin would have disqualified a person, and since everyone is born in sin (Rom 5:12-21) it is impossible to "obey the whole law" perfectly. This is the logic of Paul's argument.

Causes a fall from Christ and grace (5:4)

The Galatians have to choose between these two theories of justification, that of the Judaizers (justification by the law) and that of Paul's gospel (justification by faith). As I mentioned at 2:16, the word "justify" as used in this context is forensic and eschatological, referring to God on his judgment seat pronouncing us to be innocent or guilty of sin. Paul has already warned the Galatians about two consequences of choosing the first: nullifying the effect of Christ's sacrifice (v. 2) and requiring perfect observance of the law on their part (v. 3). Now he warns them that, should they make the latter choice, they will be relegated to a life of continual striving to be justified by the law. The rest of their life will have to be a constant struggle to be good enough.

Moreover, since they can never be good enough, their failure means they "have been alienated from Christ" and "have fallen away from grace." Law and grace are mutually exclusive. To opt for one negates the other. Paul is using further language of apostasy (see 1:6–9; 3:4; 4:9, 19, 30). "Alienated from" (*katērgēthēte apo*) means to "nullify," "render powerless," "wipe out," or "abolish" a thing. This reiterates Paul's point in verse 2; the Galatians have made Christ nothing and completely removed themselves from any connection to him and to his death on the cross on their behalf. To make the law the core of their salvation is to reverse what Christ has done. He has culminated the function of the law and removed it as an instrument of covenant renewal. Now they are about to detach themselves from Christ and the cross as an instrument of their salvation.

The grace of God is the basis of salvation. As Paul states in Ephesians 2:5, 8, "it is by grace you have been saved." Returning to the law rejects the new covenant established by the grace of God and states unequivocally that we are trusting ourselves and our own efforts rather than God for our salvation. If the Galatians continue down this path, they will "have fallen from grace"—from the grace of God in saving them from their sins. Those who place themselves under the umbrella of circumcision and the law in effect negate Christ and remove themselves from the grace of God, for their eternal destiny is now tied to a system in which they have to earn their own salvation rather than being able to depend on Christ and God for it. Such people commit apostasy, severing themselves from Christ and God.

THE SOLUTION: THE TRUE GOSPEL (5:5-6)

Paul shifts from speaking in the second person ("you") in verses 2-4 to using the first person ("we") in verses 5-6 to emphasize the place of the Galatians in the church. In verses 2-4 he identified them as outsiders being challenged to turn their lives around and get right with Christ. Here he addresses them as what they had been to this point: fellow believers in Christ. They were in serious danger of going all the way in terms of falling for the Judaizers' heresy (some of them likely had), but as a group they were not yet there, so Paul addresses them still as brothers and sisters in Christ (as he had done in 1:2, 11, 19; 3:15; 4:12, 28, 31). At the same time he is telling them why those who committed the apostasy of verses 2-4 would no longer have any part with Christ and God. Only those who have found the righteousness that comes "through the Spirit ... by faith" belong to Christ.

Righteousness through the Spirit (5:5)

There is a strong eschatological cast to this verse, speaking as it does of the Christian life in which we "eagerly await by faith the righteousness for which we hope." Paul uses "righteousness" here not with reference to our past and/or present reality, though believers have already attained a right standing with God. He is speaking in this verse about the final state of righteousness we will attain in heaven. A literal translation of the Greek is "the hope of righteousness"[2] that we are "eagerly awaiting through the Spirit by faith."

---

2. This "hope of righteousness" does not mean "the hope that comes from [past] righteousness" but rather "the hope that consists of [our future] righteousness."

While this is forensic or legal righteousness (the same as the "justification" of v. 4) rather than ethical righteousness, we do not already possess it, for it is still a future hope for which we are waiting.[3] This must relate to the day of judgment when we give account to God and receive our final reward in heaven. At that time God will confirm our justification and receive us into our eternal home.

We live in the hope of that day, and we participate in it now "through the Spirit by faith." The Spirit comes to us at conversion (3:2–5) as the seal and deposit guaranteeing "our inheritance until the redemption of those who are God's possession" (Eph 1:13). The Spirit is the One who guides and empowers us so that we can live in the present in light of the future. Our part is to allow God's salvation to take root in us and the Spirit to work in us "by faith." This is how we live victoriously. The Spirit gives us strength to face our difficulties, and we appropriate that strength by faith. This is how we can, even in the midst of present painful trials (Heb 12:11), find ourselves "eagerly waiting" for that which provides a "living hope" (1 Pet 1:3).

Faith expressed through love (5:6)

Here Paul explains why circumcision cannot suffice to make us right with God. The truth, he says, is that "in Christ Jesus neither circumcision nor uncircumcision has any value." The only thing "that counts is faith expressing itself through love." This expands the "by faith" of verse 5. Faith appropriates that right standing with God that Christ has made possible and then guides our responses throughout the Christian life. We are first justified by faith (not by the law, v. 4) when God declares us to be right with himself in his court of law. Then we continue to live by faith

---

3. Forensic or legal righteousness refers to God's judicial decision on his judgment seat to declare us right with himself. Ethical righteousness refers to our decision to live out his righteousness in our daily conduct.

through the process of sanctification. This happens as we live rightly before God, again by faith. Finally, we enter the eternal heaven and receive our final righteousness—all by faith.

Circumcision is not a part of this process. Along with the law it has been removed from the equation by Christ and no longer counts as part of the covenant process. It does not matter whether one is circumcised (like Jews) or not (like Gentiles). Both groups of believers stand before God by grace through faith, not by works.

What does matter is ethical righteousness, "faith expressing itself through love." Love is a work, so it is possible to say that love is the instrument through which faith works itself out. However, the important point is that faith, not love, is the source. Love is the outworking of faith. We will see this again in 5:22, where love is listed as a "fruit of the Spirit." For the believer filled with faith and the Spirit, love is the result rather than the source of righteousness.

Many have linked this with the idea of the "new creation" in Paul, as in 6:15, below: "Neither circumcision nor uncircumcision means anything; what counts is the new creation." In this we are part of the "new humanity" created in Christ (Eph 2:15), and we look forward to a "new heaven and new earth" (Rev 21:1). Love is the primary characteristic that defines the new humanity, and it is the outworking of faith and the Spirit in us. The true relationship between faith and works is found in Ephesians 2:8-10: "For it is by grace you have been saved ... not of works. ... For we are God's handiwork, created in Christ Jesus to do good works." We are saved by faith, not works, but true faith must and will result in works (love).

PAUL WARNS ABOUT THE DANGER OF THE FALSE TEACHERS (5:7-12)

This section concludes 4:12-5:12, which centers on the demand of freedom from the law and the critical issue of freedom in Christ versus the slavery that stems from following the law. Until this point Paul has dealt with the theological problem; here he turns to

the perpetrators of the heresy, the Judaizing false teachers themselves. The Galatians, he argues, dare not follow the demands of
these dangerous men to submit to the Mosaic ordinances, lest they
lose their standing with Christ. These opponents of truth want to
derail the Galatians, but they will pay for their sins. The Galatians
should follow the example of Paul and be faithful to Christ, even
if that means persecution. Paul wishes that these agitators who
are so enamored with cutting off the foreskin would go all the way
and cut off their genitalia in a kind of poetic justice!

THEIR INSIDIOUS INVASION OF THE GALATIAN CHURCHES (5:7-9)

Returning once again to the early years of the Galatian church,
Paul remembers that time when "you were running a good race"
and the church in Galatia was both growing and remaining faithful to Christ. The Spirit was at work in their midst, and they were
models of the Christian walk. But more recently they had begun
to falter. When the Judaizer heretics arrived and demanded that
the Galatian believers follow the law, many began to listen and
buy in to their lies.

Paul uses one of his favorite metaphors, the races from the
Olympic and Isthmian games, to depict the problem (see also
1 Cor 9:24-26; Phil 2:16; 2 Tim 2:5). As I write this I am watching the
Olympics, and I am certain that, were he alive today, Paul would be
watching these wonderful competitions right along with me! He
begins the metaphor by using a rhetorical question to involve the
Galatians in identifying the culprit: "Who cut in on you ...?" They
knew the answer as well as Paul did—the Judaizers! By asking this
leading question Paul is inviting the Galatians themselves to place
blame where it belonged.

There are two images in this metaphor. The first is that of competing runners who "cut in" front during a race and cause others to
stumble, while the second has to do with obstacles placed in front
of runners to impede their progress in the race. Both images are
viable here; either way, the idea is that these hindrances would

"keep [them] from obeying the truth." The Judaizers were like an opposing racer who "cuts in" and then hinders the Galatian runners from winning the race, causing them to stumble and fail.

The key to victory is "obeying the truth." The only possible reasons for the susceptibility of the Galatians to these false teachers would have been spiritual laziness and the resultant ignorance about the truth and logic of the gospel of Christ (1:7), in contrast to the logical fallacies of the Judaizing system. The Galatians were still relatively ignorant theologically and as a result were allowing these heretics to talk them out of adhering to the truth.

Certainly the "truth" about which Paul was talking was the gospel truth he was proclaiming, but today we could also apply this to obeying God's truths as recorded for us in his word. In our day failure to obey the truth might look like becoming a member of a cult or following certain false teachers into either a materialistic Christianity (the prosperity gospel) or a secular lifestyle. There is an absence of teaching in too many of our churches. We need to get back to Acts 2:42, where teaching was the first pillar of the church!

In verse 8 Paul condemns these Jewish Christian agitators and makes a judgment call against those who were hindering the Galatian churches, stating, "That kind of persuasion does not come from the one who calls you," meaning that their teaching was in no way coming from God. They were "persuading" many of the Galatians, but the result was not success in the race of life but defeat caused entirely by the obstacles that were being placed in the believers' way by these opponents. Their teaching was not bringing people to God; it was keeping them away from him!

The emphasis on God's calling goes back to 1:6, in which Paul decried those Galatians who were "deserting the one who called you to live in the grace of Christ." Paul adds here that this desertion was caused by the persuasive power of the Judaizers, and his strong statement that this power did not originate with God could be construed as an implicit charge that it actually stemmed from

Satan. It is quite common in passages on false teachers to assert demonic influence behind their "convincing" rhetoric (2 Cor 4:4, 11:13–15; 1 Tim 4:1; 1 John 4:1–3; Rev 16:14; 18:2).

In verse 9 Paul quotes a proverb to depict the spreading evil that was emanating from the false teachers' persuasion of all too many Galatian Christians. "A little yeast works through the whole batch of dough" also appears in 1 Corinthians 5:6, a passage in which Paul enjoins the Corinthians to expel from their church the man who had committed incest. In that context, the man represented the yeast that was filling the church with sin. Here the circumstances were similar; the Judaizers were like yeast permeating the church with their pernicious teaching.

Yeast was used then, and still is now, to cause dough to rise. The emphasis in the Jewish feasts of Passover and Unleavened Bread on eating bread baked without yeast prompted the Jewish association of yeast with evil in many contexts, including Jesus' condemnation of "the yeast of the Pharisees" (Mark 8:15 and parallels). Paul's point is that the false teachers' evil would continue to spread like bad dough and eventually fill God's people, pervading the church with their lies.

CERTAIN JUDGMENT FOR THEIR SINS (5:10)

Despite the persuasive power of his adversaries (v. 8), Paul remained with regard to the Galatians "confident in the Lord that you will take no other view." In fact, the same Greek word (*peithō*) lies behind both "persuasion" in verse 8 and "confident" in verse 10. One could paraphrase, "Their persuasion is not from God … [and] I am persuaded that you will not be hindered in your race by it." Many of the Galatians, in fact, had been persuaded to join the heretics, but Paul remained convinced that in the long run the Spirit would prevail and the Galatians would reject these falsehoods.

"Take no other view" is literally "think no other way" and refers to the Galatians' mindset and theological understanding. Certainly Paul has in mind their understanding of the gospel message, which reassures him that they would not ultimately be persuaded to cast off the Christian gospel in favor of heresy. The Judaizers were preaching a false gospel, and God had no part in it. The Galatians, Paul is certain, would soon realize that truth and jettison this dangerous teaching. Now it was up to them to prove Paul right and turn back to the gospel of Christ.

Whatever the Galatians did, however, would not stop divine judgment from taking place. The only question is which side the Galatians would ultimately be on—the victorious side of the faithful saints or the side of those condemned and judged by God. The indisputable fact is that "the one who is throwing you into confusion, whoever that may be, will have to pay the penalty." As in verse 7, Paul points indirectly to the guilty party, not that there was any doubt about the identity of "the one"—the Judaizers. Here again Paul wants the Galatians to acknowledge the opponent for themselves. The singular "one" could point to the leader of these heretics but more likely is collective, encompassing the movement as a whole.

Paul defines the "hindrance" from verse 7 as "throwing you into confusion." The word behind this (the participle tarassōn) means to "disturb" or "trouble" someone; Paul used the same term in 1:7 of those who were "trying to pervert the gospel of Christ." This verb is the reason many refer to these heretics as "agitators"—as those who were disturbing the Galatians with their false gospel. The Galatians, fledgling Christians that they still were, lacked a sophisticated grasp of the gospel and so were easily confused by the demand of the false teachers that they be circumcised and obey the Mosaic law.

The agitators may seem to have been winning at this point, but in reality their future judgment was certain: They would "have to pay the penalty" (literally, "bear his judgment"). Paul is pointing to the last judgment, when leaders will "give an account" to God for the quality of their ministry (Heb 13:17). Those who have been the source of vicious lies and have led the church astray will receive payback, and if there are degrees of punishment as well as degrees of reward (possible in light of Rev 20:12–13), theirs will be a particularly severe judgment.

PAUL'S OPPOSITION TO THEM (5:11)

There is some dispute regarding why Paul would feel the need to say here, "If I am still preaching circumcision, why am I still being persecuted?" Some speculate that he is speaking about a pre-Christian ministry to the Gentiles. This is possible, but we have no evidence of his reaching out to Gentiles, as a Jew, prior to his Christian conversion.

A more likely theory is that the Judaizers had accused Paul of hypocrisy because he had allowed coworkers and others to be circumcised (such as he would do with Timothy later on in Acts 16:1–3). Paul's response is that the extent of his persecution by the Jews proves that he never preached or practiced circumcision as a covenant rite. Timothy was circumcised only for the sake of his ministry with Jews, and it was well known in Jewish circles that Paul had largely stopped practicing as a Jew—though he had not done so entirely, for he would later take a Nazirite vow at Cenchreae (Acts 18:18) and perform purification rites (Acts 21:22-26). His practice was to live like a Jew when among Jews and as a Gentile when among Gentiles (1 Cor 9:19–23). He did this for the sake of ministry effectiveness, not as a lifestyle that he encouraged in others. For this reason, his Jewish opponents treated him as an apostate and persecuted him.

Paul's second response is that he could not have preached circumcision because, had he done so, "the offense of the cross" would have been "abolished." If circumcision truly did bring salvation, there would have been no need for the cross, since salvation would have been earned by works. Had this been the case Paul would not have been persecuted but would have been accepted as a member of the group. The very fact of the cross was viewed by the Jewish people as an offense in that crucifixion was considered the most degrading instrument of execution imaginable. The message of the cross was even more of a "stumbling block" (1 Cor 1:23) in that it symbolized the human inability to earn salvation by one's own effort.

The cross was a scandal to self-righteous humanity. Still today we long to believe that we can enter heaven based on our own essential goodness and through our own good works. The cross tells us in no uncertain terms that this yearning can never come to fruition, reminding us that Christ has paid the penalty for our sins and that there is no way to be saved apart from Christ and the cross (Acts 4:12). This is and will always be unacceptable to human pride and a deep affront to human works-righteousness.

PAUL'S WISH FOR THEM (5:12)

Paul concludes by expressing a sarcastic wish (using a strong wordplay) that those "troublemakers" (NLT) who were "cutting in" on the Galatian runners (v. 7) might "cut off" (NIV: "emasculate") their own members (genitalia). They had troubled the church with their demands that the Galatians circumcise themselves (1:7; 5:10), and now he expresses the desire for them to go the next step and use that same knife to "castrate themselves" (one meaning of this verb). This would have been poetic justice with a real twist! The wordplay is similar to that of Philippians 3:2 but here involves a much stronger image. There Paul calls the Judaizers who were demanding circumcision (peritomē) the "mutilators of the flesh" (katatomē), while here he in effect taunts them to mutilate themselves. Another possible meaning of this image stems from Deuteronomy 23:1, where we are told that a person who has been emasculated was not allowed to "enter the assembly of the LORD." This, then, could also have entailed the offending Galatians' removal from the Christian assembly.

As several interpreters have pointed out, Paul is claiming that these Judaizers are little more than pagans in a new guise. Theirs is a fleshly religion that has nothing to do with the God of the

Bible. Since the new era had arrived, and the Messiah had come and brought with him God's final salvation—a salvation that is by faith rather than works—any attempt to go back to the old covenant reality constitutes a rejection of the covenant God and is nothing more than another brand of pagan works-righteousness.

———

In his letter thus far Paul has spent a lot of time disproving his opponents and their theology, and in this section he has shown that their so-called "freedom" is exactly the opposite. They negate Christ in favor of works, with the twin results of slavery and apostasy. Today many continue to make the same tragic mistake, believing that when they are "free" to choose their own method of salvation by works they become truly liberated. Christians need to fully understand this terrible error, for our own "good works" enslave us in a never-ending cycle of deeds that can never ultimately save us. We can never do them well enough.

The language of apostasy dominates this section, and that introduces a huge debate: Can true believers lose their salvation? The Arminian side of the issue, named after the Dutch theologian Jacobus Arminius, says that they can, basing its contention on passages like Hebrews 6:4-6; 10:26-31; James 5:19-20; and 2 Peter 2:20-22. The Calvinist side, following the Genevan Reformer John Calvin, insists that they cannot on the basis of passages like John 6:38-40, 10:27-29; Romans 8:30-39; and 1 Peter 1:5. There is insufficient space for me to present here a full-fledged discussion of the two sides. I am more convinced by the Arminian interpretation of these passages, but several of my closest friends are Calvinist. With its stark warnings about falling away, it would seem as if Galatians fits more closely into the Arminian camp, but several Calvinist scholars identify Paul's warnings here as the means by which God prevents his people from falling into apostasy. In the end, each reader will have to decide for herself.

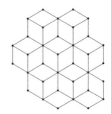

FREEDOM IN LOVE AND BY THE SPIRIT (5:13–24)

This begins the next major section of the letter. The first half dealt with Paul's response to the charges of his Jewish Christian opponents that he was only a pseudo-apostle (answered in 1:6–2:21) proclaiming a false gospel (answered in 3:1–4:11). Paul asserted in response that he had received his apostolic commission directly from Christ and that his was the gospel of Christ, centered on faith rather than on the works of the law. In the second half of the letter Paul turned his attention to the freedom true believers enjoy in Christ, and he has just argued that Christian liberty entails freedom from the enslaving power of the law (4:12–5:12). By its very nature it must be separate from circumcision and the Mosaic law. Now Paul begins to develop the connection between Christian liberty and life in the Spirit (5:13–6:10). The dominant themes here are the practical manifestations of the Spirit in the daily conduct of the believer and the centrality of love among the fruits of the Spirit.

LOVE HOLDS A CENTRAL PLACE IN THE CHRISTIAN LIFE (5:13–15)

Paul has made his case against the false theology of his opponents. He has shown that salvation comes only by faith and not by circumcision or the works of the law. He has challenged the Galatians to turn away from slavery under the law and instead to seek the freedom that comes only in Christ. He realizes, however, that people who have been raised as pagans might easily misconstrue liberty for libertinism and turn to immorality, so now he has to clarify what he means by Christian liberty (vv. 13–15). Freedom in Christ is freedom in the Spirit, so they must realize it means living in the Spirit rather than the flesh as shown especially by the fruit of the Spirit (vv. 16–24). The answer to the flesh is the vertical centrality of the Spirit and the horizontal centrality of love operating at the center of the church.

THE MEANING OF FREEDOM: LOVE, NOT LIBERTINISM (5:13)

The conclusion from the previous section on freedom in Christ is Paul's ringing declaration that "you, my brothers and sisters, were called to be free." The Greek here begins with "for freedom you were called," alluding to 5:1, which asserted that "for freedom Christ has set us free." The point is that freedom in Christ is the very basis for Christian conduct. This freedom has both a negative side (freedom *from* the powers of evil) and a positive side (freedom *to* live for God in the Spirit). Negative freedom includes freedom from the law, which enslaves us under the control of sin (4:1–3). Paul primarily centers here on the positive side, the outworking of Christian liberty in a community characterized by love. In Christ we are all called to live out our freedom in community relationships.

Before he can get into this, however, he must make a critical clarification: "Do not use your freedom to indulge the flesh." These are former Gentiles/pagans, so Christian liberty could easily be corrupted to become libertinism and used as an excuse to "indulge the flesh." The Greek word for "flesh" (*sarx*) can be neutral, meaning simply the physical, finite human body, but in passages like this its thrust is negative, an implied reference to sinful human tendencies and sensual desires. Both here and in Romans 8:1–13 we see a flesh versus Spirit dualism, which the Jews referred to as the "two impulses"—the tendency toward good (*yetzer hatob*) and the tendency toward evil (*yetzer hara'*). Indulging the flesh includes a type of slavery, called "sexual addiction" in our day, in which a person is under the control of immoral impulses. We could also expand "indulging the flesh" to include materialism and the pleasure principle broadly defined, but here Paul primarily has in mind sexual sins.

The flesh must be under control before the Christian can experience true freedom. When that happens, we can begin to "serve one another humbly in love." Paul's strong statement here might be better translated "through love be slaves to one another." Paul spent the last couple of chapters developing the antithesis between freedom and slavery, but now he uses "become slaves" in a positive sense. This fits with his imagery in Romans 6:15–23, where he develops the theme that Christ has liberated us from the enslaving power of sin so that we might become slaves of God and of righteousness. Here he asserts that Christ has freed us from sin and the law to enable us to become slaves to each other.

This voluntary enslavement takes place "through love," which at its core stems from a desire to serve another person. By nature love is reciprocal, as seen in the added "one another." The Christian community is meant to be defined by love, as Jesus pointed out at the beginning of his farewell discourse in John 13–17. He commanded his disciples to "love one another," adding, "By this everyone will know that you are my disciples, if you love one another" (John 13:34–35). Churches need to make a concerted effort to work at this with all they have, for this type of loving service to others does not come easily in any human society, let alone in the self-centered culture of our day. Moreover, this community-serving love is a major evangelistic tool that will attract love-starved sinners, many of whom experience far too little positive attention or reinforcement outside the family of Christ.

LOVE AS THE FULFILLMENT OF THE LAW (5:14)

The reason ("for") the command to love in verse 13 is so critical is that "the entire law is fulfilled in keeping this one command"—a reference to Leviticus 19:18. At first glance this assertion seems hypocritical; Paul has throughout this letter argued that we should not put our hope in keeping the law, and now he points to that which fulfills the same law. Yet this is perfectly in keeping with what he has been arguing all along. In Matthew 5:17–20 Christ declared that he himself fulfills the law, and here we see that Christian love functions in the same way. This is why the law has ended (Rom 10:4). It has been fulfilled in Christ and in the new dynamic of love that he brought with him and that is centered on him. This has nothing to do with obeying the law and everything to do with the culmination of the law in Christ and the new level of love he has initiated in the church.

The point about "the entire law" being fulfilled echoes Matthew 22:34–40, where Jesus stated that the whole law is summed up in love for God (Deut 6:5) and neighbor (Lev 19:18). The first principle sums up the first table of the Ten Commandments (the side relating to God), while the second encapsulates the second table (the side relating to other people). Paul's point is the same here. Love serving others is at the very the heart of the social side of the law. Paul is arguing that when we are justified by faith we become members of God's family—the children of God, as well as members of Christ's body, the messianic community. That community is governed by love and self-sacrificial service to one another, and the command in Leviticus to "love your neighbor as yourself" is the definitive statement of this dynamic. "Neighbor" is to be understood widely, as inclusive of all other people, both believer and nonbeliever, and "as yourself" carries two connotations: We ought to both love others as deeply as we love ourselves and to love them as being in a sense part of our basic selves, since all humanity has been created in the image of God.

Still, what does it mean to say that Christian love "fulfills" the law? Paul brings up this same point in Romans, where he twice asserts that "whoever loves others has fulfilled the law" (Rom 13:8, 10). There is also present here the idea is **eschatological** completeness. Christ, in this new age he has inaugurated, has brought a new set of relationships, centered on love, that has completed the law and brought it to fulfillment. The law was intended to produce a new relationship with God and with others, and it is love in Christ that culminates that purpose.

Warning about Conflicts (5:15)

The opposite of love is dissension, and the language Paul uses here to describe it is strong. The image behind "bite and devour one another" is that of a pack of wild animals taking down and savagely tearing apart their prey. There is no evidence of dissension in the Galatian church, though disagreement over the issue of the **Judaizers** undoubtedly caused some tension. Paul may have included this warning to point out the polar opposite of love. Love is essential because it acts as an antidote to this kind of conflict.

Throughout history conflict has always been problematic in God's community, composed as it is of fallible human beings who struggle to get along. There are a number of passages in the New Testament reflecting conflict among Jesus' disciples (Mark 9:33-34; 10:41-45), Christian leaders (Acts 15:35-37; Gal 2:11-14; Phil 4:2-3), or people in the church (Acts 6:1-7; Rom 14:1-15:13; 1 Cor 1:10-13; Phil 2:1-3), and there is also a fair amount of teaching on the topic of dissension (Matt 5:23-25; 18:15-18; Rom 12:17-21; Jas 3:1-12).

Paul is warning that discord creates an atmosphere of internal warfare that can end up destroying a church. This is one of Satan's most effective ploys: Get the people of God squabbling with each other, and let them tear each other apart. Any of us who has spent time in a church can tell story after sad story about instances in which this has taken place. Churches that have experienced this kind of conflict are usually ineffective for years afterward, and some never recover. Conflict management is an absolutely essential topic of teaching in every congregation.

LIFE IN THE SPIRIT IS OPPOSED TO
LIFE IN THE FLESH (5:16-24)

A church dominated by love and mutual service will be a church in which the Spirit is central. In this section Paul demands the practical manifestation of the Spirit in daily conduct. He demonstrates this negatively, enumerating those fleshly works that are to be avoided (19-21), as well as positively, delineating those fruits of the Spirit that are to be exemplified in the church (22-23). As the Spirit takes over and empowers the church, its members are able to conquer the flesh and live victoriously together in love.

ANTITHESIS BETWEEN FLESH AND SPIRIT (5:16-18)

With his "so I say" Paul adds a new point to his discussion, bringing in his signature motif of flesh-Spirit dualism. He here provides the thesis statement for this entire section, providing God's answer to the problem of the flesh in verse 13: the power of the Spirit to overcome the flesh.

The Spirit opposed to the desires of the flesh (5:16-17a)

Paul's point is eminently practical: "Walk by the Spirit, and you will not gratify the desires of the flesh." It is a mathematical certainty that the extent to which we depend on the Spirit is the extent to which we will defeat the flesh. This is the meaning of Christian liberty. As we yield more and more to the Spirit we are freed from the self, as dominated by the flesh, and liberated to live a life that matters.

The verb "walk" is central to both testaments as a way to speak about the general conduct of one's life. In Genesis 17:1 God told Abraham, "Walk before me faithfully and be blameless." This became one of the primary themes for depicting the life of the people of God, as in Exodus 18:20 ("the way in which they must walk and what they must do," esv), Deuteronomy 5:33 ("walk in obedience to all that the Lord your God has commanded you"), and Psalm 84:11 ("no good thing does he withhold from those whose walk is blameless"). In the New Testament the terminology is carried over into Paul's teaching (Rom 6:4; 8:1, 4; 1 Cor 7:17; Eph 2:10; 4:1; 5:2). Life in the Spirit must be manifest in our daily conduct.

When the Spirit dominates our conduct, the flesh (our sinful tendencies) will of necessity diminish in power over us. Believers who follow the command to "walk in the Spirit" reap the benefits of a prophetic promise: "You will not gratify fleshly desires." Allow me to reiterate: The more the Spirit is in control, the less power the flesh will have to tempt us. This is an incredible promise, but we must acknowledge at the same time that the flesh is so strong that it is difficult for us to yield fully to the Spirit. The areas in which the Spirit reigns within us are those areas in which we are victorious, while the areas in which we ignore the Spirit are those in which we experience defeat. Satan and his minions are equal opportunity invaders. They attack in every area of our being and look for cracks in the walls of our spiritual lives, exploiting every weakness. We must work hard at detecting and remaining particularly vigilant with regard to our vulnerable areas.

The conflict is presented in verse 17a: "For the flesh desires what is contrary to the Spirit, and the Spirit what is contrary to the flesh." The Spirit and the flesh are polar opposites within us. An important term, appearing also in verse 16, is "desire" (*epithymia*), which in itself is neutral, denoting a human wish. But in contexts like this it carries a negative connotation, referring to the evil cravings of the flesh. In verse 16 Paul had in view specific desires, but here in verse 17 he highlights a general characteristic of the flesh—its opposition to the Spirit. Paul states the point both ways for emphasis: The flesh and the Spirit are at war with one another, and everything the flesh wants is opposed to what the Spirit desires.

The conflict between flesh and Spirit (5:17b–18)

Opposition becomes conflict in this second part of verses 16–18, as Paul states, "They are in conflict with each other, so that you are not to do whatever you want." The intents and desires of the one battle against those of the other. What, precisely, does Paul mean when he says believers are not to do whatever they want? There are several options:

1. Due to the conflict between flesh and Spirit, we cannot in our own power do what the Spirit wants us to do. This understanding is reminiscent of Romans 7, where Paul in great detail says that because of the flesh he is unable to accomplish anything he wants to do or think, concluding, "What a wretched man I am! Who will rescue me from this body that is subject to death?" (Rom 7:24). The flesh keeps intervening and forcing him to do the opposite of what his spiritual desires want. The problem is that the Spirit is absent from Romans 7 (though hardly so in Romans 8!), so the two passages are not really parallel.

2. The opposite interpretation would be to understand "whatever you want" as primarily the will of the flesh. This would make it more of a positive statement, asserting that the Spirit intervenes and infuses us with strength, enabling us not to do what the flesh desires. Flesh and Spirit are at war in the first clause, and in the second the Spirit takes over and defeats the flesh. However, there is no contextual indication that the Spirit is the subject of the second clause. While this interpretation is appealing, there is not enough evidence to indicate that this is what Paul is saying.

3. Some take this as an equal battle, one in which there is no clear winner. In this view Paul is highlighting the battle itself, acknowledging that the result is an impasse. The "so that" indicates result, as neither side could fulfill its desires. While quite possible, this neither satisfies the reader nor fits the context of verses 16–18.

4. In a slight modification to the third option, the opposition between the Spirit and the flesh demonstrates that we must become proactively involved, refusing to remain neutral in the battle. If we give in to the flesh, it will indeed keep us from the Spirit, and vice versa. Both exert power over us, and both are operative in our lives. We can no longer sit on the sidelines, doing "whatever we want," for the flesh will dominate us unless we take decisive action. Paul wants believers to recognize this battle and begin allowing the Spirit to take control. The war is real, and we must actively turn to the Spirit, lest we suffer defeat.

This last option seems to be the best interpretation within the context. The battle is not neutral, and we dare not remain so either. We must take sides, proactively letting the Spirit take control.

Paul concludes by providing resolution to the conflict (v. 18), beginning with an adversative "but" (de). "If," he begins, instead of allowing the flesh to dominate "you are led by the Spirit, you are not under the law." The Spirit must overcome the flesh, and believers must share in that victory. The conflict of verse 17 is framed by the path to victory in the Spirit in verses 16 ("walk by the Spirit") and 18 ("led by the Spirit").

So the battle and possible defeat in verse 17 are resolved by the victory proclaimed in verse 18. Verse 16 stresses our part as we conduct our lives under the Spirit, while verse 18 highlights the Spirit's part as he guides us in walking according to God's will. Several interpreters have compared this passage to Isaiah 63:11-14, which relates how the Spirit of Yahweh directed the steps of the Israelites through the Red Sea and gave them rest. The Spirit is like our spiritual GPS, directing our path along the journey of life.

One point of these verses is to remind us that we are indeed at war. This spiritual warfare is infinitely more serious than any human wars, for eternity is at stake. In this war the Spirit provides the only path to victory. As in Ephesians 6:10-12, we are called to "put on the full armor of God"; it is only after we have done so that we can take our stand against Satan and find the victory.

Another point is that being under the Spirit means that we are "not under the law." At first glance Paul's point could be misconstrued as saying that when we are under the Spirit's control we are not under human laws and are free to do whatever we think the Spirit wants us to do. That is a serious error, for Paul is talking not about human laws but about the Mosaic law. Spirit-led freedom doesn't imply that we are free to live above the laws of the land we call home. Paul means that God's people live in a new salvation-historical age of the Spirit (see 3:1–5, 14), not in the old covenant period of the law. Since we have the Spirit, it is wrong and dangerous for us to subject ourselves to that old covenant law, for that would mean we have rejected the Spirit and the new age of Christ to return to the Old Testament period. To go there would be to leave behind God, Christianity, and the Spirit and to cease being a Christian.

THE DEEDS OF THE FLESH (5:19–21)

These next verses juxtapose the works of the flesh (19–21) and the fruit of the Spirit (22–23), showing them to be polar opposites. Paul begins, "The acts of the flesh are obvious," meaning that anyone can easily discern and identify what kind of conduct is inherently wrong from a moral standpoint. The most hardened sinners know instinctively what stands against God and the rest of society. Even if they rationalize their own sins against others to the point of becoming psychopathic, they are acutely aware when someone else has done them wrong.

The deeds enumerated (5:19–21a)

What follows is one of the vice lists that occur frequently in the New Testament letters (Rom 1:29–31; 1 Cor 5:9–11; 6:9–10; Eph 4:31; 5:3–5; Col 3:5; 1 Tim 1:9–10; 6:4–5; 2 Tim 3:2–4; Titus 1:7; 1 Pet 4:3;

Rev 21:8; 22:15). Their purpose is to identify behavior that displeases God and is inappropriate for his people. Paul's list here consists of sexual sins (numbers 1-3), sins involving worship (4-5), and social sins dealing with relationships (6-15).

1. Sexual immorality (*porneia*) is the general term for sexual sin. In the **Hellenistic** world such behavior was expected and rampant, though that was not the case in Jewish society. This made ministry among Gentiles difficult, as it took a while for Gentile converts to understand the Christian aversion to sexual libertinism. Given this reality, Paul began his discussion of this topic in 1 Thessalonians 4:1, 3: "We instructed you how to live in order to please God. ... It is God's will that you should be sanctified [and] ... avoid sexual immorality." Gentile converts needed to know that it was God and not just Christian leaders who mandated this (proper) conduct.

2. Impurity (*akatharsia*) considers sexual sins from the perspective of Jewish purity laws, meaning that in God's eyes this behavior renders one "unclean." Paul often lists these first two terms together (as in Eph 5:3; Col 3:5) to emphasize that sexual deviancy renders one unfit to stand before God or to worship him. People who commit such sins are defiled in the eyes of God.

3. Debauchery (*aselgeia*) is overt sensuality, a complete absence of restraint and decency, both in appearance and in lifestyle behavior. The debauched are party people, binge drinkers, potheads—those who openly flaunt their wild living and even live to offend others. In our day this kind of behavior is often on display among popular musicians and other celebrities, with one "star" after another grabbing headlines with their outrageous antics.

4. Idolatry (*eidōlolatria*) refers to the worship of the false gods of the pagans and can be extended to include anything that takes priority over God in our lives ("no other gods before

me," Exod 20:3), as in Colossians 3:5 and Ephesians 5:5, where greed is labeled idolatry. This is the basic sin in Scripture: a refusal to worship the one true God and a preference for humanly devised deities.

5. Witchcraft (*pharakeia*) is sorcery, which consists of practices that try to manipulate natural forces through supernatural means for selfish ends. It is often condemned in Scripture (as in Exod 7:11; 8:14; Isa 47:9, 12; Rev 18:23; 21:8), and in Acts 19:19 the success of the gospel in Ephesus was demonstrated when many of the sorcerers who had been converted held a public burning in which they destroyed their magic scrolls.

6. Hatred (*echthrai*) is that enmity between people that destroys relationships. It is the first of eight terms describing sins that bring conflict and disrupt the social cohesion of the church. Hatred is the basic emotion that foments discord and here is presented as plural, probably referring to actions that display enmity toward others.

7. Discord (*eris*) is the result of the previous item, hatred, and refers to strife or quarreling between parties, leading to division in the church (see Rom 13:13; 1 Cor 1:11; Phil 1:15; 1 Tim 6:4).

8. Jealousy (*zēlos*) is often translated "zeal" when it has a positive thrust, but in vice lists like this it refers to a self-centered passion that stems from wanting what others have and feeling more deserving of it than they are. Jealousy, like hatred," is one of the basic sins that contribute to poor social harmony in a group (Rom 13:13; 1 Cor 3:3; Jas 3:14, 16).

9. Fits of rage (*thymoi*) is one of the two primary terms for anger (with *orgē*) and as a plural refers here to outbursts of wrath that bring strife to the church. The term is often used of the wrath of God, but in this context it is human anger directed at others (as Luke 4:28; 2 Cor 12:20; Eph 4:31; Col 3:8).

10. Selfish ambition (*eritheia*) is presented as one of the basic sins of dissension that divided the Philippian church in Philippians 2:3 (with "vain conceit"), and as a major sin of the tongue in James 3:14, 16. It is a self-centeredness that is willing to divide the group in order to gain praise and power for oneself.

11. Dissensions (*dichostasiai*) are actions that cause infighting and bring discord and divisions to the group (Rom 16:17).

12. Factions (*hairesis*), the Greek term from which "heresy" is derived, refers to the divisiveness that causes warring parties to form groups, such as the Pharisees, Sadducees, and Essenes among the Jews or the conflicting parties named in Corinth (1 Cor 1:10–17). This is the only instance in which Paul refers to "dissensions" and "factions," leading some to think that this was a particular problem among the Galatian churches.

13. Envy (*phthonoi*), often connected to "jealousy" (Rom 1:29; Phil 1:15; 1 Tim 6:4), denotes that self-centered emotion that wishes one could have what others possess. Jealousy can be understood as an emotion that arises from envy, with envy as the desire itself. This is a common sin today, as most of us are prone to eyeing with envy others who have more than we do. Envy is a refusal to accept with satisfaction what God has given us and be satisfied.

14. Drunkenness (*methai*) is the first of two words for a depraved lifestyle. It does not refer just to those who drink too much but describes wild parties involving binge drinking and carousing. This and the next term are often paired (Rom 13:13; see 1 Pet 4:3) and together describe a kind of abandon that fits our day every bit as much as Roman times.

15. Orgies (*kōmoi*) describes the debauchery and the drinking bouts, above, combined into wild and raucous partying. The term was often used of religious festivals in honor of

the pagan gods but came to be used of any excessive party in which the carousing got out of hand.

Such actions dishonor both God and his people and desecrate all that is holy and good, and Paul's added "and the like" shows that this list is representative rather than exhaustive. Either way, the lengthy list reflects a continuing significant need for godliness among the Galatians, as indeed is true for every one of us.

Warning: no inheritance (5:21b)

Paul ends the vice list with a serious warning that repeats his earlier teaching to the Galatians, probably referring back to his first missionary journey. Vice lists often end in warnings, and this particular warning is that "those who live like this will not inherit the kingdom of God." Two passages in Paul's other letters are strikingly similar: 1 Corinthians 6:9–10 ("Neither the sexually immoral nor idolaters ... will inherit the kingdom of God") and Ephesians 5:5 ("No immoral, impure, or greedy person ... has any inheritance in the kingdom of Christ and of God").

The concept of an inheritance awaiting the people of God has a rich history, beginning with the promise of the land in the Abrahamic covenant (Gen 15:7–8, 28:4) and then again during the exodus (Exod 23:30; 32:13). In the Prophets this was extended to the restoration of Israel and the new exodus after the exile (Isa 9:8; 65:9; Ezek 47:13, 21–23). Finally, in the New Testament, inheritance language depicted the eternal inheritance awaiting the faithful (Matt 5:5; 19:29; Eph 1:14, 18; Col 3:24; Heb 6:12; 9:15).

The kingdom of God is seen throughout the New Testament as both present (God's reign inaugurated in Jesus' first coming and a present reality in this world) and future (God's coming reign in the new heavens and the new earth). In those passages on the future kingdom it is clear that our sins will keep us out of God's eternal kingdom unless they are forgiven in Christ.[1] Paul's warning

---

1.   In addition to the passages above, see 1 Cor 15:24, 50; 1 Thess 2:12; 2 Tim 4:1, 18.

is severe, for it means the loss of eternal life with God in heaven and implicitly refers to eternal punishment for the Galatians' terrible sins.

Today we must continue to help people understand that a basically good life will not suffice to get us into heaven. This is one of the most important points most will ever hear. We cannot be justified before God by our moral conduct, which will never be good enough since every one of us has committed several of the sins in Paul's list within the past few days alone! Without faith in Christ these fleshly deeds will doom us to an eternity of suffering; it is time to turn to him in faith *right now*!

THE FRUIT OF THE SPIRIT (5:22–24)

Vice lists are often followed by virtue lists, as is the case here. Vices are the product of the flesh, the tendency to sin that hampers every one of us. Virtues, in contrast, are the product of the Spirit, and this is a good thing, for if our own strength were their sole source they would be sporadic and half-hearted at best. The agricultural image of fruit provides the perfect metaphor. God plants the seed, and it is he who produces the crop, as Jesus made clear in his parables of the sower, the weeds, and the mustard seed in Matthew 13.

The fruit enumerated (5:22–23)

The emphasis is entirely on the work of the Spirit, not on the personal cultivation of good qualities. We do not just work at these issues and improve; we rely on the Spirit to produce these virtues in us. This does not mean that we are not to strive to improve ourselves in these areas but simply that we are to do so while depending on the Spirit's work in us. As throughout this letter, we grow in these qualities not by works but by faith, which are the product not of human effort but of divine empowerment. There is no discernible order in the nine qualities here, though it is clear that love is first because it is the foundation for all the others.

1. Love (*agapē*) is the apex of the virtues. Of faith, hope, and love "the greatest of these is love" (1 Cor 13:13), and Jesus stated forcefully, "By this everyone will know that you are my disciples, if you love one another" (John 13:35). Love among believers is the outworking of the love within the Godhead that is poured out into the lives of Christians (John 13:34; 15:12; 17:11). Such love proceeds from Father (Rom 5:8; 8:39; Eph 1:4–5) and flows to us through the Son (Rom 8:35; 2 Cor 5:14) and finally through the Spirit's work in us, causing us to love one another (Rom 12:10; 13:8-10; 1 Cor 13).

2. Joy (*chara*) is that highly elusive quality for which every human being is searching in this life. Sadly, most seek it in places that can never produce it—in areas like possessions, sex, or high-octane lifestyles. This searching is fruitless because earthly pleasure, when made an end in itself, is ultimately both unsatisfying and demeaning. Scripture teaches that true joy stems from God and from our relationship with him. This is the key to being able to follow that otherwise impossible command in James 1:2: "Consider it pure joy … whenever you face trials of many kinds." Such an approach seems incomprehensible until we realize that joy is not necessarily the equivalent of happiness. We are happy when things go the way we want them to, but we have "pure joy" only when we recognize that God is in charge and that he will work even in and through our trials for our good (Rom 8:28). Joy is God-centered and the result of faith in him.

3. Peace (*eirēnē*), closely linked with joy in Romans 14:17 and 15:13, refers to that inner tranquility of spirit that stems from reconciliation with God (Rom 5:1), which is achieved by the cross (Eph 2:14-17). It is a sense of well-being and trust in the future through a deep relationship with the

Triune Godhead. When such a relationship is operative this "peace of Christ" rules in the church and in each of its members (Col 3:15).

4. Forbearance (*makrothymia*) refers to that patience or long-suffering shown by God toward sinners (Rom 2:4; 1 Pet 3:20) and toward fallible Christians (2 Pet 3:15). Since we have experienced God's forbearance, we in turn can show the same quality to those around us (2 Cor 6:6; Col 3:12; 2 Tim 4:2). Paul defined it well in Ephesians 4:2: "Be patient, bearing with one another in love."

5. Kindness (*chrēstotēs*), or graciousness and generosity, stems from God's own kindness and grace in bringing sinners to repentance and then to salvation (Rom 2:4; 11:22; Eph 2:7; Titus 3:4). Our experience of God's kindness imbues us with strength and provides for us a model to follow in showing the same kindness to each other (2 Cor 6:6; Col 3:12).

6. Goodness (*agathōsynē*), at times translated "generosity," denotes much the same quality as the previous term: a gracious, kind, and good spirit shown to others (Rom 15:14; Eph 5:9).

7. Faithfulness (*pistis*) results from faith in God and refers to a person on whom others can depend, one who sticks by others in their time of need. The term occurs especially in Paul's Pastoral Letters (1 Tim 4:12; 2 Tim 2:22; Titus 2:2, 10). In a context like this, centering as it does on one's relationship with both God and the community, this quality originates in our total trust in God as it leads to our faithful behavior toward God and those around us.

8. Gentleness (*praütēs*) stems from a humble spirit and is exemplified best by Jesus, who is "gentle and humble in heart" (Matt 11:29). In particular the word depicts the manner and spirit in which we are to correct others, both unbelievers (2 Tim 2:25, "opponents must be

gently instructed") and believers (Gal 6:1, "restore that person gently").

9. Self-control (*enkrateia*) is a quality manifested by those who lead disciplined lives (Acts 24:25; 2 Pet 1:6) and have gained control over the "deeds of the flesh" outlined in verses 19–21. Several interpreters think that Paul intends this as a direct contrast to the drunkenness and carousing of verse 21. It is also possible that he cites this last because it is the tool by which we conduct ourselves by the Spirit rather than by the flesh—the all-purpose behavioral safeguard by which the believer lives out the other virtuous qualities enumerated above.

Paul concludes this virtue list by stating, "Against such things there is no law." It is possible that his intention here is "against such people"—referring to those who exhibit these qualities—but more probable that he means "against such things," a reference to the fruit of the Spirit. Either way, the simplest explanation for this declaration is that the law would never negate or warn against any such quality. In other words, both law and Spirit are in favor of these virtues. Yet some expositors hold a different view, that the law in itself is unable to produce such qualities. Both these options make sense, but the general tenor of this letter would favor the latter, in that law and Spirit are antithetical to one another. Moreover, the point of verse 14, that love fulfills or completes the law, also supports this second option. The fruit of the Spirit culminates the law and takes the lives of God's people to another level.

The crucifixion of the flesh (5:24)

In keeping with the second option, above, that the law is unable to produce the fruit of the Spirit, Paul turns here to the question of defeating the deeds of the flesh to make room for the fruit of the Spirit. Christians who "belong to Christ Jesus" are the redeemed who have been purchased by his blood and have become bondslaves of Christ. One with Christ in his death, they "have crucified the flesh with its passions and desires." This does not imply that they themselves have done the crucifying, as though the saints possess the strength to do this. It is their union with Christ alone that makes this possible.

Galatians 2:20 provides a key perspective, proclaiming that we have been "crucified with Christ" at the time of our conversion. Our old nature has been nullified or rendered powerless (see 2 Cor 5:17; Eph 4:22-24); it is no longer an internal controlling force but an external power invading us and trying to take over. It works in our lives through the flesh—that sin tendency within us. Paul's point here is that sin's power has been broken and that as we identify with Christ and his death we render current temptation powerless in our lives. Paul's declaration that both "the passions and [the] desires" of the flesh have been crucified stresses the complete victory that is possible for us. The two somewhat synonymous terms together indicate the yearnings of our fleshly nature. We can be victorious over them by the Spirit, who provides "the way to escape" when we are tempted (1 Cor 10:13).

———

The two most immoral periods of human history arguably took place during the time of the Roman Empire and in our own day. We are reliving the evil period with a similar society in which rampant craving for pleasure is expected and even considered normal. In this age defined for many in the West by the pursuit of pleasure and the avoidance of pain, the problem is the same as that which Paul describes here in 5:13-24: When people, even Christians, think of freedom, their minds immediately interpret it as license to think, do, and say whatever they want, no matter how sinful. Paul presents two solutions in this section to the problem of the flesh: the power of the Spirit and the cohesive strength of love within the believing community. It is only when these are operating in the church that victory over the flesh can result.

Paul establishes the conflict between the flesh and the Spirit as concretely as possible by providing representative lists, first of the deeds of the flesh and then of the fruit of the Spirit. These vices and virtues are so clearly polar opposites of one another that no reader can fail to see that the one set will destroy us and the other fulfill our deepest needs. We must reject the one and pursue the other, not just to please God but also to bring happiness and satisfaction into our lives. We do so by putting to work the benefits of our "crucifixion with Christ." Through dying in Christ to sin and the flesh we gain the strength to live in the Spirit and find victory over our depraved earthly tendencies.

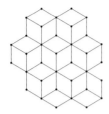

LIVING LIFE BY THE
SPIRIT (5:25–6:10)

We have now come to the final part of this third major section
of the letter, which deals with freedom from the law and in the
Spirit (4:12-6:10). Paul began the section by emphasizing the radical antithesis between slavery under the law and freedom in
Christ (4:12-5:12), proving not only that the law enslaves a person
under the dominion of sin but that the person who chooses life
under the law has rendered Christ null and void and has become a
non-Christian. The immediately preceding section (5:13-24)
showed that the life of freedom in Christ is lived under the Spirit
and involves the rejection of fleshly deeds in favor of the fruit of
the Spirit. In other words, the life of freedom in the Spirit is to be
lived out in daily relationships.

These verses, many of them well known, continue the emphasis on freedom in the Spirit and the new messianic community.
Paul deals with the restoration of errant brothers and sisters and
the theme of humility versus conceit, ending with a central call
for doing good to all. At first glance there seems to be a lack of
cohesion in these ethical commands, yet Paul is organizing them
around his primary theme—life in the Spirit—and showing how
that life must work itself out in the messianic community. When
the church is "in step with the Spirit," it truly becomes the family

of God. The people are a community humbly living for each other, so that all benefit from the unity developed step-by-step.

PAUL TELLS HOW TO KEEP IN STEP
WITH THE SPIRIT (5:25–6:5)

The first verse of this section develops the thesis that governs all of it: "If we live in the Spirit,[1] let us keep in step with the Spirit." Paul is challenging the Galatians to prove by their lives that they are indeed living in the Spirit. Their gullibility in the face of the Judaizing false teachers has cast doubt on the maturity of their church, so this is a key challenge.

THE BASIS: ABSENCE OF CONCEIT (5:25–26)

Paul begins this section with "if," a condition of fact indicating his confidence that they would do what he asked—though they still needed to get their act together.

The key to spiritual victory is to be "in" the Spirit. There is difference of opinion on this, with many interpreters believing that this refers to *means* (living "by" the Spirit), as in 5:16, "walk by the Spirit." My view, however, is that in this context *sphere* seems to be the better thrust. That is, living in the Spirit means living every day and in every way in the sphere of the Spirit's empowering presence. There is double meaning in "live," for it refers both to life in this world, in the daily conduct of each believer, and to the new life in the Lord: the spiritual life we also live in this world.

Believers will demonstrate the centrality of the Spirit in their daily life when they "keep in step with the Spirit." This in essence goes back to 5:16, "walk by the Spirit," and to 5:18, "led by the Spirit." The

---

1. I prefer this to the NIV's "Since we live by the Spirit." It is a true conditional, telling the Galatians that they needed to demonstrate by their actions that they were indeed living in the Spirit. Also, I take the dative *pneumati* as referring to sphere ("in") rather than to means ("by"). I will develop this in the next paragraph.

verb used here is *stoichōmen*, which was used in a military context
for marching in line. In the three other times the term is used in
the New Testament it conveys the idea of following in step with
expectations (Acts 21:24; Rom 4:12; Phil 3:16). As God's army ("Lord
of hosts" in the Old Testament means "Lord of heaven's armies")
we must march in line with the Spirit, our commanding officer.
We are now part of the new creation, and we follow in step with
the new age of the Spirit by following his lead in everything we do.

When the Spirit is truly the guiding presence in our lives, we
will be focused on him rather than on ourselves. This means that
we will not allow ourselves to "become conceited." Our outlook is
no longer to be inward (focused on ourselves) but outward (focused
on the Spirit). As Bill Bright, the founder of Campus Crusade,
pointed out in his "Four Spiritual Laws," there simply is no room
for two beings on the throne of our lives. If we are crucified
with Christ, the ego—the "I"—can no longer live (2:20) but has
to die and be replaced by Christ and the Spirit in control of our
lives. Arrogant pride (no oxymoron!) must be done away with. In
Philippians 2:3 the NIV translates the noun form of this word,
kenodoxia, as "vain conceit," and a literal translation is "vain glory"
(*kenos + doxa*)—the meaningless glorification of the self. It is amaz-
ing how easily people with a bit of talent or wealth can elevate
themselves to the status of a god. The only thing truly good in us
is that which glorifies God rather than self.

A conceited person almost invariably causes conflict in a community. The proud, by elevating themselves over the others around
them, all too often end up "provoking and envying one another."
The focus is on the cause (envy) and its result (provocation). Pride
leads to envy, which produces conflict. "Provoke" (*prokaleomai*) is a
word used in athletic contexts with the idea of challenging another
to a contest of strength. When our focus is on self and on earthly
glory, we never can have enough and are always dissatisfied and
envious. The athlete with the bronze medal envies the one with

the gold medal, and the athlete with one gold medal envies the one who has two or three.

The great football coach Vince Lombardi was fond of saying, "Winning isn't everything; it's the only thing." This mindset finds its way all too often into church or scholarly contexts. The conceited leader places victory over truth and ends up splitting the group into warring factions.

THE CORPORATE SIDE: STRENGTHENING THE SAINTS (6:1-3)

The opening "brothers and sisters" of chapter 6 marks a change of perspective. In verses 25-26 Paul's focus was on each believer as an individual relating to the Spirit and rejecting the tendency toward pride that we all share. Now Paul shifts to the corporate side of the Christian life and looks at believers as part of a family with responsibilities to one another. The first verse stresses the negative side, restoring those who have fallen into sin. Verse 2 looks at the positive, helping those who have fallen on hard times. In verse 3 Paul addresses the opposite of those who bear other's people burdens, those whose concern is only for themselves.

The restoration of sinners (6:1)

This verse emphasizes our responsibility for one another. This is often forgotten in our modern era of rampant individualism, but God expects believers to be involved in each other's lives. We are to share and care for one another, and the restoration process is supposed to begin whenever we become aware that one of our spiritual siblings is struggling.

The conditional "if" here is different in meaning from the "Since" in 5:25 (*ean* rather than *ei*). It denotes a true condition that suggests possibility rather than actuality, pointing to a situation that is not expected for a believer—being "caught in a sin." The verb (*prolambanō*) means to be surprised by an unexpected event. There may be a hint of a military takeover, as one is overtaken and entrapped by an opposing force. That which catches the person by surprise is a "sin." Literally, this refers to a "trespass" (*paraptōma*), a New Testament term often used of ethical sins. Paul perhaps chose it because of the image it conveys of falling out of step with God's demands. At any rate, sin seems to have caused one of the brothers to fail to keep in step with the Spirit (v. 25).

The Greek uses *pneumatikoi* ("you who are spiritual"), and the NIV has properly paraphrased this as "you who live by the Spirit." Yet Paul does not mean that only the leaders or the "spiritual members" of a church should do this. All of us are Spirit-led (though I admit this applies to some more than to others), and Paul is saying every one of us should be engaged in helping our fellow siblings in the Lord to grow spiritually. All of us have received the Spirit (3:2, 5, 14), and all believers alike both walk in the Spirit and are led by the Spirit (5:16, 18). This means all of us are sufficiently Spirit-empowered to jointly engage in this ministry.

The task is to "restore them gently" in their walk with the Lord. To "restore" (*katartizō*) is to return a thing to its proper order, to calibrate it to its proper condition—in this case with God. Paul's idea here was that this individual had been damaged or placed out of joint and needed to be brought back to a useful condition (Heb 12:12–13). This was to be done "gently" or "in a spirit of gentleness" (the same term Paul cited as the eighth fruit of the Spirit in 5:23, above), used also in 2 Timothy 2:25 for "gently instructing" opponents in the church. Such hurting individuals are to be restored not just to the Lord but also to the other people in the church, and the importance of gentleness cannot be overstated. The purpose is to help them, not to beat them down, and lovingkindness and compassion must be operative at every stage. Several interpreters have noted the connection between this verse and Jesus' words in Matthew 18:15–18 about the discipline of offending church members. This would correlate with the first stage of that process, when we go to the person and try to bring about repentance, restoration, and reconciliation.

We find it is relatively easy to help when our fellow Christians are struggling financially or materially (v. 3) but very hard to do so when the issue involves a spiritual battle with sin. We are afraid we will be charged with judging them, but Paul did not call for judgment. Judging can occur only when we are feeling superior and looking down on another, but Paul is calling for a loving concern for them on a spiritual level, in keeping with Hebrews 3:13: "Admonish[2] one another daily, as long as it is called today, so that none of you are hardened by sin's deceitfulness." Paul's demand is that we care enough when we see someone being defeated by sin to get involved and restore them spiritually.

In this process of restoration it is essential to be attuned to oneself as well as concerned for the fallen friend. In bringing someone to repentance it can be tempting to approach them with feelings of superiority and to be guilty of the sin of pride (as in v. 1). It is also possible, in dealing with someone else's sin, to be tempted to fall into the same sin. There can be a continuous, reciprocating cycle here of need and of help. I will help you today as I see you falling prey to Satan's snare, and I want you to help me tomorrow when I myself am being so tempted. The key is humility and gratittude on both sides of the equation. We need each other at all times.

Bearing one another's burdens (6:2)

While this verse could be interpreted as repeating the admonition of verse 1, with the "burden" being sin, it is more likely that Paul intends a wider application, with the "burden" referring to the trials and difficulties of life, including every type of problem and struggle we face. The readers are pictured as servants bearing the accumulated burdens for others. The community is engaged in congregational care as its members assist one another.

---

2. This is a better translation than "encourage" in this context of correcting sin in someone else's life.

In so doing they "fulfill the law of Christ." Some translations (like the NLT) take this as an imperative: "In this way obey the law of Christ." However, it more likely has a future thrust: "In this way you will fulfill the law of Christ," showing the future effectiveness of community goodwill. To "fulfill," as in 5:14, has to do with **eschatological** completeness: Love in the church culminates all that was intended in the old covenant. Here, however, it is "the law of Christ" that comes to completion.

There are two possible understandings of this phrase. First, it could refer to Christ as the final interpreter of the Mosaic law, with Christ's "law" a reference to Paul's understanding and teaching of it. Second, it could refer to the law (Torah) of the Messiah, the final teaching of Jesus in the gospel that is distinct from the Mosaic law and yet completes it. While the first option is possible, the teaching of this letter makes it unlikely that the "law of Christ" would be linked with the Mosaic ordinances. This means the "law of Christ" likely refers to love as the fulfillment of the Mosaic law in Christ. It is Christ's law of love that is completed in bearing the burdens of others.

This does not mean that love is the sole content of the law of Christ, for this law includes all of the ethical teaching of Christ, as indeed the ethical implications of the gospel in Paul and others. So both love and right living before God are essential. Love not only fills up all that is included in Christian ethics but provides the motivation for ethics—life in the Spirit.

Absence of pride (6:3)

This section is framed with warnings against pride, in 5:26 and here, where the self-serving types are told, "If anyone thinks they are something when they are nothing, they deceive themselves." Paul is not suggesting that we are worthless, for every human being has been created in the image of God and is of infinite worth in God's eyes. He is speaking of self-perception. To "think we are something" means to bask in our own false sense of importance, to place ourselves at the top of the church's ladder of success and believe ourselves to be superior to others. We dare not, as in Romans 12:3, "think of ourselves more highly than we ought" but rather are to think with "sober judgment" and take our rightful place as servants of the church. We must develop a proper sense of worth and realize that *apart from Christ* we are indeed worth "nothing." In Christ each one of us is worth everything!

There is no place in the church, and especially in Christian leadership, for those who think they are better than anyone else. When we allow ourselves an inflated sense of our own importance, we "deceive ourselves," ignorant of the reality that everything we do that is worthwhile is God's work, not our own. Part of the problem is that gifted Christian leaders are so often told how great they are that they start believing it. We must realize that all the good we do takes place through the Spirit in us, not as a result of our personal gifts, which are specific tools at the Spirit's disposal for his use.

The disciples learned the nature of Christian leadership the hard way in their terrible reactions to Jesus' predictions of his death. After the first (Mark 8:31-33) Peter had the gall to rebuke Jesus for identifying himself as the suffering servant, to which Jesus responded, "Get behind me, Satan!" After the second (Mark 9:30-37), instead of reflecting on the message the disciples began to argue over who among them was the greatest. Jesus told them, "Anyone who wants to be first must be the very last, and the servant of all." After the third (Mark 10:32-45), instead of internalizing what Jesus was saying James and John asked whether they could sit on his right and left hands in the kingdom. Jesus replied, "Whoever wants to be first must be slave of all." They were concerned only for themselves and had to learn that greatness in the kingdom comes only through servant leadership.

Allow me to reiterate: Everything we accomplish is done only by the grace of God and through the empowering presence of the Spirit. All the good we do is for the glory of God and never for our own glory. We are nothing apart from Christ, and what we accomplish is great only to the extent that God and his Spirit are working in and through us his good work.

THE INDIVIDUAL SIDE: TESTING ONE'S OWN ACTIONS (6:4–5)

Verse 3 is all about self-examination, about making certain we don't have an overinflated view of our own worth and place in the church. Verses 4–5 tell us how that examination should proceed. However, they seem almost to clash with verse 3, appearing to suggest that we should indeed boast about ourselves. The key is to understand the contexts. Verse 3 is all about our relationship to others, while verses 4–5 are about our relationship to God.

In verse 4 Paul asks every believer to "test" or "examine" their lives carefully and deeply, since they will give account to God. We dare not think more of ourselves than is appropriate. Our "own actions" equate to the sum total of our deeds. Some interpreters see this primarily as the work of ministry (v. 6), but that restricts Paul's meaning too much, as it almost certainly encompasses all that we do in life. He enjoins us to test the quality of our entire life and all our deeds, asking ourselves whether we are living for God, for others, or for self.

The goal seems strange: to "take pride in themselves alone, without comparing themselves to someone else." Ordinarily being proud of oneself is thought a sin, but again we need to look at the context. "Pride" is *kauchēma*, "boasting," and the Greek is literally translated "then they will have boasting in themselves alone and not in another." There are a couple of ways to take this: The terminology could mean that we are to restrict our boasting to our own work rather than to that of others, as in the NRSV (also NASB, ESV): "All must test their own work; then that work, rather than their neighbor's work, will become a cause for pride." Or it might mean that we are to consider our own work in isolation, without comparing it to what others do, as in the NLT (also NIV, NET): "Pay careful attention to your own work, for then you will get the satisfaction of a job well done, and you won't need to compare yourself to anyone else."

This is a difficult determination, but the second rendering seems slightly better and more in keeping with Paul's theology and style. The time of boasting is probably at the final judgment rather than in the present. Paul is saying that we cannot stand before God and try to look good by making comparisons with others ("Look, Lord—I was so much better than this other person"). We stand on our own, and the quality of our work will be judged individually. I should neither feel inferior because someone else is a better scholar than I am or superior because I am more accomplished in this area than someone else. I am to look to the gifts God has given me and strive with them to be *the best I can be*, rather than ranking myself as better or worse than others around me. Paul asks us to be satisfied with whatever gifts God has given us and to use them to the best of our ability and strength, without worrying about those around us.

Verse 5 provides the basis for such self-examination: "For each one should carry their own load." All people will stand before God and give account for their own actions—and for no one else's. Therefore, as they assess their work at the present time they should center only on themselves and what God wants for and from them, not judging others or comparing themselves (either favorably or unfavorably) with those around them. The imagery behind "carrying a load" is similar to that of "bearing one another's burdens" in verse 2, though the contexts are different. Verse 2 deals with afflictions in the present, while verse 5 looks ahead to the future day of judgment. In the former we share the daily struggles of life, while in the latter we present the sum total of our lives before God at the final judgment. There we are judged on the basis of what we ourselves have done with the gifts and resources God has given us.

DOING GOOD CONSTITUTES KEEPING IN
STEP WITH THE SPIRIT (6:6-10)

Seemingly out of the blue Paul turns to the issue of caring for Christian leaders. Several commentators place this section with verses 1-5 as a specific example of "bearing one another's burdens" in verse 2. That makes sense, but I feel that verse 6 fits better with the section in verses 7-10 on doing good to others. This larger passage (5:13-6:10) centers on life in the Spirit, a critical aspect of which is the ministry of helping. If believers are truly concerned for others this must include the leadership of the church, so Paul mandates that the "instructors" themselves should be cared for, that the saints need to "share all good things with their instructor."

FINANCIAL SUPPORT FOR CHRISTIAN LEADERS (6:6)

The members of the congregation ("the ones receiving instruction") are expected to support their leaders; the verb "share" (*koinōneitō*) is often used in Paul of financial sharing with others (Rom 12:13; 2 Cor 8:4; Phil 4:15). "Share all good things" in this context, then, refers specifically to meeting the financial needs of the teachers. There are several passages relating to this issue, such as Luke 10:7 ("The worker deserves his wages"); 1 Corinthians 9:3-12 ("the right of support"); 1 Corinthians 9:14 ("those who preach the gospel should receive their living from the gospel"); and 1 Timothy 5:17-18 ("Do not muzzle an ox"). The early church wished to free its leaders of material pressure so as to enable them to effectively teach the word and lead the flock. This is every bit as important today, and the leaders in turn must hold themselves responsible for the quality of their teaching and leadership.

It is important to notice that the pastoral role here, as is often the case in the New Testament, centers especially on the teaching office. In the list of core church ministries in Acts 2:42, teaching is first, and in the early church "instruction in the word" and in theology was at the apex of the needs of the church. In our day this understanding of pastors has fallen on hard times. All too many pastors prefer topical rather than Bible-centered expository sermons, and there is too little teaching that takes place in the average church. Paul would be mortified!

FINAL JUDGMENT: REAPING WHAT WE SOW (6:7–8)

In Galatians 6:3 Paul had warned the Galatians about the self-deception behind human pride. Here he makes the same point, using a prohibition, "Don't be deceived," as he does on two other occasions (1 Cor 6:9, 15:33). As many interpreters point out, all three are in passages dealing with our final inheritance when we will stand before God and give an account of our lives.

Paul is not accusing the Galatians of ignorance but is stressing an important truth by rhetorically warning them against being deceived. "Mocking" God is showing contempt or scorn for the things of God. For the Galatians this had to do with a lifestyle that displeased God and scorned the teaching about their responsibility to live in light of Christ's return. People can "mock" God verbally but can also do so by ignoring his demands and living for themselves rather than for him.

To show the importance of being aware of the final judgment, Paul uses an agricultural proverb that would have been well known in the first century—"A man[3] reaps what he sows"—illustrating that what we do to others will return to us in kind. In 2 Corinthians 9:6 he cited the same maxim in the context of financial giving, so many interpreters think of this as a continuation of his emphasis in verse 6 on supporting Christian leaders. While related to that injunction, Paul is now expanding the focus to every area of life. His point is that we will all be judged by God on the basis of how we have lived our lives, as we will see in verse 8.

---

3. The reason the NIV uses "man" rather than "person" is that in the ancient world a farmer would always have been a man.

This is the basic definition of Christian ethics: Whatever we do to others we are actually doing to God, since they have been created in his image, and God will return to us what we have sown—reward for the good we have done and judgment for the evil (Matt 25:40, 45).

Verse 8 makes explicit for Paul's readers the meaning of the proverb. It begins with *hoti* (not translated in the NIV), which can be causal ("because") but here is explanatory and would best be translated "namely" (or "that is"). This was intended to help the Galatians understand the meaning of the sowing and reaping of verse 7 and to link the imagery to the flesh-Spirit contrast that dominates this section. We all have a choice as to whether to spend our lives pleasing the flesh or the Spirit. When we make that choice, however, it is essential that we understand the ramifications.

If our life goal is to gratify the flesh, we are not the people of God but belong to this world (called "the present evil age" in 1:4) and are living for its temporary rewards. This goal of maximizing pleasure and minimizing pain is commonly called "the pleasure principle." If we live by this principle we will indeed receive its rewards; many live for drunken parties and carousing (5:21a), and that becomes almost all they have. As soon as one party is finished they are planning the next, for there is no lasting satisfaction in this pursuit. One of the saddest aspects of our internet culture is that all of us can see, and often are attracted to, the lives of the "jet set." We can see the glamour, but the accompanying emptiness remains hidden from view.

The future effects of living by the pleasure principle are the emphasis here in this verse, for we are told that such people will reap "destruction"—the loss of everything, including their eternity with God. Hebrews 10:27 states this powerfully (in a context of apostasy): All that remains for them is "a fearful expectation of judgment and a raging fire that will consume the enemies of God." It is important for us to realize that "destruction" (literally, "corruption") does not equate to annihilation. The unsaved will live on, but everything for which they have been living will be destroyed, and their eternity will be spent in the lake of fire (Rev 20:13–15).

However, the promise for those who live to please the Spirit is glorious. They will reap not only a rich and satisfying present existence but, of infinitely greater importance, eternal life. Note the progression of the imagery related to the Holy Spirit in Galatians: We at conversion "receive the Spirit" (3:2, 14) and then live a life in which we "walk by the Spirit" (5:16) and are "led by the Spirit" (v. 18). With this we are enabled to exhibit "the fruit of the Spirit" (vv. 22–23) and "walk in step with the Spirit" (v. 25). As a result we can please the Spirit and reap the eternal rewards of the Spirit-filled life (this verse). We are saved by grace through faith, but the quality of our life still matters. To choose earthly pleasure over God has drastic consequences, and God demands that we not only have faith but live faithfully. Our works do not save us, but they are indispensable evidence that we have been saved.

Life in the Spirit: Doing Good (6:9–10)

These last two verses in the section provide a summary statement, stressing the positive side of the admonition in verses 7–8 (in fact, of all of 5:13–6:8): the consequences of doing good. The Galatians needed to sow good deeds, and when they did so they would reap a "harvest" of rewards. Life in the Spirit at the community level will always include good works as the faithful "bear one another's burdens" (v. 2) and take care of their leaders (v. 6). The "good" of which Paul speaks here is primarily sharing our resources to care for the needs of others.

The danger is to "become weary" and then to "give up" in terms of caring, about which Paul also warns about in 1 Thessalonians 3:13: "Never tire of doing what is good." This may well have been an issue based on both the central problem of seeking earthly pleasure and a spiritual laziness of the kind expressed in Hebrews 5:11; 6:12. The Galatians needed to fight such worldly tendencies and center on what God had called them to do: Share with each other and do good. The goal of the messianic community has always been that there be "no needy persons among them"; this was exemplified in the early church in Jerusalem, where "no one claimed that any of their possessions was their own, but they shared everything they had" (Acts 4:32, 34), and it remains the goal for the church of our day as well (the reason for a church to develop and maintain a program of congregational care).

As we have seen, the harvest time is the final judgment. This is stated elsewhere in the parable chapter of Matthew that includes the productive crop (Matt 13:23) and the harvest by the angels, where the evildoers are cast into the fiery furnace while the righteous shine like the sun (Matt 13:41-43, 49-50). We usually think of the final judgment as that time when sinners will be cast into eternal punishment, but it will also be the time when the saints will face God and give an account of their lives—it will be a time of reward as well as punishment. Here Paul details the reward aspect, when God will repay us for all our sacrifices and for the good we have done in our lives.

Since the harvest is coming, Paul calls on the believers in verse 10 to "make the most of every opportunity" (Eph 5:16) to "do good to all people." Once again, this indicates material and financial help. I believe that we are at the core of the doctrine of rewards here. There are, I believe, degrees of rewards based on the extent to which we have allowed God to guide us into a life of glorifying him and doing good for others. Our model is the shrewd manager in Jesus' parable (Luke 16:1-13) that contrasts the crooked manager, who is shrewd at looking out for himself, and the "people of the light" who are shrewd at using their resources to help others. Every dollar used to help others is banked in heaven and will come back to us as eternal reward. The principle is that whatever we do for others will be repaid to us as eternal reward. Whatever is spent on ourselves, on the other hand, is temporary earthly reward and gone forever.

Paul then defines two levels of giving: "Do good to all people, especially those who belong to the family of believers." We are to love every neighbor (5:14) but to retain a special affection for our brothers and sisters in Christ. The image of the church as a family, or household, stems from Israel as the house of God (Num 20:29 ESV). In the early church the same image was used to describe the new Israel as God's household (1 Tim 3:15; 1 Pet 2:5). The emphasis is on a special responsibility for our spiritual family. In my home church we have a care ministry for which we regularly take a special offering. This ministry has two foci: benevolence for all in the community and congregational care for those who worship regularly in our church. One-third of the giving goes to the benevolence fund and two-thirds to the members of the congregation. It works exceedingly well.

———

This is a fitting conclusion to an incredible passage that could be labeled a case book both on ethical responsibility in the church and on our responsibility before God at the final judgment. God has placed each of us in a community that we are to consider a family. The members of that community are our brothers and sisters in Christ, and we are all responsible for each other. In the spiritual realm that means that we are responsible for one another's growth in Christ, caring enough to admonish another when we observe someone moving away from him and seeking to restore each other. In the physical realm we are to care for each other's needs and help whenever a fellow saint is struggling financially or materially. Life in the Spirit includes the material as well as the spiritual needs of believers. Each of us is a whole person, meaning that we are material as well as immaterial, body as well as Spirit. Therefore, to be in step with the Spirit means to care, as he does, for one another's holistic needs.

There is no place in the church for self-centered Christians who place themselves above everyone else. We are to be humble servants who exhibit the fruit of the Spirit and care deeply for all within our community. As part of God's family and spiritual siblings of each other, we are to be deeply involved in each other's lives. We love one another in Christ, meaning that we share and care in concrete ways so that all needs are met.

Underlying all of this is the doctrine of rewards. God takes note of everything that we sacrifice to help our fellow saints, as well as people in the community outside our church, and when we stand before God we will reap a harvest of rewards for our "doing good." In our day Paul's proverb is reiterated in a similar maxim: "Pay it forward." We need to realize that when we buy things for ourselves in the secular marketplace we enjoy them for a time before they are gone and have to be replaced. The heavenly reward, in contrast, is eternal and will never fade away.

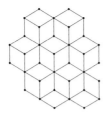

CONCLUDING THOUGHTS (6:11–18)

In the vast majority of Paul's New Testament letters the conclusion follows **Hellenistic** letter-writing patterns and contains final greetings from his associates, news regarding his current situation, prayer requests, instructions, travel plans, and a closing benediction. The situation in the Galatian churches, however, was so desperate that Paul felt the need to dispense with the niceties and summarize the arguments of the letter. He had taken a similar approach in the opening section, omitting the thanksgiving and intercessory prayer in order to get right to the point. These departures from his norm served a rhetorical purpose and were intended to alert the readers to the critical nature of the Judaizing heresy.

Each section of these closing thoughts is intended to emphasize anew the dangers of declaring circumcision and the Mosaic law to be necessary for salvation (vv. 12–13) while ignoring the centrality of the cross for everything Christian (v. 14). Paul here stresses the new creation and the elevation of the readers in Christ (v. 15) and promises God's special mercy only on those who "follow this rule," becoming part of God's new creation in Christ by faith (v. 16). This deeply theological conclusion is steeped in the salvation-historical reality of the new age of salvation. These are the final days, in which God is bringing this evil world to its end and establishing a new Israel and a new family that will inhabit this new creation.

PAUL'S SIGNATURE SHOWS THE IMPORTANCE OF THE CONCLUSION (6:11)

By beginning with "see" (*idete*) Paul draws attention to the fact that he is taking up his reed pen and signing his own letter to authenticate it. This was common practice in the ancient world, as officials would dictate to an **amanuensis**, or scribe, and then personally sign the letter to validate it and verify whom it was from. Paul mentions this often (1 Cor 16:21; Col 4:18; 2 Thess 3:17; Phlm 19), but this is the only place in which he adds the highly personal note "See what large letters I use." This points to his poor eyesight (see the commentary on 4:13–15), though it isn't clear why he is stressing that issue again here. Most interpreters agree that the "large letters" also emphasize the importance of what he is saying. He is using the first-century equivalent of an oversized, bold font to demand that his readers pay close attention to the points of verses 11–18, saying in effect, "These points are 'written large' so you will look at them carefully."

PAUL MAKES HIS CLOSING EXHORTATIONS (6:12-15)
THE DANGER OF THE CIRCUMCISION GROUP (6:12-13)

These two verses impugn the motives and purposes of the **Judaizers**. It was not really in the interest of truth or for the sake of the salvation of the Gentiles that these people were "compelling" (NLT: "trying to force," used also in 2:3, 14) the Galatians to become circumcised, and Paul words his indictment against them strongly: They "want to impress people by means of the flesh," meaning that they were essentially showing off and seeking praise for their piety. Theirs was not a heavenly motivation or a desire to please God but a fleshly incentive, a desire to be lauded by appreciative Jewish compatriots.

Their erroneous motivation (6:12)

There were two motivations here: first to impress their Jewish neighbors and, second, to make certain that they didn't face the same level of persecution experienced by many of the Gentile Christians. Some scholars have surmised that the opposition to the early Christians was primarily from the Zealots, but that is unlikely, for there is no evidence for narrowing down the opposition to a single Jewish group. It was general and widespread.

It was also severe at times. Paul described his own early persecution of the saints when he told Agrippa how he had "opposed" Jesus and his followers, throwing many into prison, trying to force them to deny Jesus, and even "casting his vote" for the death of many (Acts 26:9-11). In 2 Corinthians 11:23-27 Paul described the persecution and suffering he himself endured after becoming a Christian.

Paul clarifies that this persecution was "for the cross of Christ." The Jews as a group could not conceive of a Jewish Messiah apart from circumcision and the Mosaic law, and so the Christian Messiah was highly offensive to most of them. The Judaizers gave in to that pressure, and Paul is calling them on this tactic. If anyone had a right to make this comment, it was Paul, who had both perpetrated and received persecution. But Paul's condemnation here goes far beyond an indictment for their caving in under pressure, for by trying in a roundabout way to avoid persecution the Judaizing "Christ-followers" were actually denying the cross of Christ and replacing it with circumcision. That constituted heresy and apostasy—a ploy to replace salvation by faith in Jesus Christ and the cross with fleshly obedience to human rules.

Their sinful purpose (6:13)

On the surface it would appear as though Paul's declaration that "not even those who are circumcised keep the law" is a contradiction in terms, since circumcision is a component of law-keeping.

However, in using the term "the circumcised" Paul has in view not all Jews but specifically the Judaizers,[1] who were ostensibly Christians. Paul features the opponents in this context; the "circumcision party" is the focus of this entire section. This could mean that the Judaizers were keeping the law from erroneous motives (v. 12) or that they were allowing their Gentile followers to maintain a lax lifestyle in relation to the whole law. While this latter explanation is possible, it seems better in light of Romans 2:17–24 to point out the obvious truth that the Judaizers themselves were failing to keep the law perfectly. It is certain that they at times broke the very laws to which they were insisting on compliance, unintentionally demonstrating that the Mosaic law could never solve the human sin problem and effect salvation. One could paraphrase as "not even the circumcision party keeps the whole law perfectly."

The purpose of their ministry among the Gentiles was also wrongheaded. The Judaizers wanted the Galatians to be circumcised in order "that they may boast about your circumcision in the flesh." They were interested neither in serving God nor in seeking salvation for the Galatians but only in self-aggrandizement, in trying to look good in the eyes of their Jewish countrymen. Jesus pronounced this same indictment against the Pharisees in Matthew 23:5–7 on the basis of their desire to be seen by others as pious and important. Like the Pharisees, the Judaizers were "like whitewashed tombs" (Matt 23:27–28), looking beautiful on the outside but spiritually dead inside. Note the play on words here: They were filled with pride in the fleshly prize (circumcision) they were displaying for all to see, while at the same time they had devised a fleshly religion devoid of God's presence.

---

1. Some alter this slightly, seeing it as a reference to Gentile converts who were being circumcised, but that is unlikely here, as it does not fit the details of verses 12–15.

The True Basis for Pride (6:14-15)

What was the basis for pride in Paul's own life—those deeds that demonstrated his human accomplishments or the work that Jesus had accomplished on the cross? He answers that question both here and in Philippians 3:4-6, where he reviews his Jewish pedigree and then replies, "Whatever were gains to me I now consider loss for the sake of Christ." It was Christ and Christ alone who mattered to Paul and must matter to us—not how important we are or what impressive feats we may have accomplished.

The centrality of the cross and the crucified life (6:14)

The Judaizers had replaced the cross with the works of the law and in so doing had developed a works righteousness that had no place for justification by faith through the cross. Paul's Jewish "Christian" opponents were boasting in all the wrong things (v. 13), and he wanted to make certain he could never be accused of the same. Paul restricts his boasting severely: "May I never boast except in the cross of our Lord Jesus Christ." The cross is the ultimate proof of God's reversal of human pride and status. Crucifixion was the most painful and shameful death imaginable, and God chose it to be the mode of salvation. Jesus had to die in our stead and to bear our "curse" (Gal 3:10-14) as the atoning sacrifice for our sins. Paul uses the full title, "Lord Jesus Christ," to stress this significance of the cross, for on it Jesus was crowned as royal Messiah and Lord of all.

The significance of the cross is the only legitimate reason for boasting on the part of the believer, for through it, as Paul says, "the world has been crucified to me, and I to the world." This recalls Galatians 2:19-20, where Paul asserted that he had "died to the law" and been "crucified with Christ." Both there and here this idea is linked to the "new creation" in Christ (6:15). At the incarnation the decisive switch occurred: The old covenant system was consummated and abolished, replaced by the new covenant in

Christ. Salvation by faith in the cross of Christ replaced the need for observance of the law. Not only was the role of the law terminated, but in Christ Paul died—was indeed crucified!—to the world.

The "world" here is not just the inhabited sphere of human beings. Paul is using it as a symbol for the realm of sin and evil, as in "the powers of this dark world" (Eph 6:12) and "the whole world is under the control of the evil one" (1 John 5:19). The world is that sphere controlled by sin and antithetical to Christ's followers (Jas 4:4; 1 John 2:15-17). When the believer unites with Christ, she unites to his death and is thereby "crucified to the world."

The centrality of the new creation (6:15)

Whether one is circumcised is now completely irrelevant in light of the new world order introduced by Christ and the cross. This rite was part of the old covenant system, which was fulfilled and completed in Christ, so that the act of circumcision no longer has covenantal implications but is now part of "the world" (v. 14), and all Christians have died to it in terms of any salvific significance. Paul had already stated this in 2:19 ("died to the law") and 5:6 ("neither circumcision nor uncircumcision has any value"). All differences—racial, ethnic, economic, gender, and social—have broken down in Christ, and oneness pervades all relationships in him (Gal 3:27-29).

Paul now states the key point to this section: "What counts is the new creation." A literal translation would be more succinct: "but a new creation." New creation theology provides some of the most exciting truths in the New Testament. It begins in John 1:3-5, where we read that Christ was the agent of the original creation (v. 3) but now has brought into this world a new creation of spiritual life and light in God's salvation (vv. 4-5). In 2 Corinthians 5:17 this new creation is entirely salvific: "If anyone is in Christ, [they are part of a] new creation." The new convert is recreated as part of a new world and a new reality. In Ephesians 2:15 Christ has "created in himself one new humanity out of two" (Jew and Gentile), so the new creation contains a new humanity as a result of Christ and the cross.

This new creation has been inaugurated and is in the process of becoming at the present time, but when Christ returns it too will be culminated and eternity ushered in (Rom 8:18–22). Newness constitutes the new eon in Christ, so Paul asks "Why would anyone wish to go back to the inadequate old eon when the new has come?"

PAUL MAKES A PRAYER-WISH FOR THE NEW ISRAEL (6:16)

For those "who follow this rule" Paul utters a prayer-wish, an **eschatological** promise of divine blessing. "Follow" is "keep in step," the same word as in the command to "keep in step with the Spirit" in 5:25. The "rule" is what Paul had enunciated in verses 14–15, the centrality of the cross in the new creation. Most interpreters agree that this entails the new creation having supplanted circumcision and the law, so that Paul is exhorting the saints to stop following the law and to center entirely on the new humanity of which they were a part in Christ.

The prayer-wish is for God's "peace and mercy" to rest upon them. Yet this is a conditional promise, for only those who obey God with respect to "this rule" will experience his peace and mercy. In fact, the whole letter is framed by conditional statements: the negative warning regarding God's curse in 1:8–9 and the positive promise regarding God's peace and mercy in 6:16. The Galatians' reaction to Paul's demands to reject the Judaizers' false teaching would determine whether they would face God's curse or receive his promise. Paul intended this promise of peace to assuage the chaos caused by the Judaizers, and the promise of mercy was based on the present justification and future acceptance into heaven that would reward the faithful.

The faithful are here called "the Israel of God." Interpreting this phrase is quite difficult, as there are two distinctly different ways to translate this verse. The question is whether those "who follow this rule" and "the Israel of God" are two different entities (the church and ethnic Israel) or the same entity (the church). The NIV translation, "Peace and mercy to all who follow this rule—to the Israel of God" favors both phrases, referring to the church as composed of Jews and Gentiles. The CSB translation favors seeing these as two separate groups, thus "May peace come to all those who follow this standard [the church], and mercy even to the Israel of God [ethnic Israel]."

Word order could favor the two-group option (literally, "peace upon them and mercy also upon the Israel of God"), but the message of the book definitely points toward "the Israel of God" being the church as the true Israel. It is hard to conceive, after all that Paul has written against the works of the law, that he would be pronouncing a blessing on the Jewish people. If this is summing up the message of the book, then the emphasis would be on the reversal of the Jew-Gentile disparity and the union of all peoples in Christ. Faith alone can be the basis of peace and mercy, and Paul would only be pronouncing God's mercy on believing Israel. Paul is calling his readers to the cross and the peace with God it alone can produce, which means the NIV translation is definitely the correct view.

PAUL PROVIDES PROOF OF HIS MINISTRY:
THE MARKS OF JESUS (6:17)

This final sentence of the letter (apart from the benediction) begins with *to loipon*, which could be translated "finally," but which in this context more likely has a temporal thrust, "from now on." Paul has proven the Judaizers not only wrong but extremely dangerous, and it should have been clear to the Galatians that to continue to follow them would have constituted apostasy. So (from this point on into the distant future) Paul commands, "Let no one cause me trouble." He is thinking not of his Jewish Christian opponents, who would continue to proclaim their false message, but of the Galatians, whose present spiritual state, with so many starting to follow the Judaizers, is extremely painful for him. But he is convinced that his arguments will have an effect on the Galatians—that they will stop heeding the Judaizers and turning to the law. Thus he will no longer have to be "troubled" about their relationship to God.

Paul grounds his reassurance (*gar*, "for") in this: "I bear on my body the marks of Jesus." This is not simply symbolic language; he is certainly speaking of actual physical marks (Greek: *stigmata*). There have been many suggestions throughout history concerning what these marks might have been. Some of the suggestions are unlikely, including (1) circumcision; (2) a mark on his body, such as the shape of a cross or a fish, to signify that he was a Christ-follower; (3) a tattoo similar to the kind designating a slave; or (4) a religious tattoo pointing to the wearer's dedication to his or her patron god. Paul has spoken against circumcision throughout the letter and would hardly intend that here, and the other three would go against the strictures spelled out in Leviticus 19:28, "Do not ... put tattoo marks on yourselves."[2]

Most likely these marks were the scars, disfigurements, or other physical markings remaining from the beatings, stonings, and shipwrecks Paul had endured in the process of bringing the gospel to the Gentiles (see the list in 2 Cor 11:23–27). Paul had been "bearing" his own cross for Christ (Luke 14:27 uses the same verb

---

2. Paul rejected the law as an instrument of salvation but was free to follow that law in the same sense as the Jewish Christians in Romans 14:1–15:13 who practiced the food and purity laws as a matter of personal piety. So Paul and most Jewish Christians would have heeded Leviticus 19:28.

as here for "carry their own cross and follow me") and could point to his extensive sacrifices and suffering for the cause of Christ, while the Judaizers, who had been avoiding persecution at all costs (6:12b), had no such marks.

PAUL CLOSES THE LETTER WITH A BENEDICTION (6:18)

Most of Paul's letters conclude with a prayer like this one for the grace of God to be poured out on the saints. This closing is especially close to the form in Philemon 25 and Philippians 4:23 ("The grace of the Lord Jesus Christ be with your spirit"). As in verse 14 Paul employs the full title, "Lord Jesus Christ," to stress the lordship of Christ over the church. His prayer-wish that Christ's grace "be with your spirit" stresses the personal and spiritual nature of the saints' relationship with Christ. This is not a long-distance relationship but one that takes place at the deepest part of our being.

There is also stress on the family of God. Only here in Paul's benedictions does he say "*our* Lord Jesus Christ," and he adds "brothers and sisters" to the customary blessing. Both of these additions stress that the Galatians had joined Paul, his team, and all of the believing Jews as part of the family of God. They were a part of the new humanity in the new creation (Eph 2:14–15; Gal 6:15), citizens of heaven (Phil 3:20), and members of the new family of God who had been united with Christ and with each other. The final unusual addition is "amen," which ratifies and sealed the benediction as a prayer ("so be it") for the Galatian Christians and provides a fitting end to the letter.

———

This conclusion also draws together the great relevance of this letter's message for the modern church. We don't face exactly the same heretical opponents, but there are far more cults and satanic delusions in our world than there were in Paul's day. We need to be every bit as alert as Paul was for those who would twist truth to their own ends and lead people astray to their destruction. Heretical cult leaders in our time have the same motivations of human pride and the same desire for fame and fortune, as well as for the avoidance of persecution and hard times. Like the Galatians, we must become familiar with theological truth and be able to recognize when people are straying from it. Let me ask you a serious question: How long would it take a heretic with charisma and a command of Scripture to lead your own church astray, and how many within your congregation would be aware and concerned enough to recognize and combat the false teaching?

We also must be deeply committed to the cross and to justification by faith. Works righteousness keeps sneaking to the forefront in too many churches, leading them to replace the gospel with good works and do away with evangelism in favor of social concern and fellowship. These external issues must never be allowed to supplant the internal reality of faith in Christ as the core of everything we are and do. The unequivocal and unmistakable message of Galatians lies at the epicenter of the Christian faith: We are all sinners saved only by faith in the Christ who became the substitute for us and bore our sins on the cross. The works-oriented salvation of Paul's Judaizer opponents was heresy, and to follow it constituted apostasy. In our day, we must be carefully attuned to so-called Christian movements that in reality depart from the clear gospel message and deeply endanger the church.

Our purpose is simple yet profound: We are to keep the cross central and maintain a lifestyle that is "crucified to the world"— that considers itself dead to the world's values and goals. We are part of a "new creation," no longer pursuing self-centered goals and sacrificing eternal realities for the fleeting pleasures of this life. We also seek a balanced life, enjoying the world in which God has placed us while centering on God, the Giver. Our goal must be to live for God's mercy and within God's peace.

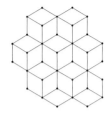

GLOSSARY

amanuensis A scribe or secretary hired to write letters in the
    ancient world.
apocalyptic Refers to truths about the coming of the last
    days, which God has hidden from past generations and
    is now revealing to his messianic community.
chiasm A stylistic device used throughout Scripture that
    presents two sets of ideas in parallel to each other,
    with the order reversed in the second pair. Chiasms
    generally are used to emphasize the element or
    elements in the middle of the pattern.
christological Relating to the New Testament's presentation
    of the person and work of Christ, especially his
    identity as Messiah.
eschatological (adj.), eschatology (n.) Refers to the last
    things or the end times. Within this broad category,
    biblical scholars and theologians have identified more
    specific concepts. For instance, "realized eschatology"
    emphasizes the present work of Christ in the world
    as he prepares for the end of history. In "inaugurated
    eschatology" the last days have already begun but have
    not yet been consummated at the return of Christ.

Hellenism (n.), Hellenistic (adj.) Relating to the spread of Greek culture in the Mediterranean world after the conquests of Alexander the Great (356–323 BC).

Judaizers Label commonly used to identify a group of teachers who, in contradiction to Paul's gospel, encouraged Gentile Christians to observe the Jewish law and undergo the rite of circumcision. (The term "Judaizers" itself does not appear in the Bible.)

proleptic Refers to the presentation of a future act as though it has already been accomplished.

Septuagint An ancient Greek translation of the Old Testament that was used extensively in the early church.

Shekinah A word derived from the Hebrew *shakan* ("to dwell"), used to describe God's personal presence taking the form of a cloud, often in the context of the tabernacle or temple (e.g., Exod 40:38; Num 9:15; 1 Kgs 8:10–11).

Shema A Jewish confession of faith composed of Deuteronomy 6:4–9; 11:13–21; and Numbers 15:37–41.

soteriological Relating to the broad doctrine of salvation, including such subjects as atonement, justification, and sanctification.

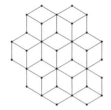

BIBLIOGRAPHY

Bruce, F. F. *The Epistle to the Galatians: A Commentary on the Greek Text*. New International Greek Testament Commentary. Grand Rapids: Eerdmans, 1982.

Dunn, James D. G. *The Epistle to the Galatians*. Black's New Testament Commentary. London: Continuum, 1993.

Fee, Gordon D. *Galatians*. Pentecostal Commentary. Dorset, England: Deo, 2007.

Fung, Ronald Y. K. *The Epistle to the Galatians*. The New International Commentary on the New Testament. Grand Rapids: Eerdmans, 1988.

George, Timothy. *Galatians*. The New American Commentary 30. Nashville: B&H, 1994.

Hansen, G. Walter. *Galatians*. The IVP New Testament Commentary Series. Downers Grove, IL: InterVarsity Press, 1994.

Longenecker, Richard N. *Galatians*. Word Biblical Commentary 41. Dallas: Word, 1998.

Martyn, J. Louis. *Galatians: A New Translation with Introduction and Commentary*. Anchor Bible 33A. New York: Doubleday, 1997.

Mohrlang, Roger, and Gerald L. Borchert. *Romans and Galatians. Cornerstone Biblical Commentary 14*. Carol Stream, IL: Tyndale House, 2007.

McKnight, Scot. *Galatians*. The NIV Application Commentary. Grand Rapids: Zondervan, 1995.

Moo, Douglas J. *Galatians*. Baker Exegetical Commentary on the New Testament. Grand Rapids: Baker Academic, 2013.

Morris, Leon. *Galatians: Paul's Charter of Christian Freedom*. Downers Grove, IL: InterVarsity Press, 1996.

Oakes, Peter. *Galatians*. Paideia Commentaries on the New Testament. Grand Rapids: Baker Academic, 2015.

Schreiner, Thomas R. *Galatians*. Zondervan Exegetical Commentary on the New Testament. Grand Rapids: Zondervan, 2010.

Stott, John R. W. *The Message of Galatians: Only One Way*. The Bible Speaks Today. Downers Grove, IL: InterVarsity Press, 1986.

Wilson, Todd. *Galatians: Gospel-Rooted Living*. Preaching the Word. Wheaton, IL: Crossway, 2013.

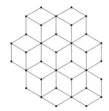

SUBJECT AND AUTHOR INDEX

and justification, 70
by the law, 132, 161–62
salvation history, 8, 15–17,
     20–21, 71–72
and Abraham, 82, 88, 97, 100–
     01, 153
and Christ, 23, 30, 78, 93, 96–97,
     110–12, 117–26, 149, 162
and eschatology, 33, 150–51,
     164–65, 178, 211–12, 217
and Isaac, 153
and the law, 76, 85, 93, 97–98,
     101–04, 111–12, 120, 132–34,
     149, 162
and the Spirit, 81–84, 97–98, 120,
     125, 128, 132, 152, 183, 196
Samaria, 43
Sanders, E. P., 7–8
Sarah, vs. Hagar, 145–52
Satan, 28, 131–32, 183, 199
  and church conflict, 80, 83, 178
seed, of Abraham, 99–100, 117–19
self, and salvation, 75–78,
     115, 196–97
self-control, 191
self-examination, 202–03
servant. See slave
sexual immorality, 184
Shekinah. See glory: of God
Shema, 107
signature, of Paul, 212
sin
  and the curse, 92
  dying to, 76–78, 191–93
  and the flesh, 184–87
  judgment on, 169–71
  and the law, 72–76, 105–06, 162
  in motives, 213–14
  and restoration, 197–98
  sexual, 176, 184
  slavery to, 109–12, 125
Sinai, and Hagar, 149–50

sinners
  Gentiles as, 69
  Jews as, 73–74
  restoration of, 197–99
slave
  of Christ, 29
  Paul as, 44
slavery, spiritual, 52–53, 121–30,
     134, 145–59, 173–76
slaves
  in the church, 116
  of one another, 176
Son, of God, 16, 78, 125–28. See
     also Christ
sons, of Abraham, 146–48
sonship, and Christ, 113–
     15, 127–30
sowing, imagery of, 205–06
Spirit, 16, 102–03
  and Christian freedom, 17
  vs. the flesh, 85–86, 153–54, 175,
     179–92, 206–07
  and the Galatians, 83–84, 87
  and Isaac, 148
  and life, 207–09
  living by, 194–98
  promise of, 97–98
  and righteousness, 164–65
  the sending of, 128–30
spit, and evil spirits, 138
status, unimportance of, 54
stigmata, 219
stoicheia, 123–25, 131
stoichōmen, 196
substitution, 96–97
suffering
  eternal, 187–88
  of the Galatians, 86
synagogues, Paul in, 39
Syria, Paul in, 42–43, 46–49

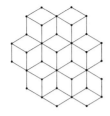

INDEX OF SCRIPTURE AND OTHER ANCIENT LITERATURE

Old Testament

New Testament

Other Ancient Literature